DERRIDA, LITERATURE
AND WAR

Philosophy, Aesthetics and Cultural Theory
Series Editor: Hugh J. Silverman, Stony Brook University, USA

The *Philosophy, Aesthetics and Cultural Theory* series examines
the encounter between contemporary continental philosophy
and aesthetic and cultural theory. Each book in the series
explores an exciting new direction in philosophical aesthetics
or cultural theory, identifying the most important and pressing
issues in continental philosophy today.

Also available:
Foucault's Philosophy of Art, Joseph J. Tanke

Forthcoming:
The Literary Agamben: Adventures in Logopoeisis, William Watkin
Philosophy and the Book, Dan Selcer

Series contact information:
Prof. Hugh J. Silverman, Philosophy, Stony Brook University
Stony Brook, New York 11794-3750 USA
hugh.silverman@stonybrook.edu

http://ms.cc.sunysb.edu/~hsilverman/

DERRIDA, LITERATURE AND WAR

ABSENCE AND THE CHANCE OF MEETING

SEAN GASTON

continuum

Continuum International Publishing Group

The Tower Building	80 Maiden Lane
11 York Road	Suite 704
London SE1 7NX	New York NY 10038

www.continuumbooks.com

The Publishers acknowledge permission to reprint extracts from
Paul Celan's "Die hellen Steine" and "Radix, Matrix" in Paul Celan,
Die Niemandsrose © 1963 S. Fischer Verlag, Frankfurt am Main, and
the translation by John Felstiner in *The Selected Poems and Prose of
Paul Celan* © 2001 W.W. Norton, New York.

British Library Cataloguing-in-Publication Data
A catalogue record for this book is available from the British Library.

ISBN 10: HB: 1-8470-6552-X
PB: 1-8470-6553-8
ISBN 13: HB: 978-1-8470-6552-0
PB: 978-1-8470-6553-7

Library of Congress Cataloging-in-Publication Data
Gaston, Sean.
Derrida, literature and war: absence and the chance of meeting /
Sean Gaston.
p. cm. – (Philosophy, aesthetics and cultural theory)
Includes bibliographical references and index.
ISBN 978-1-84706-552-0 (hb) – ISBN 978-1-84706-553-7 (pb)
1. Derrida, Jacques. I. Title. II. Series.

B2430.D484G385 2009
194–dc22
2008048768

Typeset by Newgen Imaging Systems Pvt Ltd, Chennai, India
Printed and bound in Great Britain by The Cromwell Press Group

CONTENTS

LIST OF ILLUSTRATIONS

PREFACE

This work is concerned with Jacques Derrida's criticisms of a tradition that attempts to calculate on absence, to hold on to alterity as an assured and absolute resource. It explores Derrida's attempts to resist the ruses and traps of this tradition through not foreclosing the chances of the chance meeting. It also argues that in times of war literary narratives of the chance encounter can be seen as a possibility of an "other" of war. This frail possibility, constantly tempted by the absolute or pure claim to ethics or to a literary ideality, leaves us with the chances of literature as a series of intervals that seem to last a lifetime.

From his earliest work, Derrida had warned against calculating *on* absence as a gathering-back towards presence, whilst reiterating that one cannot avoid calculating *from* absence. The first part of the book addresses this injunction against calculating on absence as a secure or self-evident resource of difference, otherness and authenticity. It starts by marking the posthumous fortieth anniversary of the publication and reception of Derrida's own work, *Of Grammatology* (1967). How does one mark such an anniversary, most of all after the death of Jacques Derrida in 2004, without calculating on absence? In his own readings of Rousseau, Sartre and Blanchot, Derrida evokes the always compelling and always bizarre experience of an inherited dis-inheritance, a gaining or possession of a dispossession that is always more and less than the alternative of either presence or absence.

The book then turns to Derrida's early readings of Husserl and to Giorgio Agamben's recent attempts, in part inspired by Heidegger, to harness and hold on to the "darkness" of Aristotelian potentiality as an absolute resource or pure possibility for alterity and creativity. In his own readings of Aristotle, as much as Heidegger celebrated Aristotle's recognition of the many ways of being, he still privileged a gathering-back towards a "full guiding meaning". Derrida, on the other hand, argued both for the ethics of an oscillation between "shadow and light" and what he called *la chance de la rencontre*, the chances or mischances of the chance encounter. In terms of his own relationship to the work of Heidegger, and in contrast to a tradition of reading from Descartes to Heidegger, Derrida insists that there must always be the possibility of a mischance in the chance encounter or meeting. There must be a calculating from absence, a risk of not meeting and a possibility of conflict, to avoid the encounter being reduced to either the assurance of meeting or the confidence of not meeting. For Derrida, there must always be the chance of (not) meeting.

The second part of the book examines the concept of war and the chances of literature. Starting with Derrida's reading of Democritus and Epicurus and the difference between *la chance de la rencontre* and the *rendezvous*, and looking at Hume, Thackeray, Celan, Foucault and Deleuze among others, the book focuses on the relation between the chance encounter or duel (another meaning of the French word *rencontre*) and war. It traces this relation in some of the principal writings on war from the late-eighteenth century to the early twentieth century: Schiller's *Wallenstein* (1799), Clausewitz's *On War* (1832), Tolstoy's *War and Peace* (1865–1869), Conrad's "The Duel" (1908), Freud's "Thoughts for the Times on War and Death" (1915). It also follows representations of the duel in the post-Napoleonic narratives of Kleist, Stendhal, Lermontov, Turgenev, Dostoyevsky, Chekhov and Joseph Roth. The duel can always lead to the outbreak of hostilities but it is also a chance of meeting that cannot be reduced to a concept of war.

As Conrad remarked, in the midst of a global war without end, Napoleon fought a "duel against the whole of Europe". The book ends by examining the relation between war, sovereignty and the chances of the duel. Derrida suggests that the state-run imposition of anonymity, especially in times of war, relies on a sovereign attempt to leave either the enemy nameless or to name without rest what cannot be named. This is most apparent in the political and literary representation of the animal. As the works of Tolstoy, Bulgakov and S. Y. Agnon attest, literature confronts us with a vulnerable and unassailable anonymity as the index of an unavoidable (not) meeting without name.

The Melbourne based photographer Jane Brown has offered her own reading of this work with seven photographs, providing beyond the written text another series of intervals and chance meetings. Responding to the different narratives in the book on the wars of the Napoleonic period, she travelled to Belgium and Russia in 2007. These journeys produced the remarkable photos of the translucent and billowing curtains in the Hermitage (Chapter 2) and of the tourists walking in the great square outside the Winter Palace, near the column honouring Tsar Alexander I (Chapter 3). If you look closely in this last photograph, you can see figures in the foreground dressed in historical costume. Though she took many photos of the monument marking the site of the battle of Waterloo, she also brought back three extraordinary images from Belgium: the imperial toy horse from a shop window in Brussels (Chapter 7); the two glassy-eyed stuffed zebras from that disturbing remnant of Belgium's own imperial misadventures, the Royal Museum of Central Africa in Tervuren (Chapter 6); and, finally, a photo from a shop window taken in Antwerp, which at first glance could be seen as some kind of aquatic animal, though in fact it is a hat on a stand (Chapter 1).

The remaining two photographs were also taken on this journey across Europe: the castle of Kronberg in Elsinore with its cannons still pointing out to sea (Chapter 5), and a statue of a woman in the National Archaeological Museum of Athens, a figure divided by strong horizontal and vertical lines whom we only see at an oblique angle from the back (Chapter 4). Each photograph can be taken as an oblique commentary: the bizarre image of the hat on the stand and the diaphanous curtains in the Hermitage appear at moments when the text is discussing Rousseau's use of the word "bizarre" or the very different responses of Derrida and Agamben to the concept of the diaphanous. The toy horse comes in a chapter on the animal (the horse, the wolf, the dog) in literary works. The castle at Elsinore evokes obvious references to Shakespeare, while the cannons recall that this was also a place of war. The disturbing photo of two zebras – disturbing not least because it seems that one zebra is stuffed and one could be alive – appears at the moment when Conrad's characters in "The Duel", who have become strange twins or doubles in their inexplicable fifteen-year duel, can only see each other as animals. At the same time, each photograph says something about the chances of (not) meeting: of the figure with her back to us, of the reflections of images behind and in front of glass, of cannons pointing out to an empty sea, of a crowd of people seemingly arranged in a set pattern that can only be random.

These photographs, and their place in this work, were also informed by both of us reading a largely unknown text by Derrida, "Demeure, Athènes" (1996). In this short work, Derrida responds to a series of photographs taken in Athens by Jean-François Bonhomme. Derrida is fascinated by a photo from the Acropolis in which a camera is standing on a tripod not far from the photographer, who is sitting down and seems to be asleep. The photographs by Jane Brown in this book also tell us of the photographic experience. They are a series of snapshots, of moments, of intervals or intermissions that remain and linger on and on and cannot help but reflect the conditions of their own possibility: the diaphanous curtains on the windows of the Hermitage, the toy horse in the shop window and, most starkly, the hat on stand in the window that looks like some sort of animal, and reveals the reflected image of the photographer. As Derrida remarks on the photos of Athens, these images – as a reading of the strained relation between absence, chance, literature and war – leave us with *"un gout d'éternité désespéré"*, a hopeless taste of eternity.[1]

7 February 2008

ABBREVIATIONS

AD   Jacques Derrida, *Adieu: To Emmanuel Levinas* (1997), trans. Anne Pascale-Brault and Michael Naas (Stanford: Stanford University Press, 1999).

AdF   Jacques Derrida, *L'archéologie du frivole* (Paris: Galilée, 1990 [1973]).

AF   Jacques Derrida, *The Archaeology of the Frivolous: Reading Condillac* (1973), trans. John P. Leavey, Jr. (Pittsburgh: Duquesne University Press, 1980).

AM   Martin Heidegger, *Aristotle's Metaphysics Θ 1–3: On the Essence and Actuality of Force* (1931), trans. Walter Brogan and Peter Warnek (Bloomington: Indiana University Press, 1995).

AN   Joseph Conrad, "Author's Note" (1920), in *A Set of Six* (London: Dent, 1954), v–ix.

ATT   Jacques Derrida, "The Animal That Therefore I am (More to Follow)" (1997), trans. David Wills, *Critical Inquiry* 28 no. 2 (2001), 369–418.

ATV   Jacques Derrida, "At This Very Moment in This Work Here I Am" (1980), in *Psyche: Inventions of the Other, Volume I*, trans. Ruben Berezdivin and Peggy Kamuf, ed. Peggy Kamuf and Elizabeth Rottenberg (Stanford: Stanford University Press, 2007), 143–90.

AU   Jacques Derrida and Giovanna Borradori, "Autoimmunity: Real and Symbolic Suicides" (2001), in *Philosophy in a*

Time of Terror: Dialogues with Jürgen Habermas and Jacques Derrida, trans. Giovanna Borradori (Chicago: University of Chicago Press, 2003), 85–136.

BGE   Friedrich Nietzsche, *Beyond Good and Evil* (1886), in *Basic Writings of Nietzsche*, trans. Walter Kaufman (New York: Modern Library, 1968).

BT   Martin Heidegger, *Being and Time* (1927), trans. John Macquarrie and Edward Robinson (Oxford: Blackwell, 1990).

C   Jacques Derrida, "Cartouches" (1978), trans. Geoff Bennington and Ian McLeod, in *The Truth in Painting* (Chicago: University of Chicago Press, 1987), 183–247.

CA   Thomas Hardy, *The Mayor of Casterbridge* (1886), ed. Keith Wilson (London: Penguin, 2003).

CD   Jacques Derrida, "Cinquante-deux aphorismes pour un avant propos" (1987), in *Psyché: Inventions de l'autre*, 2 vols (Paris: Éditions Galilée, 1998–2003), II: 121–30.

CF   Jean-Jacques Rousseau, *Confessions* (1770), trans. Angela Scholar, ed. Patrick Coleman (Oxford: Oxford University Press, 2000).

CHM   Jacques Derrida, "Cogito and the History of Madness" (1964), in *Writing and Difference*, trans. Alan Bass (Chicago: University of Chicago Press, 1978), 31–63.

CP   Stendhal, *The Charterhouse of Parma* (1839), trans. Margaret R. B. Shaw (London: Penguin, 1958).

CTD   Francis Bacon, *The Charge Touching Duels* (1613), in *Francis Bacon: The Major Works*, ed. Brian Vickers (Oxford: Oxford University Press, 2002), 304–13.

DA   Jacques Derrida, "Demeure, Athènes", in Jean-François Bonhomme, *Athènes à l'ombre de l'acropole* (Athens: Olkos, 1996), 39–64.

DE   Jacques Derrida, "Désistance" (1987), trans. Christopher Fynsk in *Psyche: Inventions of the Other, Volume II,* ed. Peggy Kamuf and Elizabeth Rottenberg (Stanford: Stanford University Press, 2008), 196–230.

Des   Jacques Derrida, "Désistance" (1987), in *Psyche: Inventions de l'autre*, 2 vols (Paris: Éditions Galilée, 1998–2003), 201–38.

DEV   Fyodor Dostoyevsky, *The Devils* (1871), trans. David Margashack (London: Penguin, 1971).

DF   Jacques Derrida, "Différance" (1968), in *Margins of Philosophy*, trans. Alan Bass. (Chicago: University of Chicago Press, 1982), 1–27.

DFT   Jacques Derrida, *Demeure: Fiction and Testimony* (1998), trans. Elizabeth Rottenberg (Stanford: Stanford University Press, 2000).

Dlg   Jacques Derrida, *De la grammatologie* (Paris: Les Éditions de Minuit, 1967).

DMR   Jacques Derrida, "'Dead Man Running': *Salut, Salut* – Notes for a Letter to '*Les Temps Modernes*'" (1996), in *Negotiations: Interventions and Interviews 1971–2001*, trans. Elizabeth Rottenberg (Stanford: Stanford University Press, 2002), 257–92.

DRJ   Jacques Derrida, "Dereliction of the Right to Justice (But what are the 'sans-papiers' lacking?)" (1996), in *Negotiations: Interventions and Interviews 1971-2001*, trans. Elizabeth Rottenberg (Stanford: Stanford University Press, 2002), 133–44.

E   Jacques Derrida, "Envois" (1980), in *The Post Card: From Socrates to Freud and Beyond*, trans. Alan Bass (Chicago: University of Chicago Press, 1987), 1–256.

EAD   Jacques Derrida, *États d'âme de la psychanalyse: L'impossible au-delà d'une souveraine cruauté* (Paris: Éditions Galilée, 2000).

EHO   Jacques Derrida, *Edmund Husserl's Origin of Geometry: An Introduction* (1962), trans. John P. Leavey, Jr. (Lincoln: University of Nebraska Press, 1989).

EidM   Martin Heidegger, *Einführung in die Metaphysik* (1935) (Frankfurt am Main: Vittorio Klostermann, 1983).

EJ   Jacques Derrida, "Edmond Jabès and the Question of the Book" (1964), in *Writing and Difference*, trans. Alan Bass (Chicago: University of Chicago Press, 1978), 64–78.

EM   Jacques Derrida, "The Ends of Man" (1968), in *Margins of Philosophy*, trans. Alan Bass (Chicago: University of Chicago Press, 1982), 109–36.

EX   *Exodus*, in *The Five Books of Moses*, trans. Everett Fox (New York: Schocken, 1992).

F   Democritus, "Fragments", in *Early Greek Philosophers*, ed. Jonathan Barnes (London: Penguin, 1987), 244–88.

FeS   Jacques Derrida, "Force et signification" (1963), in *L'écriture et la différence* (Paris: Éditions du Seuil, 1967), 9–49.

FMC   Thomas Hardy, *Far From the Madding Crowd* (1874), ed. Rosemarie Morgan and Shannon Russell (London: Penguin, 2003).

FS   Jacques Derrida, "Force and Signification" (1963), in *Writing and Difference*, trans. Alan Bass (Chicago: University of Chicago Press, 1978), 3–30.

FT   Jacques Derrida, "Fifty-two Aphorisms for a Foreword" (1987), in *Psyche: Inventions of the Other, Volume II*, trans. Andrew Benjamin, ed. Peggy Kamuf and Elizabeth Rottenberg (Stanford: Stanford University Press, 2008), 117–26.

FWT   Jacques Derrida and Elisabeth Roudinesco, *For What Tomorrow . . . Dialogue* (1989–1990), trans. Jeff Fort (Stanford: Stanford University Press, 2004).

G   Jacques Derrida, *Glas* (1974), trans. John P. Leavey Jr. and Richard Rand (Lincoln: University of Nebraska Press, 1986).

GS   Jacques Derrida, "'Genesis and Structure' and Phenomenology" (1959), in *Writing and Difference*, trans. Alan Bass (Chicago: University of Chicago Press, 1978), 154–68.

GSD   Jacques Derrida, *"Geschlecht* I: Sexual Difference, Ontological Difference" (1983), in *Psyche: Inventions of the Other, Volume II*, trans. Ruben Bevezdivin and Elizabeth Rottenberg, ed. Peggy Kamuf and Elizabeth Rottenberg (Stanford: Stanford University Press, 2008), 7–26.

HD   Mikhail Bulgakov, *The Heart of a Dog* (1925), trans. Michael Glenny (London: Vintage, 1968).

HE   Jacques Derrida, "Heidegger's Ear: Philopolemology (*Geschlecht* IV)" (1989), in *Reading Heidegger: Commemorations*, ed. John Sallis, trans. John Leavey Jr. (Bloomington: Indiana University Press, 1992), 163–218.

HF   Dominique Janicaud, *Heidegger en France* (2001), 2 vols (Paris: Hachette, 2005), II.

HH   Jacques Derrida, "Heidegger's Hand (*Geschlecht* II)" (1985), in *Psyche: Inventions of the Other, Volume II*, trans. John P. Leavey Jr. and Elizabeth Rottenberg (Stanford: Stanford University Press, 2008), 27–62.

HOE   David Hume, *The History of England* (1754–1762), intro. William B. Todd, 6 vols (Indianapolis: Liberty Classics, 1983).

HOT   Mikhail Lermontov, *A Hero of Our Time* (1841), trans. Paul Foote (London: Penguin, 2001).

I   Edmund Husserl, *Ideas: General Introduction to Pure Phenomenology* (1913), trans. W. R. Boyce Gibson (New York: Collier, 1962).

IJD   Derrida, Jacques, and Dominique Janicaud, "Interview with Jacques Derrida" (1999), *Heidegger en France*. 2 Vols. (Paris: Hachette, 2005) II: 89–126.

IM   Martin Heidegger, *Introduction to Metaphysics* (1935), trans. Gregory Fried and Richard Polt (New Haven: Yale University Press, 2000).

IMP   Jacques Derrida, "Implications: Interview with Henri Ronse" (1967), in *Positions*, trans. Alan Bass (Chicago: University of Chicago Press, 1981), 1–14.

IRH   Alexandre Kojève, *Introduction to the Reading of Hegel* (1937–1938), ed. Raymond Queneau and Alan Bloom, trans. James H. Nichols (Ithaca: Cornell University Press, 1991).

JA   Jacques Derrida, "Ja, or the *faux-bond* II" (1975–1977), in *Points . . . Interviews 1974-1994*, ed. Elisabeth Weber, trans. Peggy Kamuf (Stanford: Stanford University Press, 1995), 30–77.

JO   Jacques Derrida, "Ja, ou le faux-bond" (1975), in *Points de suspension: Entretiens*, choisis et présentés par Elisabeth Weber (Paris: Éditions Galilée, 1992), 37–81.

K   Heinrich von Kleist, "The Duel" (1811), in *The Marquise of O – and Other Stories*, trans. and intro. David Luke and Nigel Reeves (London: Penguin, 2004), 287–320.

LC   Jean-Jacques Rousseau, *Les confessions* (1770), ed. Alain Grosrichard, 2 vols (Paris: Flammarion, 2002).

LO   Jacques Derrida, "LIVING ON. Border lines", in *Deconstruction and Criticism*, trans. James Hulbert (New York: Continuum, 1979), 75–176.

LRD   Maurice Blanchot, "Literature and the Right to Death" (1949), in *The Work of Fire*, trans. Charlotte Mandell (Stanford: Stanford University Press, 1995), 300–44.

LSB   Jacques Derrida, "Le souverain bien – ou l'Europe en mal de souveraineté" (2004), *Cités* 30 (2007): 103–40.

M   Jean Paul Sartre, *Les mots* (1964) (Paris: Gallimard, 2006).

MAJ   Jacques Derrida, "Majesties" (2002), in *Sovereignties in Question: The Poetics of Paul Celan*, ed. and trans. Thomas Dutoit and Outi Pasanen (New York: Fordham University Press, 2005), 108–34.

MC   Jacques Derrida, "My Chances/*Mes Chances*: A Rendezvous with Some Epicurean Stereophonies" (1982), trans. Irene Harvey and Avital Ronell in *Psyche: Inventions of the Other, Volume I*, ed. Peggy Kamuf and Elizabeth Rottenberg (Stanford: Stanford University Press, 2007), 344–76.

MF   René Descartes, *Meditations on First Philosophy* (1641), trans. John Cottingham, intro. Bernard Williams (Cambridge: Cambridge University Press, 1986).

MH   Jacques Derrida, "La main de Heidegger (*Geschlecht* II)" (1985), in *Psyche: Inventions de l'autre*, 2 vols (Paris: Galilée, 1998–2003), II: 35–68.

MOM   Immanuel Kant, *The Metaphysics of Morals* (1797), in *Practical Philosophy*, trans. Mary J. Gregor (Cambridge: Cambridge University Press, 1999).

MPP   René Descartes, *Méditations sur la philosophie première* (1641), in *Oeuvres philosophiques*, ed. Ferdinand Alquie, 2 vols (Paris: Garnier Frères, 1967).

MT   Martin Heidegger, *Aristoteles, Metaphysik Theta 1-3: Vom Wesen und Wirklichkeit der Kraft* (1931) (Frankfurt am Main: Vittorio Klostermann, 1981).

O   Jacques Derrida, "Otobiographies: The Teaching of Nietzsche and the Politics of the Proper Name" (1979–1982), trans. Avital Ronell in *The Ear of the Other*, ed. Christie McDonald, (Lincoln: University of Nebraska Press, 1988), 1–38.

OG   Jacques Derrida, *Of Grammatology* (1967), trans. Gayatri Chakravorty Spivak (Baltimore: Johns Hopkins University Press, 1976).

OP   Giorgio Agamben, "On Potentiality" (1986), in *Potentialities*, ed. and trans. Daniel Heller-Roazen (Stanford: Stanford University Press, 1999), 177–84.

OS   Jacques Derrida, *Of Spirit: Heidegger and the Question* (1987), trans. Geoffrey Bennington and Rachel Bowlby (Chicago: University of Chicago Press, 1989).

OT   Jacques Derrida, *On Touching – Jean-Luc Nancy* (2000), trans. Christine Irizarry (Stanford: Stanford University Press, 2005).

OTL   Nietzsche, Friedrich, "On Truth and Lie in an Extra-Moral Sense" (1874), in *The Portable Nietzsche,* ed. and trans. Walter Kaufmann (London: Penguin, 1982), 42–7.

OU   Jacques Derrida, *"Ousia* and *Grammé*: Note on a note from *Being and Time"* (1968), in *Margins of Philosophy,* trans. Alan Bass (Chicago: University of Chicago Press, 1982), 29–63.

OW   Carl von Clausewitz, *On War* (1832), ed. and trans. Michael Howard and Peter Paret (Princeton: Princeton University Press, 1989).

OWP   Jacques Derrida, "Outwork, Prefacing" (1972), in *Dissemination,* trans. Barbara Johnson (Chicago: University of Chicago Press, 1981), 1–59.

OY   S. Y. Agnon, *Only Yesterday: A Novel* (1945), trans. Barbara Harshav (Princeton: Princeton University Press, 2000).

PA   Jacques Derrida, "Pas" (1976), in *Parages*, nouvelle édition revue et augmentée (Paris: Éditions Galilée, 2003), 17–108.

PF   Giorgio Agamben, "The Passion of Facticity" (1988), in *Potentialities*, ed. and trans. Daniel Heller-Roazen (Stanford: Stanford University Press, 1999), 185–204.

PG   Jacques Derrida, *The Problem of Genesis in Husserl's Philosophy* (1953–1954), trans. Marian Hobson (Chicago: University of Chicago Press, 2003).

PIO   Jacques Derrida, "Psyche: Invention of the Other" (1984), trans. Catherine Porter in *Psyche: Inventions of the Other, Volume I*, ed. Peggy Kamuf and Elizabeth Rottenberg (Stanford: Stanford University Press, 2007), 1–47.

PSS   Jacques Derrida, "Psychoanalysis Searches the States of Its Soul: The Impossible Beyond of a Sovereign Cruelty (Address to the States General of Psychoanalysis)" (2000), in *Without Alibi*, ed. and trans. Peggy Kamuf (Stanford: Stanford University Press, 2002), 238–80.

RJ   William Shakespeare, *The Most Excellent and Lamentable Tragedy of Romeo and Juliet* (1595), in *The Norton Shakespeare, Based on the Oxford Edition,* ed. Stephen Greenblatt and others (New York: Norton, 1997).

RM   Joseph Roth, *The Radetzky March* (1932), trans. Joachim Neugroshchel, intro. Nadine Gordimer (London: Penguin, 1995).

RS   Jacques Derrida, "The Reason of the Strongest (Are there Rogue States?)" (2002), in *Rogues: Two Essays on Reason*, trans. Rachel Bowlby (Stanford: Stanford University Press, 2005), 1–114.

RVR   Irina Reyfman, *Ritualized Violence Russian Style: The Duel in Russian* Culture and Literature (Stanford: Stanford University Press, 1999).

S   Aristotle, *On the Soul*, trans. J. A. Smith in *The Complete Works of Aristotle*, ed. Jonathan Barnes, 2 vols (Princeton: Princeton University Press, 1984), I; Greek text: *On the Soul*, trans. W. S. Hett (Cambridge, MA: Harvard University Press, 1986).

SA   Joseph Conrad, *The Secret Agent* (1908), ed. John Lyon (Oxford: Oxford University Press, 2004).

SB   Jacques Derrida, "Shibboleth: For Paul Celan" (1986) in *Sovereignties in Question: The Poetics of Paul Celan*, ed. Thomas Dutoit and Outi Pasanen (New York: Fordham University Press, 2005), 1–64.

Sch   Jacques Derrida, *Schibboleth – pour Paul Celan* (Paris: Éditions Galilée, 1986).

SM   Jacques Derrida, *Specters of Marx: The State of the Debt, the Work of Mourning, and the New International* (1993), trans. Peggy Kamuf (London and New York: Routledge, 1994).

SMD   Michel Foucault, *"Society Must be Defended": Lectures at the College de France, 1975-1976* (1997), ed. Mauro Bertani and Alessandro Fontana, trans. David Macey. (London: Allen Lane, 2003, 51).

T   David Hume, *A Treatise of Human Nature: Being an Attempt to Introduce the Experimental Method of Reasoning into Moral Subjects* (1739–1740), ed. L. A. Selby Bigge and P. H. Nidditch (Oxford: Oxford University Press, 1978).

TD   Joseph Conrad, "The Duel" (1908), in *A Set of Six* (London: Dent, 1954), 166–266.

TEL   Jacques Derrida, "Telepathy" (1981), trans. Nicholas Royle in *Psyche: Inventions of the Other, Volume I*, ed. Peggy Kamuf and Elizabeth Rottenberg (Stanford: Stanford University Press, 2007), 226–61.

TM   Plato, *Timaeus*, trans. R. G. Bury (Cambridge, MA: Harvard University Press, 2005).

TPP   Immanuel Kant, "Toward Perpetual Peace" (1795), in *Practical Philosophy,* trans. Mary J. Gregor, intro. Paul Guyer (Cambridge: Cambridge University Press, 1999), 311–51.

TS   Jacques Derrida, "To Speculate – on 'Freud'" (1975–1980), in *The Post Card: From Socrates to Freud and Beyond*, trans. Alan Bass (Chicago: University of Chicago Press, 1987), 257–409.

TSZ   Friedrich Nietzsche, *Thus Spoke Zarathustra* (1885), ed. Adrian Del Caro and Robert B. Pippin, trans. Adrian del Caro (Cambridge: Cambridge University Press, 2006).

TT   Sigmund Freud, "Thoughts for the Times on War and Death" (1915), in *The Standard Edition of the Complete Works of Sigmund Freud*, trans. James Strachey (London: The Hogarth Press, 1962), XIV: 273–300.

TUR   Ivan Turgenev, *Fathers and Sons* (1862), trans. Rosemary Edmonds, intro. Isaiah Berlin (London: Penguin, 1972).

VeM   Jacques Derrida, "Violence et métaphysique: Essai sur la pensée d'Emmanuel Levinas" (1964), in *L'écriture et la différence* (Paris: Éditions du Seuil, 1967), 117–228.

VF   William Makepeace Thackeray, *Vanity Fair: A Novel without A Hero* (1847–1848) (London: Penguin, 1985).

VK   Carl von Clausewitz, *Vom Kriege: Hinterlassenes Werke* (1832), ed. Werner Hahlweg (Bonn: Ferd. Dümmlers Verlag, 1952).

VM   Jacques Derrida, "Violence and Metaphysics: An Essay on the Thought of Emmanuel Levinas" (1964), in *Writing and Difference*, trans. Alan Bass (Chicago: University of Chicago Press, 1978), 79–153.

W   Friedrich Schiller, *Wallenstein* (1799), in *The Robbers and Wallenstein*, trans. F. J. Lamport (London: Penguin, 1979).

Wa   Friedrich Schiller, *Wallenstein* (1799), in *Werke und Briefe* 4, ed. Fritjof Stock (Frankfurt am Main: Deutscher Klassiker Verlag, 2000).

Wall   G. W. F. Hegel, "On Wallenstein" (1800–1801), trans. Ido Geiger, *Idealist Studies* 35 nos. 2–3 (2005), 196–97.

WCT   Martin Heidegger, *What is Called Thinking?* (1951), trans. Fred D. Wieck and J. Glenn Gray (New York: Harper and Row, 1968).

WD   Thomas Hardy, *The Woodlanders* (1887), ed. Patricia Ingham (London: Penguin, 1998).

WEC   Jacques Derrida, "The 'World' of the Enlightenment to Come (Exception, Calculation and Sovereignty)" (2002), in *Rogues: Two Essays on Reason*, trans. Pascale-Anne Brault and Michael Naas (Stanford: Stanford University Press, 2005), 118–60.

WH   Jacques Derrida, "Why Peter Eisenman Writes Such Good Books" (1987), ed. Peggy Kamuf and Elizabeth Rottenberg in *Psyche: Inventions of the Other, Volume II*, trans. Sarah Whiting, (Stanford: Stanford University Press, 2008), 104–16.

WL   Maurice Blanchot, "War and Literature" (1971), in *Friendship*, trans. Elizabeth Rottenberg (Stanford: Stanford University Press, 1997), 109–11.

WP   Leo Tolstoy, *War and Peace* (1865–1869), trans. Richard Pevear and Larissa Volokhonsky (London: Vintage, 2007).

ZUK   Sigmund Freud, "Zeitgemässes über Krieg und Tod" (1915), in *Das Unbewußte: Schriften zur Psychoanalyse* (Frankfurt am Main: S. Fischer Verlag, 1960), 185–214.

PROLOGUE

A SERIES OF INTERVALS

Before Timaeus begins to recount "the origin of the Cosmos" in Plato's dialogue, Critias tells his "genuine history", his true story (*alētheinòn lógon*) of Atlantis, which Socrates – that mime artist and mimic of the first order – insists is "not an invented fable" (*mē plasthénta mūthon*).[1] Critias has heard it from his grandfather Critias, who had been told by his father Dropides, who had in turn heard it from Solon himself, that when Solon was in Egypt a priest had spoken to him of Athens's great past in the age of Atlantis. Critias then reports that his grandfather had acknowledged that the record (*lógos*) of this true narrative (*alētheinòn lógon*) – which is constructed on a series of genealogical and geographical intervals that leave out the father (grandson–grandfather–great-grandfather–Solon–Egyptian priest) – has not survived, "owing to the lapse of time" (*dià dè khrónon*) (*TM,* 21d). An eternity has passed, and all that we now have is a narrative without a logos handed down as a *series* of regular irregular intervals.

Critias goes on to relate how the Egyptian priest ridiculed the brevity of Solon's genealogy of ancient history as "he tried to calculate the periods of time" (*peirasthai diamnēmoneúōn toùs khrónous arithmein*) (*TM,* 22b). You Greeks "remember but one deluge", the Egyptian says, "though many had occurred previously" (*pollōn émprosthen*) (*TM,* 23b). Your stories "are little better than children's tales" (*paídōn brakhú ti diaphérei múthōn*), and you have missed the repeated "destruction (*pollō pthorá*) of the things on the earth", which "recurs at long intervals" (*dià makrōn khrónōn gignoménē*)

1

(*TM,* 23b, 22d). Your stories, your eternally childish and naive fictions, are no more than a response to a series of intervals that have lasted an eternity.

"What particular name could we assign to a general science ending nowhere [*à aucune région*]?" Derrida asks in his reading of Condillac in *The Archaeology of the Frivolous* (1973).[2] How does one register the beginning of a series *of* intervals, of a seriality of gaps and lapses, of a narrative of absence and chance meetings in times of war? Can one begin with the first interval before the series has begun? Or does one start with what already needs to come both before and after to be identified as a *series*? And can one start if this relation, determined by what precedes and succeeds, is constituted by nothing more than a pause, an intermission that seems to last an age, an eternity even? (*AF,* 38–9, 42–3). For the Egyptian priest in the *Timaeus,* the impossible origin of fiction, of stories and narratives without end is found in the recurrent intervals of destruction (διαφθορα). These repeated elemental destructions, *diapthorà*, have sustained the earth, have secured its ancient genealogies to this very moment, the moment of a genealogy without the father (*TM,* 22d).

When it comes to the snapshot of the relation today between philosophy, literature and war, one has to keep in mind what Derrida called in "Demeure, Athènes" (1996), the inexhaustible temptation for "the instant [that] gathers us once and for all" (*DA,* 43). As Derrida writes, this is the "very desire of philosophy": the "destruction of delay [*retard*]" (*DA,* 45, 59). It is the ruses and traps of this "desire of philosophy" for the snapshot that one has to resist in thinking about the relation between literature and war, or what I will call the (mis)chance of *la chance de la rencontre.* It is also far too easy to dismiss this temptation by constructing a frail architecture, a seamless series of perfectly calibrated escape clauses that proclaim a magisterial indifference, a theoretical slight of hand founded on an empirical presumption. For Derrida, the challenge is always to "think the instant again starting from the delay", to read and think of the snapshot – of a photograph or apparent representation of "war" – as a series *of* intervals (*DA,* 46).[3] Such a reading and thinking could, he suggested, become "the enigmatic thought of the *aiōn* (the full interval of a duration, an incessant spacing of time, one sometimes also calls eternity)" (*DA,* 46).[4] The *aiōn* can be seen as a duration or interval that lasts a lifetime: a series of snapshots that last a lifetime – and more.

For Derrida, this raises the problem "of the fortuitous encounters, of the *tukhē* that collects them on the way, there where they find themselves by chance". The chance meetings or duels between philosophy, literature and war constitute a moment that draws itself out of itself, a moment that drags on, that lingers beyond itself and is repeated in a series of regular–irregular intervals (*DA*, 47). This series of intervals or chances can also be seen as the possibility of a lifetime, of a time of life, of experience and its others, of fiction and its others. As Derrida suggested, like Socrates waiting to see the sails from the headlands to announce his death sentence, "this time is not calculable, nor the delay, because navigating takes a long time and the winds are sometimes, unforeseeably, contrary" (*DA,* 50). For Derrida, it is always a question of "a hopeless taste of eternity" (*un goût d'éternité désespéré*) (*DA*, 60).

Condillac was convinced that in a discriminated sequence "metaphysics as such must *develop* and not *degrade* the metaphysics of natural instinct" (*AF,* 38). What law, Derrida asks, could there be to account for this sequence, this series set out and sequenced by a natural interval that remains "in the midst of going away"? (*AF,* 53). X *must* be found in Y, even though X is of an entirely different order from Y. Or rather, as Derrida suggests, X and Y are never entirely different enough to be absolutely different. As Hillis Miller observes, "it seems that X repeats Y, but in fact it does not."[5] A series *of* intervals – of a lifetime, of the relation between philosophy, literature and war – would not even register the X and Y, only the intervals *between* X and Y.

For Condillac, Derrida argues, it is perhaps less a question of "a determined object", such as the *object* X and the *object* Y that follows it, as much a question of "the very project" of X and Y being treated *as* a series of intervals (*AF,* 61). This is not merely a throwing against (ob-ject), but also a throwing in front on behalf of what is out in front (pro-ject). The relation of two ob-jects, X and Y – say "literature" and "war" – is already pro-jected, already not only found *in* a series of intervals, but also finding itself *as* a series of intervals. *In* and *as* a series of intervals, the relation between "literature" and "war" is "at once the example and the discovery of this, the production of one of these events and the concept of this law" (*AF,* 61). "Literature" and "war" cannot keep the *possibility* of their relation out of the instance of their relationship. In *and* as a series of intervals, the would-be objects are projected, in a *Geworfenheit* if you like, beyond the security of either rupture or development, and find themselves in the (mis)chance of an intermission that goes on and on.

As Condillac suggests, any account of a series of intervals is more a running after, a list that can never catch up, that can only alter and wander away from "the natural order of ideas" (*AF*, 86). For Rousseau, it is precisely the invention of the natural that takes so much time. Some philosophers, he notes in the *Discourse on the Origin of Inequality* (1755), "begin by giving the strongest persons government over the weaker ones, and straightaway introduced government without thinking of the time that had to elapse before the words 'authority' and 'government' could have meaning among men".[6] In the *Confessions* (1770), Rousseau touches on the need to think of this elapse of time when he describes his last months with Madame de Warens: "There was, by the grace of heaven, an interval, a short and precious interval, which came to an end through no fault of mine and which I need not reproach myself I misused."[7] The autobiographical interval, the confessed interval, is *only* recognized retrospectively: it cannot be seen as an interval when it is taking place, when it is present. It is only when it has been superseded that it can become "a short and precious interval". Rousseau gives this unrecognizable interval, this interval that cannot be present-to-itself, both a lingering absence and a recuperating restorative presence. "This is where my life's brief happiness begins," he writes, "this is where those moments belong, tranquil but fleeting, which give me the right to say that I had lived" (*CF*, 221).

As Rousseau's work suggests, one of the temptation among others in accounting for a series of intervals is the natural history of the Proustian moment, or the moment that quite simply lasts forever, the moment that takes on all the authority of a continuum. As Blanchot noted in *Faux pas* (1943),

Of these states, Proust took care to highlight all that, by detaching them from ordinary life, gives them a privileged nature. It is a matter of involuntary impressions, linked by chance, of such an immediate power of effect, such a decisive ravishing strength, that they immediately dissipate any anxiety about the future, any intellectual doubt, and make death indifferent.

Stopping to save everything, Proust leaves us with a time that is always losing itself and finding itself timeless. Such moments of the past that secure the future, Blanchot argued, continually affirm "the fortuitous resolution of anguish in order to eternalize it and free himself from all anxiety."[8]

One can contrast this eternity of the Proustian interval to Blanchot's description in *L'entretien infini* (1969) of *la chance de la rencontre* in André Breton's work. The chance of the chance encounter breaks the presumption of continuity: it affirms the surrealist rupture or interval of one unforeseen moment and one unplanned place. But treated in this way, the chance or interval can *only* register itself in relation to the presumption of continuity. The chance of the interval must also contend with a plurality, Blanchot argues, with differing levels, spacings and relations that cannot be directed towards a gathering-back or returned to a unity. As Blanchot writes, "*la rencontre nous rencontre.*" The encounter encounters us. The chance encounter or duel retains the (mis)chance of meeting. It meets us – we do not meet it. The one moment of encounter is always more than a single moment for us. It is already a series of other moments. The one place of encounter is already displaced, disjointed. There is always a distance – or what Blanchot calls the neutral unknown, the neutrality of the stranger (*le neutre de l'inconnu*) – in the intervals of the chance encounter. The chance encounter is not a point: it is a gap, a gap that moves. It is always a *series* of intervals that resonate *within* a single chance encounter, giving rise to a sense of unreality or, rather, to no longer being able to separate reality and the narratives of fiction.[9] It is the possibility – and the inevitability – of war stories and the becoming of literature.[10] The relation between literature and war is a series of intervals.

In his reading of Rousseau in *Of Grammatology* (1967), Derrida associated the "interval in general" with the unavoidable supplement, the inescapable insufficiency of an addition, an extra, that displaces, replaces and exceeds. He opens his discussion of "The Interval and the Supplement" by noting that Rousseau only "divided" the *Essay on the Origin of Languages* "into chapters belatedly": Derrida is interested in this spacing of the work – this retrospective introduction of a series of intervals – that cannot be confined to a unified architectonics.[11] For Rousseau, he argues, "the growth of music, the desolating separation of song and speech" is founded on – and founders on – the introduction of intervals (and of chapters). Rousseau writes: "In proportion as it was perfected, melody imperceptibly lost its ancient energy by imposing new rules upon itself, and the calculation of intervals was substituted for the subtlety of inflections."[12] The "science of intervals" separated music from the mother tongue (*OG,* 199). For Rousseau, there should be, as there once was, an art without intervals, without "the calculable and analogical regularity of intervals" (*OG,* 213–14).[13] For Derrida, on the contrary, when it comes to "a science of series and intervals", "none of the terms of this series can, being comprehended within it, dominate the economy of differance or supplementarity" (*OG,* 210, 315).

At the end of his reading of Condillac, Derrida remarks: "Philosophy deviates [*s'écarte*] from itself and gives rise to the blows [*coups*] that will strike it nonetheless from the outside [*portés du dehors*]" (*AF,* 132; *AdF,* 142–3). In his interview in the aftermath of the attacks in America on 11 September 2001, Derrida returned to this far-reaching blow (*le coup porté*) as part of a series of intervals that cannot be closed-off or shut down.[14] For Derrida, the trauma of the far-reaching blow lasts beyond its proper term, or the term of the proper, because the past always has a future:

> We are talking about a trauma, and thus an event, whose temporality proceeds neither from the now that is present nor from the present that is past but from an im-presentable to come. [. . .] Imagine that the Americans and, through them, the entire world, had been told: what just happened, the spectacular destruction of two towers, the theatrical but invisible deaths of thousands of people in just a few seconds, is an awful thing, a terrible crime, a pain without measure, but it's all over, it won't happen again, there will never again be anything as awful or more awful than that.[15]

The blow never finishes, nor can it ever be isolated, closed down or closed-off from a series: the trauma, the possibility of the past always risks the mischances of a worst future that is yet to come. We are trying to finish off what lasts forever, to put a halt to what lives on *as* a series of intervals. Derrida says:

> I assume that mourning would have been possible in a relatively short period of time. Whether to our chagrin or our delight, things would have quite quickly returned to their normal course in ordinary history. One would have spoken of the work of mourning and turned the page, as is so often done, and done so much more easily when it comes to things that happen elsewhere, far

from Europe, or the Americas. But this is not at all what happened. There is traumatism without any possible work of mourning when evil comes from the possibility to come of the worst, from the repetition to come – though worst. Traumatism produced by the *future*, by the *to come*, by the threat of the worst *to come* rather than by an aggression that is "over and done with." (*AU,* 97)

For Derrida, the far-reaching blow will always be a series of intervals because, "the missing resist the work of mourning, like the future, just like the most recalcitrant of ghosts. The missing of the archive, the ghost, the phantom – that's the future" (*AU,* 189 n. 9).

As is well known, in his influential lectures on Hegel in the late 1930s Alexandre Kojève placed great emphasis on Hegel's seeing Napoleon after the battle of Jena in 1806 as he was finishing the *Phenomenology of Spirit* (1807). According to Kojève, history ends as absolute knowledge – and dispenses with the far-reaching blow as a series of intervals – with Hegel's "conception" of Napoleon as the completely "satisfied" man, the man who alone has become individualized as a universality.[16] As Kojève writes: "It is because Hegel hears the sounds of the battle that he can know that History is being completed or has been completed, that – consequently – *his* conception of the World is a *total* conception, that *his* knowledge is an *absolute* knowledge" (*IRH,* 44).

As Derrida noted in *Demeure: Fiction and Testimony* (1998), Hegel wrote a letter to Niethammer on Monday 13 October 1806, the day the victorious French occupied Jena. In his letter he is chiefly worried about his manuscript, which may be lost or burnt after the French arrive. As Derrida suggests, it is this concern for the preservation of his writing, for his works that will survive, that will remain and live on after him, which provides the context for his first account of seeing Napoleon:

I have had such worries about sending off [*envois*] the manuscript last Wednesday and Friday, as you can see by the date. – Last night at around sunset I saw the gunshots fired by the French [. . .] I saw the Emperor – the spirit of the world – leave the city to go on reconnaissance; it is indeed a wonderful sensation to see an individual who, concentrated in a single point, sitting on a horse, extends over the world and dominates it . . . given what is happening, I am forced to ask myself if my manuscript, which was sent off Wednesday and Friday has arrived; my loss would indeed be too great; the people that I know have suffered nothing; must I be the only one?[17]

The sighting of Napoleon marks not so much the Kojévian end of history, as an interval in a series that cannot avoid all the mischances and risks of a suspended and indefinite destination that has still yet to be reached.[18] "Napoleon" is not the end of the Hegelian series, rather he marks what Derrida called *la restance*, the remainders of a series of intervals that have not yet arrived, and *la survivance*, a living-on or living over that cannot be contained within the Hegelian colonization of absence.[19]

Reading Hegel, perhaps as Hegel wanted to be read, Kojève uses "Napoleon" as the possibility for what stands at the end, above and outside the series. For Derrida, "Napoleon" is not as much "outside the series", as "the remainder of the series".[20] As he writes in "Cartouches" (1978), within and beyond Hegelianism, Derrida remains discouraged – attending to what can neither be "outside the series" nor give itself to "repetition *in series*". The "remainder of the series" would be a "series without model", an "outside the series in the series", "a serial interlace", a "series of out-of-series", "a series without family" and "a putting-into-series": a series *of* intervals (*C*, 198, 202, 210, 221, 223).[21]

How then would one read the series outside-the-series of war and peace? As Derrida noted in *Adieu: To Emmanuel Levinas* (1997), "War and peace are also too often thought to form a symmetrical pair of concepts. But give to one or the other of these two concepts a value or position of originarity, and the symmetry is broken."[22] How does one think war and peace without calculating on the other of war as a pacifying resource for all our dreams of a time without war, of an eternity that has no interruptions, no intervals and no mischances? Is there a series between a bringing together that does not tie-itself-into-one and a war without end, a war that hopelessly suicidally kills until it can form a single, uninterrupted knot, and tie-itself-into one, for eternity?[23]

Tolstoy's *War and Peace* (1865–1869) presents itself as a series of intervals, of brief chapters, that punctuate both times of war and times of peace from 1805–1812, and later 1813–1820. Represented through a series of intervals, the times of war and peace are both relative: while the battles go on in one place – even the burning of

Moscow – there are always other places where there is no fighting. As a series of intervals, "war" and "peace" take place at the same time. Tolstoy also challenges the concept of "war and peace" that is shaped and guided by what stands outside of this series of intervals. This is most apparent in his treatment of Napoleon. Echoing Stendhal and the youthful adoration of Fabrizio del Dongo in *The Charterhouse of Parma* (1839), Tolstoy finally allows Prince Andrei to meet Napoleon in the aftermath of the battle of Austerlitz.[24]

Awed by "the genius of Napoleon", before the battle Prince Andrei had asked General Dolgorukhov, who had just met Napoleon, "what is Bonaparte like? What impression did he make on you?"[25] General Dolgorukhov, who has misjudged Napoleon's feigned reluctance to fight, tries to undermine the Emperor's claims to sovereignty by describing him as being no more than "a man in a grey frock coat" (*WP*, 259). In his treatise *On War* (1832), Clausewitz gets around the problem of Napoleon's status as a monarch among European monarchs by calling him the "Emperor of the Revolution", a title which captures much of the incongruous and unsurprising sovereignty of Bonaparte.[26] After the battle of Borodino, in his role as narrator and commentator Tolstoy himself writes:

> A commander in chief is never in those conditions of the *beginning* of some event, in which we always consider events. A commander in chief always finds himself in the middle of a shifting series of events, and in such a way that he is never able at any moment to ponder all the meaning of an ongoing event. (*WP*, 825)

While General Dolgorukhov's heavy-handed "putting-into-series" does not reflect Napoleon's strategic skill – he is not just one of a series of French soldiers – it does prefigure the chance encounter between Napoleon and Prince Andrei after the Russians have lost the battle.

Prince Andrei's meeting with Napoleon is also part of a series outside-the-series, as it happens almost at the same time as Nikolai Rostov's chance sighting of the Tsar at the end of the battle. Rostov's own sighting of the Tsar before, during and after the battle can be described as a series of intervals. The first interval, while on parade before the battle, is marked by "a feeling of self-forgetfulness, a proud awareness of strength, and a passionate attraction to him who was the cause of this solemnity" (*WP*, 245). The sovereign fills this singular and seemingly never to be repeated moment: Nikolai feels himself to be nothing more than "an insignificant speck." The entire army seems a dead body before the arrival of the passing spirit of the sovereign:

> Before the approach of the sovereign, each regiment, in its speech-lessness and immobility, seemed a lifeless body; but as soon as the sovereign drew level with it, the regiment came alive and thundered, joining the roar of the entire line which the sovereign had already passed. (*WP*, 246)

Animating and sustaining the passing moment, filling and giving life to the interval, for Nikolai the sovereign becomes a mirror that determines the duration of the interval. "Seeing that smile, Rostov involuntarily began to smile himself and felt a still stronger love for his sovereign" (*WP*, 246). It is a sovereign interval.

Rostov experiences this sovereign interval in all its force three days later in this second of the series of his chance encounters with the sovereign, a chance encounter that takes on all the resonance and hope of a planned *rendezvous*:

> Rostov did not remember and did not feel how he ran to his place and mounted his horse. His regret over his non-participation in the action, his humdrum mood in the circle of usual faces, instantly went away, and all thought of himself instantly vanished: he was wholly consumed by the feeling of happiness that came from the nearness to the sovereign. He felt himself rewarded by this nearness alone for the loss of that day. He was as happy as a lover who has obtained a hoped-for rendezvous. (*WP*, 254)

At the end of the battle, in this sovereign series outside-the-series of sovereignty, Rostov is unable to approach the sovereign, to be near him, to obtain his "hoped-for rendezvous", as the Tsar sits weeping beneath an apple tree. It is a missed chance, a *rencontre* that could not be a *rendezvous*. Tolstoy writes:

> He could . . . not only could, but should have ridden up to the sovereign. And that was a unique chance to show the sovereign his devotion. And he had not made use of it. . . . 'What have I done?' he thought. And he turned his horse and rode back to the place

where he had seen the emperor; but there was no one now on the other side of the ditch. Only wagons and carriages drove along. (*WP,* 288)

When Prince Andrei encounters Napoleon, he is lying wounded on the ground after the battle. This chance meeting ends with Napoleon seeing that Prince Andrei is still alive and ordering that he be given medical attention. One could see this as a kind of resurrection: the sovereign saves Prince Andrei and brings him back to life. But there is an interval, which seems to last for an eternity, between Napoleon's "*voilà une belle mort*" and his awareness that the prince is alive. It is an interval in which the sovereign, as that which stands outside the series, becomes no more than "the buzzing of a fly". It is an absence that resists calculation towards a gathering-back, an absence registering the unavoidable mischances of the chance meeting and the interminable, indefinite and hopeless series of intervals that account for the unaccountable relation between literature and war:

"There's a fine death," said Napoleon, looking at Bolkonsky. Prince Andrei understood that it had been said about him, and that it was Napoleon speaking. He heard the man who said these words being addressed as *sire*. But he heard these words as if he was hearing the buzzing of a fly. He not only was not interested, he did not even notice, and at once forgot them. He had a burning in his head; he felt that he was loosing blood, and he saw above him that distant, lofty, and eternal sky. He knew that it was Napoleon – his hero – but at that moment, Napoleon seemed to him such a small, insignificant man compared with what was now happening between his soul and this lofty, infinite sky with clouds racing across it. To him it was all completely the same at that moment who was standing over him or what he said about him; he was only glad that people had stopped over him and only wished that those people would help him and bring him back to life, which seemed so beautiful to him, because he now understood it so differently. (*WP,* 291)

PART ONE

CALCULATING ON ABSENCE

CHAPTER 1

AN INHERITED DIS-INHERITANCE

One cannot help wishing to master absence.

(OG, 142)[1]

SANS MOT

April 2006, Paris. The Boulevard Saint Michel was closed. Policemen
stood in the side streets waiting for the demonstrators. A few students
were sitting in the empty road in front of the Place de la Sorbonne.
A huge concrete barricade had been erected at the front of the Place
to stop students occupying the Sorbonne. I had expected this, but
I was not prepared for the sight of the bricked-up entrance to the
Presses Universitaires de France, and it was only when I looked up to
the empty windows on the second floor that I realized that this great
bookshop had closed down. This bookshop, so redolent of the ambi-
ence of the new publications of the remarkable postwar generation
of French philosophers, was only waiting to become another Gap.

The bookshop La Hune on the Boulevard Saint Germain has the
extraordinary concentrated smell of fresh print and paper, and I can
only blame what follows on this inky Madeleine. On the table of new
books I found two testaments of mourning: Marie-Louise Mallet's
collection of the unfinished fragments of Derrida's *L'animal que donc
je suis*, and Hélène Cixous's *À insister – à Jacques Derrida*, written in
his absence from a 2005 conference on Derrida reading Cixous.[2]
Walking in the narrow spaces of the bookshop, I found myself pick-
ing up Sartre's *Nausea* (1938) and *Words* (1964). In 1964, as Derrida
was publishing his essays on Foucault and Lévinas, "Cogito and the
History of Madness" and "Violence and Metaphysics", Sartre was
publishing an autobiography, the death-knell of most writers and

thinkers, at least until Derrida began to take seriously Nietzsche's insistence that all works of philosophy are a kind of unconscious and involuntary memoir.[3]

"My god, already fifty years!" Derrida exclaims in "'Dead Man Running': *Salut, Salut*" (1996), marking the fiftieth anniversary of Sartre's journal *Les temps modernes*.[4] How does one mark an anniversary? Sartre begins *Nausea* without a date. "The first page" of Antoine Roquentin's notebooks, the editor tell us, "is not dated". At the start of this "*feuillet sans date*", Roquentin writes: "It would be best to write about events from day to day. To keep a journal to see clearly."[5] Roquentin has not seen clearly, and is still not seeing clearly. He wants to write about events from day-to-day in the hope that he will, one day, see clearly. Writing the journal is a wager, a bet. It is a wager on the clarity-to-come of writing from day-to-day that begins without a date, *sans date*.

Sartre's autobiography *Words* (*Les mots*) begins *without* words. For Sartre, because his father died soon after he was born, when one begins with the genealogy of the father, one begins *sans mot*. Sartre writes about his father's parents, who married under mistaken financial assumptions and – for 40 years – never spoke to one another.[6] Sartre's father, and Sartre's paternal genealogy, were conceived and produced *sans mot*, in 40 years of silence. *It was 40 years ago today!* How does one mark such an anniversary?

Sartre's father was created without words, and soon after creating his son, Jean-Baptise Sartre died. For Sartre, this absolute loss of the father, created and creating in silence, is nothing less than freedom itself. "I left behind me a young dead man," he writes, "who did not have time to be my father" (*M*, 18–19). Sartre keeps insisting that he was a child without a father – *sans date, sans mot, sans père*. For himself and on his own, he finds words and the title or heading of his project: to read and to write *les mots* without a father, without the rights and duties of a father. "I never stop creating myself; I am the donor and the receiver," he concludes (*M*, 26, 27–9).[7] Starting *sans mots*, Sartre creates himself, *and never stops becoming his own father*. Like the Platonic logos before him, which as Derrida noted, "believes itself to be its own father", Sartre never stops giving birth to himself (*OG*, 39).[8]

It is difficult to stay too long in the wonderfully concentrated ink of La Hune: its bookish air is not made for the living. I soon staggered out on to the Boulevard Saint Germain and wandered into another bookshop, the more spacious L'Écume des Pages.

Still thinking of Sartre, of starting without the date, without words, but always with the father as a self-creation, and staring at shelves of pristine books by Derrida, I opened a copy of *Of Grammatology* (1967). It was a posthumous copy, printed in November 2004, one month after the death of Jacques Derrida.

Contrary to Sartre, in *Of Grammatology* Derrida suggests that the *sans mot* can neither simply restore the father nor liberate the son (as his own father). Making a case for what he calls "the ambiguity of the Heideggerian situation", Derrida argues that one is always somewhere between containment and transgression:

> It is thus that, after evoking the "voice of being," Heidegger recalls that it is silent, mute, insonorous, wordless [*sans mot*], originarily *a-phonic (die Gewähr der lautlosen Stimme verborgener Quellen . . .)*. The voice of the sources is not heard. A rupture between the originary meaning of being and the word, between meaning and the voice, between "the voice of being" and the "*phonè*," between "the call of being," and articulated sound; such a rupture, which at once confirms a fundamental metaphor, and renders it suspect by accentuating its metaphoric discrepancy, translates the ambiguity of the Heideggerian situation with respect to the metaphysics of presence and logocentrism. It is at once contained within it and transgresses it. (*OG,* 22)

For Derrida, as much as he attempts to extricate being from the determinations of presence, from the assumption of a self-evident access to conditions of subjectivity and objectivity, Heidegger also calculates on a shifting absence that gathers itself towards the unifying forces of the logos (*OG,* 3, 10, 12, 20–4). Derrida responds to this calculating on absence by evoking a containment that also transgresses, a containment that un-contains itself. While in his later work Derrida will trace the centring resonances of "the gathering of thought" (*die Versammlung des Denkens*) in Heidegger, in *Of Grammatology* it is in his reading of Rousseau that he identifies the melancholy tradition of constantly regathering what has already dispersed.[9] Derrida writes of Rousseau's theory of language:

> The analysis of the "instruments" of language is therefore governed by the situation of pure dispersion which characterizes the state of nature. Language could have emerged only out of

dispersion. The "natural causes" by which one explains it are not recognized as such – natural – except in so far as they accord with the state of nature, which is determined by dispersion. This dispersion should no doubt be overcome by language but, for that very reason, it determines the *natural condition* of language.

The natural condition: it is remarkable that the original dispersion out of which language began continues to mark its milieu and essence. That language must traverse space, be obliged to be spaced [*s'espacer*], is not an accidental trait but the mark of its origin. In truth, dispersion will never be a past, a prelinguistic situation in which language would certainly have been born only to break with it. The original dispersion leaves its mark within language. (*OG*, 232)[10]

A decade after *Of Grammatology*, and 20 years before Derrida's long-awaited letter on Sartre marking the fiftieth anniversary of *Les temps modernes*, it was not Sartre but Maurice Blanchot, who provided Derrida with the chance to read in a different register the *sans* of *sans mot*, of the *sans père* that always ends up re-identifying the son or daughter with the father or, indeed, with the mother – and Derrida's legacy will always leave us somewhere between the "father" and the "mother".[11] In "Pas" (1976), a text published the year that *Of Grammatology* was published in America, Derrida argues that the "play (without play) of the *sans*" in Blanchot's works "disarticulates all logic of identity".[12] He goes on to examine Blanchot's strategic use of the "x *sans* x", in which the same *as* the same marks itself, re-marks itself, and is marked by the wholly other (*PA*, 84–5).

Derrida's rereading of the legacy of the *sans* can also be seen as part of his own critical response to the "fathers" of French philosophy and to the "sons and daughters" of his generation. Each generation re-marks itself as it hands itself on and is marked by the gaps that deviate and diverge in any genealogy, lineage or anniversary (*OG*, 101–2). This response is always marked not by the *sans mot* as much as the *sans cap*, by a heading out, by a going ahead that always loses its head, its head of the family.[13] As Derrida writes in "'Dead Man Running': *Salut, Salut*", when he recalls first reading *Les temps modernes* as an adolescent in Algeria:

I especially remember the ruptures, having intimately felt myself to be a convinced ally of both (Merleau, Camus, to cite just the

most spectacular), but the others that followed were also important for me. Such a genealogy! Such lineages! Such a family
without a father and without a leader and without a head! [*sans
père et sans chef et sans cap*!]. (*DMR*, 277)[14]

It was forty years ago today that Derrida taught the band to play . . .[15]
How does one celebrate the fortieth anniversary of the publication of
De la grammatologie (1967–2007) without reconstituting the head of
the family, without calculating on the absence of Jacques Derrida?
As he suggested in his 2003 paper "The 'World' of the Enlightenment
to Come (Exception, Calculation and Sovereignty)", "*both* calculation *and* the incalculable *are necessary*".[16] Calculation can never
entirely separate itself from the incalculable. We are always calculating *from* the incalculable. To begin to address the question of a
relation between Derrida, literature and war, we must first start with
the problem of calculating on absence.

ESSAI

The reception and translation of *De la grammatologie* can itself be
seen as a compelling example of this tradition of calculating on
absence. One can mark the anniversary of *De la grammatologie* by
starting with two anniversaries: 1967, the year of its publication, and
1976, the year of its translation into English. One can also begin with
two temptations, namely to speak of only one date, of one history of
publication, which hides a more profound temptation – to speak
without the date.

Of Grammatology, Gayatri Chakravorty Spivak's translation of
De la grammatologie, marks at once an indispensable part of the
history of Derrida's work in America and the English speaking
world, and it is also indicative of a remarkable Hegelian *Aufhebung*.
Spivak's long introduction, frozen in 1975, the endorsement on the
back cover from J. Hillis Miller and, most profoundly, the direction
from The Johns Hopkins University Press to put the book in the
"Literature" section of the bookshops, are all traces of the extraordinary introduction of Derrida's work in the English speaking world
30 years ago. My God, already 30 years! A book warning of the traps
and ruses of the *Aufhebung*, of the incessant colonization and appropriation of alterity, *De la grammatologie* to some extent underwent
this very process in its translation and reception in departments of

English literature, as it was caught up in ever anxious institutional battles over catching the next wave of the now.

De la grammatologie, first published in Paris in September 1967, was already one-of-three, the third in a trinity of Derrida's publications in one year in France: *L'écriture et la différence, La voix et le phénomène* and *De la grammatologie*. In America, in contrast, there was *Speech and Phenomena* (1973), and then *Of Grammatology* (1976), and finally, *Writing and Difference* (1978). Already, when it comes to thinking that it was forty years ago that *De la grammatologie* was first published, it is not a question of the "history" of one book, nor even of three books that all appeared in the same year, but of six books published over twelve years in four different places: *De la grammatologie/Of Grammatology* (1967–1978). One could also add to this proliferation of dates, two elusive and ghostly titles: Derrida's 1967 proposed doctoral thesis, *"De la grammatologie": Essai sur la permanence des concepts platonicien, aristotélicien et scolastique du signe écrit*, and his advertised, but unwritten, book from 1965–1966 on Heidegger, *La question de l'histoire*.[17]

Standing in the bookshop L'Écume des Pages and looking at the posthumous edition of *De la grammatologie*, the first thing I noticed was that while the opening words of the translation read, "The first part of this book . . .", the French reads, *"La première partie de cet essai . . ."* (*OG,* lxxxix; *Dlg,* 7). In other words, *De la grammatologie* is not a book. It is an essay, an attempt, a try, a testing out, a preliminary gesture that has no assurance of becoming a "book". *De la grammatologie* is no more and no less than an *essai*.

Published by Les Éditions Minuit, *De la grammatologie* was part of the *Collection "Critique"* created by Jean Piel in 1946 with Georges Bataille. As Derrida's first footnote on the first page emphasizes, *De la grammatologie* is an essay that begins as "the development" of an essay published in *Critique* in two parts in late 1965 and early 1966: it is an essay developing an essay (*Dlg,* 7). In this history of essays, of divided and preliminary parts, Derrida's work becomes part of a *series* of publications in the *Collection "Critique"*.

While the French edition says that the first part of the work is "the development" of an essay published in *Critique*, the English translation merely says that this first part "may be read as an essay published in the review *Critique"*, as if the first part is either simply a republication of an early essay or that this "book" itself somehow has no relation to an "essay" (*OG,* 323). *Of Grammatology* seems more than an essay: it is a book. This is all the more strange, because in her preface Spivak quotes Derrida's own well-known comments on the publication of *De la grammatologie* in an interview with Henri Ronse from December 1967, in which he says:

> In what you call my books, what is first of all put in question is the unity of the book and the unity of the "book" considered as a perfect totality, with all the implications of such a concept [. . .] One can take *Of Grammatology* as a long essay [*comme un long essai*] articulated in two parts (whose juncture is not empirical, but theoretical, systematic) *into the middle* of which one could staple *Writing and Difference*. *Grammatology* often calls upon it. In this case the interpretation of Rousseau would also be the twelfth "table" of the collection. Inversely, one could insert *Of Grammatology into the middle of Writing and Difference*, since six of the texts in that work preceded – *de facto* and *de jure* – the publication in *Critique* (two years ago) of the articles that announced *Of Grammatology*.[18]

Derrida goes on to discuss what he calls this "strange geometry" in relation to *Speech and Phenomena* (*IMP,* 4–5). For Derrida, when it comes to *Of Grammatology*, there is *plus d'un*: there is no one, always more than one *and* always more than two – a "strange geometry", which is always more and less than the geometry of a book.

When Spivak quotes and translates the last part of this 1967 interview in her introduction, she makes two ellipses in the text:

> *Of Grammatology* can be taken as a long essay articulated in two parts . . . between which one can stitch in *L'écriture et la différence*. *The Grammatology* often refers to it. In that case, the interpretation of Rousseau would be the twelfth item of the collection. Conversely, one could insert *Of Grammatology* in the middle of *L'écriture et la différence*, since six texts of the latter are anterior, in fact and in principle, to the publication . . . in *Critique,* of the articles announcing *Of Grammatology*. (*OG,* lxxix)

What are we to make of these seemingly small omissions from Derrida's interview? What silent restitution is at work here? In the first case, Spivak has taken out Derrida's parenthetical description of the joint or hinge that links the two parts of the *essai*: "One can take

Of Grammatology", Derrida had said, "as a long essay articulated in two parts (whose juncture [*soudure*, join, soldered joint] is not empirical, but theoretical, systematic)". Why did Spivak cut out Derrida's insistence that this division or cut in *De la grammatologie* is "*théoretique, systématique et non empirique"*?[19]

Since his early readings of Husserl, the qualification of the empirical had played an important role in Derrida's work. As he had first suggested in *The Problem of Genesis in Husserl's Philosophy* (1954), in attempting, on the one hand, to avoid an empiricism that denies any ideal, non-historical, objects and, on the other hand, to avoid an ahistorical Platonic idealism, Husserl is left oscillating in an irresolvable tension that will, ultimately, lead him to turn to "the Idea in the Kantian sense" as an ideal outside or beyond phenomenology.[20] Empiricism (as a historicism), denies the very possibility of the *theōria* that Derrida challenged without respite. For a critique of theorems, philosophemes and ideal objects – theorems, philosophemes, ideal objects must be possible.[21] When Derrida challenges Husserl's audacious argument for a historicity of ideal objects in his introduction to *The Origin of Geometry* (1962), he nonetheless affirms that theorems have had a profound and lasting influence.

If Spivak felt a need to erase this "theoretical" gesture in Derrida's description of *De la grammatologie* as an *essai* that is enmeshed in a strange geometry (not one book, not three books, but a *series* of essays that can cut into or interrupt the apparent linear sequence of each work), why does she then go on to delete the seemingly insignificant point that *two years* elapsed between the essays in *Critique* and the *essai* of *De la grammatologie*? Of course, this makes these two years seem very important. But I think this is not so much a question of dates, of simplifying the dates from 1965–1967 in the 1976 translation, as of Spivak's need for *Of Grammatology* to be a book, to be received as a coherent, serious, even if preliminary, book on "de-construction". In her translation, Spivak cuts out the interval between the *essai De la grammatologie* (1965–1966) and the *essai De la grammatologie* (1967), because she needs *Of Grammatology* to be a book. When she discusses the relation between the 1965–1966 "review articles" and *Of Grammatology*, it is to emphasize that we are now dealing with a book: "It is fascinating to study the changes and interpolations made in the text of the review articles as they were transformed into *the book*" (*OG*, lxxx, my emphasis). This sovereign gesture of removing the interval, of closing the gap, in the name of presenting a "de-construction" of Western Metaphysics, is a calculating on absence *par excellence*. *Of Grammatology* is an *Aufhebung* of *De la grammatologie* because it suppresses the strange geometry of Derrida's work as a series, as a series of intervals.

While Derrida writes from the first line of his work that this is not a book, and entitles the first chapter "The End of the Book and the Beginning of Writing", Spivak seems to need Derrida's work to be a book for America, for the English Departments of America. With the assistance of The Johns Hopkins University Press who, as we have seen, decided that *Of Grammatology* should be sold in bookshops in the "Literature" section, Derrida's work became part of the vanguard of a vastly complex Anglo-American institutional warfare between the fathers and sons, the mothers and daughters, the professors and patrons of "English Literature". One can see this as an example of the "recourse to literature as [a] reappropriation of presence," which Derrida warns of in his reading of Rousseau (*OG,* 144).[22]

Beyond the over anthologized "Structure, Sign and Play in the Discourse of the Human Sciences", *Of Grammatology* would become *The Book of Derrida.*[23] This particular history of translation, with "Structure, Sign and Play" first appearing in English in 1970, and *Of Grammatology* in 1976, also launched a host of academic careers and even schools founded on the "ahistorical" and "apolitical" *"il n'y a pas de hors-texte"* reading of Derrida's work. While this approach to Derrida has diminished – in no small part due to the 2003–2005 translation of his 1975–1990 essays on the politics of the institution, *Right to Philosophy* – it is worth recalling that his first work translated into English, the 1968 paper "The Ends of Man" in 1969, opens with Derrida placing the question of politics and the relationship to the institution at the centre of his work:

> Every philosophical colloquium necessarily has a political significance. And not only due to that which has always linked the essence of the philosophical to the essence of the political. Essential and general, this political import nevertheless burdens the *a priori* link between philosophy and politics, aggravates it in a way, and also determines it when the philosophical colloquium is announced as an international colloquium. Such is the case here.[24]

Derrida's first published essay, "Force and signification", appeared in *Critique* in 1963, and he would publish four more essays in

Critique in the 1960s.[25] He would also later publish *Margins – of Philosophy* and *Positions* in the *Collection "Critique."* The *Collection "Critique"* seems an eminently French, Parisian context in which to place and hold on to *De la grammatologie*. However, it is important to avoid the temptation of reducing the history of *Of Grammatology* back to its pure and authentic source, to resist this invitation to the *Aufhebung*. In a 1966 issue of *Critique* devoted to Blanchot, which appeared six months before "De la grammatologie (I)", there is an essay by Paul de Man. De Man would publish another essay on Georges Poulet in *Critique* in 1969, and Samuel Weber had an article in the 1969 double issue devoted to Walter Benjamin.[26] In other words, even in the midst of the *Collection "Critique"*, the history of *De la grammatologie* is already transatlantic. Nor was the designation of the *essai De la grammatologie* as a book confined to its American translation: on the back cover of the French edition Derrida's work is called *"ce livre"*. Everyone, it seems, except Derrida, needed *De la grammatologie/Of Grammatology* to be a book.

De la grammatologie/Of Grammatology is part of a series of intervals that mark the histories of publication, reception and translation. From his earliest work on Husserl, Derrida had warned that one must be attentive to the temptations of simply embracing a diachrony (a linear development in time, a series without singularity) or a synchrony (a timeless cut or structural moment, a one time outside-the-series) (*EHO,* 61). In "At This Very Moment in This Work Here I Am" (1980), Derrida meditated on the inadmissible hybrid of a "dia-synchrony," which he describes as a "serial *one time*, the 'several times' that will have taken place only once," a dia-synchrony that marks at once the possibility and the ruin of any pure diachrony or synchrony (*ATV,* 168). *De la grammatologie/Of Grammatology* is part of a remarkable series of publications and translations in France and America, and it is a singularity that has "taken place only once". It is also a singularity that cannot help but be repeated, that cannot help but give itself to be read, to be translated, again and again, to give itself to another day, to the day of the other. *It was 40 years ago today . . .*

MORE OR LESS: THE TRUTH

Despite the inadvertent attempts to secure *Of Grammatology* as a *resource* without resistance and to calculate *on* absence, from the opening lines Derrida insists that a grammatology must run the risk "of never being able to define the unity of its project or its object" (*OG,* 4). It is likely that Derrida already had in mind here his later critique of Heidegger's gathering or recollection of thinking. The sentence that follows on metaphysical epochs certainly gestures to Heidegger, though it begins with the methods of Descartes:

> Such a science of writing runs the risk of never being established [*voir le jour*] as such and with that name. Of never being able to define the unity of its project or its object. Of not being able either to write its discourse on method or to describe the limits of its field. For essential reasons: the unity of all that allows itself to be attempted today through the most diverse concepts of science and of writing, is, in principle, more or less covertly [*plus ou moins secrètement*] yet always determined by an historico-metaphysical epoch of which we merely glimpse the *closure.* I do not say the end. (*OG,* 4; *Dlg,* 13–14)

Today, Derrida argued in 1967, the history of metaphysics "more or less" determines concepts of science and writing. Today, this is a question of truth. In "The End of the Book and the Beginning of Writing", Derrida is concerned with that which – one can call it "writing" in double quotation marks – "no longer issues from a logos" (the great unifier) and brings about the "de-construction" "of all the significations that have their source in that of the logos", He goes on to add, "particularly the signification of *truth*" (*OG,* 10). Derrida then distinguishes the logos and the truth:

> All the metaphysical determinations of truth, and even the one beyond metaphysical onto-theology that Heidegger reminds us of, are more or less immediately inseparable from the instance of the logos, or of a reason thought within the lineage of the logos, in whatever sense it is understood: in the pre-Socratic or the philo-sophical sense, in the sense of God's infinite understanding or in the anthropological sense, in the pre-Hegelian or the post-Hegelian sense. Within this logos, the original and essential link to the *phonē* has never been broken. (*OG,* 10–11)

Within the logos, the link to the *phonē* "has never been broken": the logos and the *phonē* are always linked. But the link between the logos and truth is slightly different: "all the metaphysical determinations of truth [. . .] are more or less immediately [*plus ou moins immédiate-ment*] inseparable from the instance of the logos" (*OG*, 11; *Dlg*, 21).

Derrida gestures to the complexity of this "more or less" immediate inseparability when, after having said that the link between the *phonē* and the logos "has never been broken", he then qualifies this relation: "As has more or less implicitly been determined [*plus ou moins implicitement déterminée*], the essence of the *phonē* would be immediately proximate to that which within 'thought' as logos relates to 'meaning,' produces it, receives it, speaks it, 'composes' it" (*OG*, 11; *Dlg*, 21). In *Of Grammatology* we have to be attentive to a rhetorical strategy that is always more and less than a rhetoric: *plus ou moins secrètement, plus ou moins immédiatement, plus ou moins implicite-ment*. Derrida is bracketing (in a quasi-Husserlian sense) *and* unbracketing the determination of the concepts of the secret, the immediate and the implicit. The force of this (un)bracketing is apparent some pages later when Derrida both asserts and qualifies the domination of the Hegelian *Aufhebung*: "the *Aufhebung* is, more or less implicitly [*plus ou moins implicitement*], the dominant concept of nearly all histories of writing, even today" (*OG*, 25; *Dlg*, 40).

Always more or less implicit, never merely self-evidently implicit or not implicit, the *plus ou moins* more or less outdistances and exceeds the labour of the *Aufhebung* to harness what is not stated but understood and what is reserved but present (*EHO*, 123). This, more or less, is a calculating *from* absence. In "From Restricted to General Economy", also published in 1967, Derrida uses the *plus ou moins* and *plus et moins* to reread Bataille's use of the concept of "sover-eignty" as the absolute surpassing of Hegel:

> Sovereignty, as we shall verify, is more and less [*plus et moins*] than lordship, more or less [*plus ou moins*] free than it, for example; and what we are saying about the predicate 'freedom' can be extended to every characteristic of lordship. Simultaneously more and less [*à la fois plus et moins*] than lordship, sovereignty is totally other.[27]

Derrida constantly evokes the *plus ou moins* in *Of Grammatology* to disrupt the temptation to define the *unity* of both his project and its object, to create either the assumption of a totality to-be-refuted or an other-than-totality as an absolute resource of alterity:

It follows that not only has phoneticization never been omnipotent but also that it has always already begun to undermine the mute signifier. "Phonetic" and "nonphonetic" are therefore never pure qualities of certain systems of writing, they are the abstract characteristics of typical elements, more or less [*plus ou moins*] numerous and dominant within all systems of signification in general. Their importance owes less to their quantitative distribution than to their structural organization.

(*OG,* 89; *Dlg,* 135)

It is therefore a declared and militant Rousseauism. Already it imposes on us a very general question that will orient all our readings more or less directly [*orientera plus ou moins directement toutes nos lectures*]: to what extent does Rousseau's appurtenance to logocentric metaphysics and within the philosophy of presence – an appurtenance that we have already been able to recognize and whose exemplary figure we must delineate – to what extent does it limit a scientific discourse?

(*OG,* 106; *Dlg,* 155)

But once languages are constituted, the polarity need/passion, and the entire supplementary structure, remain operative within each linguistic system: languages are more or less close [*plus ou moins proches*] to pure passion, that is to say more or less distant [*plus ou moins éloignées*] from pure need, more or less close [*plus ou moins proches*] to pure language or pure nonlanguage.

(*OG,* 217; *Dlg,* 310)[28]

On at least one occasion, Derrida is explicit about this strategic importance of dislodging the *plus ou moins* from an assured determination of *the* "more" or *the* "less". In his reading of Levi-Strauss, he writes: "It is precisely the property of the power of differance to modify life less and less as it spreads out more and more" (*modifier de moins en moins la vie à mesure qu'il s'étend*) (*OG,* 131; *Dlg,* 191).[29] Derrida takes care here to differentiate the "power of differance" (*pouvoir de différance*) from an Aristotelian understanding of potentiality (*dúnamis*) and a Cartesian notion of extension (*extensio*).[30] We will come back to the question of using potentiality as an assured resource in the following chapter.

Derrida is aiming here at the great either-or of ontology. The supplement, he argues in the last pages of his reading of Rousseau, is "less than nothing [*moins que rien*] and yet, to judge by its effects, much more than nothing [*plus que rien*]. The supplement is neither a presence nor an absence. No ontology can think its operation" (*OG*, 314; *Dlg*, 442). *De la grammatologie/Of Grammatology* is more *and* less than a book, and this is nothing less and nothing more than Derrida's recasting or retranslating (the history of) the truth.

LA BIZARRERIE: AN UNAVOIDABLE HOSPITALITY

On the back cover of *De la grammatologie*, the write-up begins with a quote from Rousseau: "Languages are made to be spoken, writing is only used to *supplement* speech [. . .] Writing is nothing but the *representation* of speech; it is *bizarre* that one gives more care to the determining of the image than to the object."[31] After the quote, someone has commented: "*Ce livre est donc voué à la bizarrerie.*" This book – or this *essai* – is therefore devoted to the bizarre.

The well-known relation that Derrida traces between writing and speech in *Of Grammatology* is not followed to reassert the place of writing or to deny the place of speech, but to address the strangeness of the more *and* less, the *Unheimlichkeit* between speech and writing, between the *essai* and the book (*OG*, 56).[32] In addressing an unavoidable hospitality towards *la bizarrerie*, Derrida gestures to a reluctant and persistent calculating *from* absence in the works of Rousseau.

Derrida had first quoted this passage on *la bizarrerie*, taken from a fragment of Rousseau's *Essay on the Origin of Languages*, as an epigraph in his 1965–1966 article in *Critique*, and it has the same position in the *De la grammatologie* of 1967, opening the chapter on "Linguistics and Grammatology" (*OG*, 27). This quasi subtitle on the *bizarre* is then quoted or re-cited in the chapter itself, giving it what Derrida would later call an interlacing oscillation between the inside and the outside of the work.[33] This quasi-subtitle then links Saussure and Rousseau and inaugurates the important passage on the strange relation between speech and writing and the unavoidable oscillations of re-presentation:

Rousseau: "writing is nothing but the representation of speech; it is *bizarre* that one gives more care to the determining of the *image*

28

than to the *object.*" Saussure: "When one says that a certain letter must be pronounced in a certain way, one takes the image for the model [. . .] To explain this oddity [*bizarrerie*], one adds that in this case it is a matter of an exceptional pronunciation." What is intolerable and fascinating is indeed the intimacy intertwining [*enchevêtrant*] image and thing, *graphie* and *phonē*, to the point where by an effect of mirroring, of inversion and perversion, speech seems in its turn the speculum of writing, which "thus usurps the main role." Representation mingles [*s'enlace*] with what it represents, to the point where one speaks as one writes, one thinks as if the represented were nothing more than the shadow or reflection of the representer. [. . .] The reflection, the image, the double, splits open what it redoubles. The origin of speculation becomes a difference. What can look at itself is not one and the law of the addition of the origin to its representation, of the thing to its image, is that one plus one makes at least three. (*OG,* 36; *Dlg,* 54–5, trans. modified)

Over a hundred pages after he uses *la bizarrerie* to link Saussure and Rousseau to the oscillations of representation, Derrida echoes this passage in his reading of the supplement. As a replacing and displacing supplement, writing "diverts the immediate presence of thought to speech into representation and the imagination. This recourse is not only 'bizarre,' but dangerous" (*OG,* 144).[34] The movement of the supplement is *bizarre,* "because it is neither presence nor absence" (*OG,* 154).[35] It is bizarre because it gestures to an interlacing oscillation that cannot be reduced to the *alternative* of either presence or absence. Nor can it be reduced to the Heideggerian reconfiguration of "a presence sheltered in absence" (*eins ins Abwesen geborgenes Anwesen*).[36] It was forty years ago today . . . that Derrida left metaphysics and its ends limping.

It is with *Of Grammatology* that Derrida also began his long circonfessions around the problem of autobiography by interweaving the drama of the first five books of Rousseau's confessions into his reading of the *Essay on the Origin of Languages.*[37] In the *Confessions* (1770), Rousseau gives *la bizarre* a prominent role in the fault lines or extreme outcrops of his confessions, suggesting that what is most bizarre is the *narrative* of telling his story, of telling one's own story. As Rousseau observes in Book Eight, "The success of my first publications had made me fashionable. The condition in life that

I had chosen for myself excited the public's curiosity; they wanted to know this bizarre man, who courted no one and who cared for nothing except for living free and happy in his own chosen way" (*CF*, 357). It is not with Sartre, but with Rousseau that we must start, that other philosopher as novelist and autobiographer.

When his beloved Mme de Warens proposes that she and Rousseau become lovers, and first "lays down her conditions" and gives him "a week to think it over", he describes her behaviour as a "bizarre." What is bizarre to Rousseau is not that they sleep together, but that she takes this "precautionary step" and insist on "the most grave formalities" (*CF*, 190). Before and after this, Rousseau links his narrative, foreshadowing and returning to this event, by characterizing his surprising change in relationship with Mme de Warens as "bizarre". In Book Two, he warns: "there was certainly something singular in my feelings for this charming woman; indeed, they will be found in due course to have had their bizarre aspect [*des bizarreries*], which no one would expect" (*CF*, 51).[38] One page after he has described her formality and postponement over their change in relationship as bizarre, and one page before he admits that "it was as though I had committed incest", Rousseau returns to his earlier promise: "I promised that the story of my attachment to Maman would have its bizarre aspects [*j'ai promis des bizarreries dans l'histoire*]; here surely is one that no one would have expected" (*CF*, 191–2; *LC*, 238). From Book Two to Book Five, it is the story (*l'histoire*), the narrative itself, which has become "bizarre".

If the writing of his confession is bizarre, Rousseau also suggests that reading is bizarre. Reading avidly as an adolescent, Rousseau was "filled with distaste for everything that was within my reach", and it is this wonderful and disturbing dislocation from what is around him that saves him from his incomprehensible sensual desires (*CF*, 39). Only literature it seems can save us, but literature is always the ideality of an escape that also dislocates and displaces the self-evident subject. Rousseau writes:

> My troubled imagination did, however, find a way out of this curious situation, which saved me from myself and calmed my emergent sensuality. This was to dwell on situations that had appealed to me during my reading, to recall them, to vary and combine them, and to appropriate them in such a way that I became one of the characters I imagined and could envisage

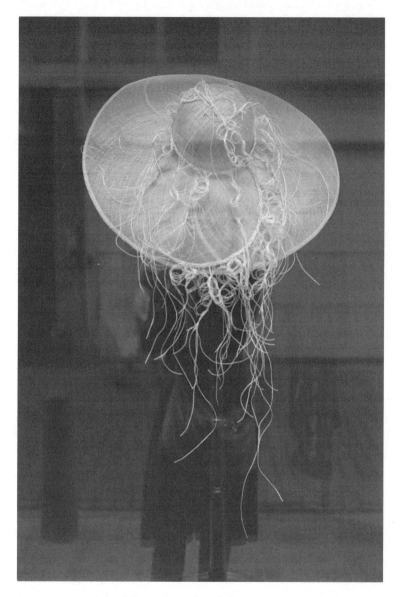

Figure 1 Antwerp, 2007 © Jane Brown 2009

myself always in some role that was dear to my heart; I managed, in other words, to place myself in fictional situations that allowed me to forget the unhappiness of my real one. This love of imaginary objects and the ease with which I became absorbed in them had the effect, eventually, of turning me against everything that surrounded me, and of confirming me in that taste for solitude which has remained with me ever since. We will see more than once during the course of my story the bizarre effects [*les bizarre effets*] of this predilection. (*CF*, 40; *LC*, 69)

Rousseau turns to reading to escape from his bizarre sensual desires, and once he is "absorbed" into what he reads, he endures and produces a new series of "bizarre effects" as he turns against the mundane world around him. He turns from the bizarre and returns to the bizarre and always finds himself in the midst of what he is reading. Once again, as with Mme de Warens, Rousseau promises and foreshadows a narrative of the bizarre. The narrative can only structure itself, give itself an apparently clear line, by turning to *and* turning away from the bizarre. This is what Derrida would later call the *fort/ da* of confession.[39]

As Maurice Blanchot observed, "desperate to write against writing", Rousseau associated writing and reading "with a power of strangeness under the threat of which he will little by little lose all stable rapport with a self". [40] The "bizarre" circumstances of the loss of his virginity, his insatiable appetite for reading, the almost moment of "incest" with Mme de Warens, do nothing to arrest this sense of having to endure, to reason *with*, to reason *from*, the unavoidable visitations of *la bizarrerie*. As Derrida suggests, *la bizarrerie* is "the 'rationality' [that] . . . no longer issues from a logos" (*OG*, 10).[41]

What is remarkable about Rousseau is that he never claims in the *Confessions* to be able to avoid the visitations of *la bizarrerie*. He attests to an unavoidable hospitality in desire, in reading, in writing, in telling one's own story. In *De la grammatologie/Of Grammatology*, Derrida gestures to a kind of unavoidable hospitality, to a hospitality that has already taken place before the good conscience of any invitation. This unavoidable hospitality is more or less the possibility of *la bizarrerie*, of a bizarre relation or narrative that cannot be reduced "to a dialectical and teleological determination of negativity", that cannot be secured as an assured resource of either presence or absence (*OG*, 40). It can, however, be discerned, Derrida suggests, by a gap (*écart*) that moves (*écarter*):

Nature is affected – from without – by an overturning which modifies it in its interior, denatures it and obliges it to be separated from itself. Nature denaturing itself, being separated from itself [*s'écartant* d'elle-même], naturally welcoming [*accueillant*] its outside into its inside, is *catastrophe*, a natural event that overthrows nature, or *monstrosity*, a natural deviation [*écart naturel*] within nature. (*OG*, 41; *Dlg*, 61, trans. modified)[42]

This "unity of nature", Derrida writes, is "shaped and undermined by a strange difference which constitutes it by breaching it" (*OG*, 198). Between nature and itself – *phusis* – there is always a moving gap "naturally welcoming [*accueillant*] its outside into its inside": a series of intervals that mark an unavoidable hospitality which exceeds our inexhaustible attempts to calculate on absence.

Of Grammatology: the histories, and narratives and anniversaries of an unavoidable hospitality that has begun neither with the father nor without the father. In marking a posthumous anniversary in the work of Jacques Derrida, the sons and daughters of this inheritance are left with neither the comfort of a paternal or maternal blessing, nor with the ease of a patriarchal or matriarchal dismissal. This anniversary is therefore devoted to *la bizarrerie*, to the terrible inherited dis-inheritance of the moving gap, of "the weight of this sad time" that gives itself neither to the presence nor to the absence of the name that is inscribed on the front cover of *De la grammatologie/ Of Grammatology*.[43]

CHAPTER 2

ABSENCE AS PURE POSSIBILITY

Thought within its concealed relation to the logic of the supplement, the concept of virtuality (like the entire problematic of power and act) undoubtedly has for its function, for Rousseau in particular and within metaphysics in general, the systematic predetermining of becoming as production and development, evolution or history, through the substitution of the accomplishment of a dynamis for the substitution of a trace, of pure history for pure play [. . .]. Now the movement of supplementarity seems to escape this alternative and to permit us to think it.

(OG, 187, trans. modified)

From his early work on phenomenology, structuralism and Lévinas's reaction against Heidegger, we can see that Derrida begins not only with a critique of the logocentrism of presence, but also with a warning against a renewed idealization of absence in which the other is equated with a unique effacement or passivity that enables a philosophical discourse, a radical ethics or even a literary theory.[1] It is in this period from 1954 to 1964, before the publication of *Of Grammatology*, that Derrida articulates the ruses and traps of calculating on absence as a pure possibility.

In his 1954 dissertation, *The Problem of Genesis in Husserl's Philosophy*, Derrida had been interested in the moment when Husserl, almost despite himself, turns back to Kant:

The whole purpose of the present work is to show how Husserl, right from the start, turns upside down the Kantian doctrine of the ideality of time and is finally obliged, after endless detours, precautions, and subtleties, to reintroduce an ideality of time in the form of a teleology. (*PG,* 189 n. 11)

In his 1962 introduction to *The Origin of Geometry* (1936), Derrida traces this moment of Husserl turning back to Kant as a turning back to Aristotle.[2]

"The geometer", Husserl argues in *Ideas I* (1913), "is not interested" in morphological concepts, in "actual forms intuitable through the sense". These "vague" forms of and from the senses are more properly the province of "the descriptive student of nature". The words of the student of nature are "*essentially and not accidentally inexact*". For Husserl, the form (morphological) and matter (hyletic) of essences are necessarily inexact, while geometrical concepts in contrast, are "exact concepts" or " '*ideal' concepts*".[3] Husserl insists that "the highly impor-tant *Kantian concept of the Idea*" should be kept "free from all contact" with these descriptive or "general concepts of the formal or material essence". This clear distinction allows him to reconstruct the phenome-nological order: "Exact concepts have their correlates in essences, which have the character of 'Ideas' in the Kantian sense. Over against these Ideas or ideal essences stand the morphological essences, as correlates of descriptive concepts" (*I,* 191).

For Husserl, because the idea in the Kantian sense is kept "free from all contact" with the form and matter of essence, it is the *pure possibility* of the phenomenological distinction between ideal essences and morphological essences. This pure possibility provides a limit, a goal, a teleology to which the inexact essences can "'approximate' more or less, without ever reaching them" (*I,* 191). The inexact will labour ceaselessly and fruitlessly to reach the exact. Derrida describes this as the movement toward "the ideal and invariant pole of an infi-nite approximation". This movement is founded on the "idealization of anticipation": the inexact can only anticipate the exact. It has no chance, or mischance, of an alternative: it is a teleology of pure pos-sibility (*EHO,* 134).

For Husserl, the inexact is always incomplete in relation to the exact. In *The Problem of Genesis,* Derrida links this "essential incom-pletion" to Husserl's analysis of temporality. He writes: "It is its essential incompletion that would be apprehended at each moment through a concrete intuition; this latter is the very movement that constitutes the pure present" (*PG,* 98). Presence is the ideality of the exact *in relation to* the "essential incompletion" of the inexact. Presence is the unification of our singular, concrete apprehension of temporality. The certainty of this incompletion is an invitation to the unity of an infinite ideality. Derrida neatly summarizes this five years later in his 1959 paper "'Genesis and Structure' and Phenomenology":

> What Husserl seeks to underline by means of this comparison between an exact and a morphological science, and what we must retain here, is the principled, essential, and structural impossibility of closing a structural phenomenology. It is the infinite opening of what is experienced, which is designated at several moments of Husserlian analysis by reference to an *Idea in the Kantian sense*, that is, the irruption of the infinite into consciousness, which permits the unification of the temporal flux of consciousness just as it unifies the object and the world by anticipation, and despite an irreducible incompleteness [*inachèvement*]. It is the strange *presence* of this Idea which also permits every transition to the limit and the production of all exactitude. (*GS*, 162)[4]

In his account in *Ideas* of the difference between the inexact and the exact, Husserl notes that these ideal concepts "express something which one cannot 'see'" (*I*, 190). As Derrida points out in his introduction to *The Origin of Geometry*, one cannot *see* the idea in the Kantian sense. Phenomenology is devoted to the problem of what appears and to "the *possibility* of its appearing" (*EHO*, 150). The idea in the Kantian sense becomes "the regulative possibility" of phenomenology. The Idea is the unseen origin of phenomenology: the *not x but the possibility of x*. This is absence as a pure possibility that can *only* reconstitute presence. Derrida will later argue in *Of Grammatology* that while this structure of absence remains a pure possibility, *as* a possibility it can also never be pure.

OMBRE ET LUMIÈRE

For Derrida, the unseen Idea in Husserl's work is a thought of the future as an "infinite unity" that makes "the Living Present" and "the phenomenalization of time" possible. This *unseen* and *thought unity*, "which never phenomenalizes itself," is the possibility – the ideal "origin" of phenomenology (*EHO*, 136–7). Absence as pure possibility becomes *darkness*. The unseen Idea, Derrida writes, takes phenomenology to a region "where darkness risks being no longer the provision of appearing or the field which offers itself to phenomenal light, but the forever nocturnal source of the light itself" (*EHO,* 137). This darkness, this absence as the *absolute resource* for the pure possibility of seeing, the idealization of anticipation and essential incompletion and the ideality of time, is absolutely necessary for phenomenology. It is with this absence as an idealized darkness that Derrida turns to Aristotle:

> It is not by chance that there is no phenomenology of the Idea. The latter cannot be given in person, nor determined in an evidence, for it is only the possibility of evidence and the openness of "seeing" itself; it is only *determinability* as the horizon for every intuition in general, the invisible milieu of seeing analogous to the diaphaneity of the Aristotlelian Diaphanous, an elemental third, but the one source of the seen and the visible: "by diaphanous I mean what is visible, and yet not visible, and not yet visible in itself, but rather owing its visibility to the colour of something else." It is thanks to this alone "that the colour of a thing is seen". (*EHO,* 138; S, 418b)

Like the Aristotelian concept of the diaphanous, which is "the invisible milieu of seeing", the unseen Idea is absence as the pure possibility, as "the one source" of phenomenology.

Derrida returns to the question of the origin as an unseen "thought unity", and an instance of the "diaphanousness of pure ideality", in "Force and Signification" (1963) (*EHO,* 106).[5] Structuralism, he argues, is still reliant on phenomenology and this renders it unable to respond "to language's peculiar inability [*impuissance*] to emerge from itself in order to articulate its origin [*dire son origine*]."[6] If "force is the other of language without which language would not be what it is," Derrida insists that one must not refer "to the *thought* of force [*la* pensée *de la force*]". The *other* of language cannot be reduced to the unassailable priority of a "thought unity" in which "all value is first constituted by a theoretical subject." The "supreme value" of such a metaphysical tradition, Derrida adds, is "diaphanousness [*la diaphanéité*]" (*FS,* 27; *FeS,* 46).

In metaphysics, force cedes its place to form, to a lightened, enlightened *form*. Derrida insists on this: the force/weakness opposition "can only be articulated in the language of form, through images of shadow and light [*par ombre et lumière*]" (*FS,* 28; *FeS,* 46). Darkness is a resource of ideality. If "force", as the other of language is to resist the role played by absence as pure possibility, it cannot be determined as a darkness. Derrida writes that

> force is not darkness [*la force n'est pas l'obscurité*], and it is not hidden under a form for which it would serve as substance, matter or crypt. Force cannot be conceived on the basis of an oppositional couple, that is, on the basis of the complicity between phenomenology and occultism. (*FS,* 28; *FeS,* 46)

In "Violence and Metaphysics" (1964), Derrida suggests that, in trying to challenge what seems to be "the ancient clandestine friendship between light and power [*la lumière et la puissance*], the ancient complicity between theoretical objectivity and technico-political possession", Emmanuel Lévinas evokes "a certain non-light [*non-lumière*] before which all violence is to be quieted and disarmed" (*VM,* 91, 85: *VeM,* 136, 126). For Derrida, in evoking this "non-light", Lévinas conjures and despite himself, holds on to "the oppressive and luminous identity of the same", until "everything given to me within light appears as given to myself by myself" (*VM,* 92–2). In an important passage, Derrida goes on to argue against both the creation of a totality-as-light and the determination of absence as a non-light that always remains itself in its pure passivity, alterity and resistance:

> If light is the element of violence, one must combat light with a certain other light, in order to avoid the worst violence, the silence and the night which precedes or represses discourse. This *vigilance* is a violence chosen as the least violence by a philosophy which takes history, that is, finitude, seriously; a philosophy aware of itself as *historical* in each of its aspects (in a sense which tolerates neither finite totality, nor positive infinity), and aware of itself, as Levinas says in another sense, as *economy*. But again, an economy which in being history, can be *at home* neither in the finite totality which Levinas calls the Same nor in the positive presence of the Infinite. Speech is doubtless the first defeat of violence, but paradoxically, violence did not exist before the possibility of speech. The philosopher (man) *must* speak and write within this war of light [*guerre de la lumière*], a war in which he always already knows

Figure 2 Hermitage, St. Petersburg 2007 © Jane Brown 2009.

himself to be engaged, a war which he knows is inescapable, except by denying discourse, that is, by risking the worst violence. (*VM*, 117; *VeM*, 172–3, trans. modified)

STOP

For Derrida, there is an unavoidable "war of light", or rather of "shadow and light", which cannot be overcome or avoided by turning to "darkness" as an absolute or pure resource. One can contrast this to Giorgio Agamben's readings of Aristotle, Heidegger and Derrida. In the midst of "On Potentiality", a lecture given in Lisbon in 1986, Agamben writes: "I would like to pause on a figure of potentiality that seems to me to be particularly significant and that appears in *De Anima*. I refer to darkness, to shadows."[7] How does one *pause* on a *figure* of *potentiality*, particularly when this figure of potentiality is "darkness" *or* "shadows"? This ability to stop seems even more fraught if one asks what is the difference between darkness (the absence of light) and shadows (relative darkness)? Agamben has turned to the question of potentiality because it has always been connected to what he calls "that part of humanity that has grown and developed its potency [*potenza*] to the point of imposing its power over the whole planet". The traditional concept of potentiality, he suggests, has been defined as an imperial power and a potency that leads to global power.

In *Glas* (1974), Derrida had warned, "what Hegel says of the structure of *Potenz* – and this will be true of the dialectical moment – explains for us how he, Hegel, meant to be read" (*G*, 105a). Hegelian *Potenz* is an extraordinary quasi-Aristotelian structure of ruptures that maintain continuity. It also describes, Derrida points out, the ability to pause, to stop:

In each particular totality, as such, the absolute totality *comes to a halt, stops itself* [s'arrête], stops its necessity. The particular totality then takes, as a part, a certain independence, a certain subsistence. To come to a halt, to stop itself, is here *sich hemmen*. *Hemmen* is often translated by inhibit, suppress. The infinite totality inhibits itself in the *Potenz*. This totality limits itself, gives itself a form [*se donne une forme*], goes out from a certain *apeiron*, suspends itself, puts an end to itself, but the delay it thus takes on itself (*hemmen* also signifies delay, defer) is the positive condition of its appearing, of its glory. Without the delay, without the suspensive and inhibiting constriction, the absolute would not manifest itself. So the delay is also an advance, progress, an anticipation on the absolute unfolding of the absolute. (*G,* 106–7a)[8]

To begin by stopping at the question of potentiality is perhaps already to have moved from the potential to the actual. What is the actuality *of* the potential? This seems to be a Hegelian – and Aristotelian – question *par excellence.*

FIRE

"To pause on a figure of potentiality", Agamben starts "from a certain *apeiron*". Aristotle, he argues, "opposed potentiality to actuality, *dynamis* to *engergia*, and bequeathed this opposition to Western philosophy" (*OP,* 178). Does Aristotle oppose potentiality to actuality? Leaving aside this problem for the moment, Agamben starts by quoting an *aporia* from Aristotle's treatise *De Anima* or *On the Soul*:

> There is an *aporia* as to why there is no sensation of the senses themselves [*dià tí kaí tōn aisthéseon aùtōn où gínetai aíhia msthēsis*]. Why is it that, in the absence of external objects, the senses do not give any sensation, although they contain fire, earth, water, and other elements of which there is sensation? This happens because sensibility [*aisthētikòn*] is not actual but only potential [*oùk éstin energeía, àllà dunámei mónon*]. (*OP,* 178; S, 417a)[9]

According to Agamben, for there to be a prior faculty of x, "we are already in the domain of potentiality" (*OP,* 178). The primary question of potentiality is how one has "a faculty". However, just after the passage from *De Anima* that Agamben quotes, Aristotle writes:

> We use the word "perceive" [*aisthánesthai*] in two [*dikhōs*] ways, for we say that what has the power [*dunámei*] to hear or see, "sees" or "hears," even though it is at the moment asleep, and also that what is actually [*ènergoun*] seeing or hearing, "sees" or "hears". (*S,* 417a)[10]

For Heidegger, as we shall see, Aristotle's great contribution to philosophy was this recognition of the "twofold" nature of being.

41

When it comes to a faculty, Aristotle argues, there is always *more than one*: perception is potential *and* actual. Aristotle goes on to write: "Hence 'sense' too must have two meanings [*dikhōs àn légoito*], sense potential, and sense actual" (*S,* 417a). When it comes to words and meanings, perception and sense are potential *and* actual.

Just before the passage that Agamben quotes, Aristotle also reminds his readers that, "sensation depends, as we have said, on a process of movement or affection from without." The *aporia* arises for Aristotle not so much from a potentiality that is on its own, as Agamben suggests, as the problem of why it is that when the "outside" does nothing, the "inside" also does nothing. This connection is perhaps more obvious in J. A. Smith's translation of *De Anima*, when the first phrase of the *aporia* ("why do we not perceive the sense themselves") is not made into a sentence in its own right, as it is in Agamben's text: "why do we not perceive the sense themselves, or why without stimulation of external objects do they not produce sensation?" (*S,* 417a). Why, Aristotle wonders, without the influence of the outside, if the inside has the capacity, the potential, does it do *nothing*?

One would have to ask, when is the "inside" ever truly on its own, without the "outside", and does Aristotle himself believe that one can pause or stop for any length of time at such a moment? For Agamben, the *aporia* of the inside that does nothing when it is on its own is indicative of the nature of the potential: "In this sense, we say of the architect that he or she has the *potential* to build, of the poet that he or she has the *potential* to write poems" (*OP,* 179). It is worth noting here that it is Agamben, and not Aristotle, who introduces the poet into the aporia of potentiality in *De Anima*. Agamben suggests that the knowledge that enables the architect or poet to have the potential to build or write also means that they can *choose* not to build or not to write. He illustrates this with a phrase from the *Metaphysics* in which Aristotle says "what is potential can both be and not be".[11] Following Heidegger, Agamben takes "the *potential not to be*" as the definition of potentiality (*OP,* 182).

For Agamben, "impotentiality" is the index and resource of absence: it is "the origin (and the abyss) of human power" (*OP,* 182). It also seems that *having* potential means that those with knowledge (and power) have the freedom, can *choose* not to be actual, can reject or resist actuality (*OP,* 179, 183). But can choice remain potential? And how can one have potential and *hold on to* potentiality?

In *De Anima*, Aristotle is a bit more reticent about the potential of potentiality: with potential knowledge the individual "can reflect when he wants to, if nothing external prevents him [*àn mē ti kolúsē tēn éksōthen*]" (*S,* 417a). What, one might also ask, is the temporality of this decision of the potential, as Agamben characterizes it? Is it a moment of ease (I always have the potential, I can always build or I can always not build), of crisis (can I build, can I not build?), or even of madness (can I build and not build, at the same time)?

Aristotle is more concerned with the problem of fire. Why, when the inside is free of the influence of the outside does the inside do nothing? Because, if the inside were able to act on its own, if it was always actual, it would die: *it would burn itself to death.* Aristotle writes:

> The power of sense is parallel to what is combustible, for that never ignites itself spontaneously [*où kaíetai autò kath' autò*], but requires an agent which has the power of starting ignition [*áneu tou kaustikou*]; otherwise it could have set itself on fire [*ékaie gàr àn éautó*], and would have not needed actual fire to set it ablaze. (*S,* 417a)

Sensation is potential, does nothing on its own, because it must be fire resistant, it must *resist* the elements within itself or it would spontaneously combust, and perception could never start.

In Aristotle's economy of the soul, exemplified as Derrida suggested by the Greek ear, there is always a buffer zone between the inside and the outside, a place of modulation, mediation and moderation that keeps the senses alive, that protects them from the extremes (too hot, too cold, too loud, too soft, too bright, too dark). There can be no direct contact between the inside and its own internal elements; there must always be "*something* in between [*metaksú*]" (*S,* 419a). The dream of a potentiality that chooses or does not choose to activate itself is the dream of *self*-combustion, a direct, visceral burning of the self. It is an auto-affective death. It is the death-dream of the architect or the poet of a self-ignition, a self-firing, of bringing forth from inside their very own fire. Calculating on absence as a pure possibility, *in the name of the poet*, Agamben returns to nature itself, to *phusis* as self-creation, to what Derrida had called in *Of Grammatology* the "recourse to literature as [a] reappropriation of presence" (*OG,* 144).[12]

For Derrida, there must always be *"something* in between", because the *resistance* of the other is the possibility of contact (*OT,* 181, 229). The Greek ear announces its continual reliance upon, and its inability to stop, "the blows from the outside".[13] The difference between Derrida and Agamben in reading Aristotle is most evident in the opening of Derrida's *On Touching – Jean-Luc Nancy* (2000):

> Let's first recall that sense, the *faculty* of sensation – the tactile faculty, for example – is only *potential* and not *actual* (*ibid.*, 417a), with the ineluctable consequence that of *itself*, it does not sense *itself*; it does not auto-affect itself without the motion of an exterior object. This is a far reaching thesis, and we shall keep taking its measure with regard to touching and "self-touching". (*OT,* 6)

The "blows from the outside", Derrida suggests, are not the possibility of auto-creation, of the poet's dream of creating or killing itself, of literature as an assured potentiality, but the possibility of invention, of the precarious *chance* of invention, of a chance meeting with invention – an invention of the other, from the other.[14]

HOLDING ON

Agamben suggests that Aristotle is primarily concerned with potentiality as a "mode of existence" in which having a "faculty means *to have* a privation" (*stereisis*). When one *has* potential, there is no need to "suffer an alteration (a becoming other) through learning" (*OP,* 179). As Aristotle observes: "Hence it is wrong to speak of a wise man as being 'altered' [*alloiousthai*] when he uses his wisdom, just as it would be absurd to speak of a builder as being altered when he is using his skill in building a house" (*S,* 417b). The potentiality that interests Agamben, the potentiality that is not "generic" as he calls it, is about *having* potential and of not being altered by the other to become potential. It is a question of holding on to potentiality as a unique privation.

As Lévinas before him, Agamben wants to hold on to what he calls a "fundamental passivity" (*OP,* 182).[15] In contrast, Aristotle himself is concerned with the problem of the relation between potentiality and actuality that could mean either the "extinction" (*pthorá*, destruction) or the "maintenance" (*sōtēría*, preservation) of potentiality (*S,* 417b). In other words, it is possible that having and maintaining potentiality is *already* an example of the transition from potentiality to actuality. For Agamben, it is indispensable that potentiality maintains itself: "*dynamis*, potentiality, maintains itself in relation to its own privation." "To be potential means: to be one's own lack, *to be in relation to one's own incapacity*" he insists (*OP*, 182). This incapacity is predicated on the assured capacity of potentiality to maintain itself *as* itself. There can be no accidents, no chance events.

In *De Anima*, these open questions – open because we are still in the *aporia* – suggest that the relation between potentiality and actuality is not one of extinction. It is rather a question of a two kinds of preservation: "transition" or "alteration" (*alloióseos*). This either-or in *De Anima* is quite extraordinary. Either the potential finds "its true self" in actuality (transition), or it finds something other than "its true self" (alteration). Aristotle then steadies his text against this strange either-or, and turns to the example of the wise man and the builder who are not altered in having and using their potential knowledge. Not being altered in this case affirms the possibility that having and maintaining potentiality is already the transition "into its true self or actuality". For Aristotle, much as time describes a dividing continuity in the *Physics*, the potential-actual relation in *De Anima* describes a non-altering transition, a development that is not a transformation.[16]

For Derrida, the abyss describes an indefinite multiplication within a structure or system, and, despite steadying his text, Aristotle responds to this *aporia* with a proliferation of either-ors (*OG*, 163). Either potentiality is not "acted upon" (*páskhein*), or there are in turn two kinds of alteration: "the change to conditions of privation [*sterētikàs diathéseis metabolēn*], and the change to a thing's disposition and to its nature [*phúsin*]". If potentiality is to be changed, and is not to become itself we can only accept the elusive distinction Aristotle draws between "conditions of privation" – or modes of existence, as Agamben calls it – and "a thing's disposition and . . . its nature". However, in both cases it is a question of a change brought about by the relation between potentiality and actuality. One has to work quite hard to hold on to potentiality in Aristotle's text.

Aristotle concludes that the non-altering transition between potentiality and actuality ends in assimilation (*S*, 418a). Agamben ends with the question of how to "*consider the actuality of the potentiality to not-be*" (*OP*, 183). For both Agamben and Aristotle, when potentiality has moved into actuality, "it *preserves itself*". Agamben ends

45

with the preservation of potentiality as an auto-salvation and auto-gift, an image that would have been worthy of Hegel, if he had ever reached the end of history: "here we are confronted with a potentiality that conserves itself and saves itself in actuality. Here potentiality, so to speak, survives actuality and, in this way, *gives itself to itself*" (*OP,* 184).

At the same time, as Agamben turns to the poets he wants to dissociate this potentiality as privation or absence as pure possibility from the whole question of not-being. Agamben wants to by-pass the *aporia* of the relation between Parmenides and Plato (the *Republic*, *Parmenides*, the *Sophist* and *Theaetetus*). He does not want to start again with the questions of *"essence"* and "what is it" (*OP,* 179). Yet he also wants to pause "on a figure of potentiality". When he says that he wants "to pause on a *figure* of potentiality", Agamben is already caught between the interlacing oscillations of potentiality and actuality. For Aristotle, matter (*húlēn*) is always potential (*dúnamis*), while form or essence (*morphēn kaì eidos*) is always actual (*entelékheia*) (*S,* 412a). Stopping at a *form* of potentiality, Agamben has already delivered the potential over to the actual. Even without Plato, for Aristotle it is not potentiality but actuality that is always the figure, the "form or essence".

Agamben does not want to start with the interminable and labyrinthine dialogue between Parmenides and Plato to be seen as the potential of Aristotle on potentiality. Derrida, in contrast, reiterates the importance of starting again with Plato. To no more than gesture to Derrida's readings of the *Republic*, and of the differences between Parmenides and Plato, in an interview from 1981 he remarks:

> From the very beginning of Greek philosophy the self-identity of the *Logos* is already fissured and divided. I think one can discern signs of such fissures of "différance" in every great philosopher: the "Good beyond Being" (*epékeina tēs ousías*) of Plato's *Republic*, for example, or the confrontation with the "Stranger" in *The Sophist* are already traces of an alterity which refuses to be totally domesticated.[17]

For Derrida, we have to start differently with Parmenides and the *Sophist*, because *De Anima* is fundamentally about how we begin (*OT,* 18). For Aristotle, we start with potentiality only because we have already started with actuality. "In the individual", Aristotle writes, "potential knowledge is in time prior [*dúnamin khróno protéra*] to actual knowledge, but absolutely it is not prior even in time [*ólōs dé où khrónō*]" (*S*, 430a). "All things", he argues, "that come into being arise from what actually is [*entelekheía óntos*]" (*S*, 431a). The potentiality of matter can be first, because it is *already* the form of "what actually is".[18] The passage that Agamben cites from *Metaphysics* 1050b to illustrate "the *potential not to be*" begins with Aristotle affirming that "actuality is prior in substantiality to potentiality" (*próteron tōousía enérgeia dunámeōs*).[19] For Aristotle, the potential is always *preceded*, is made possible, by actuality, by *ousia*: presence, substance, "*beingness* itself", as Derrida called it (*OU*, 40). This is the great ruse or trap of absence as pure possibility.

In *Metaphysics* 1050b, Aristotle is concerned primarily with the difference between what is eternal (*áidios*) and what is perishable (*phthártós*). The potential can only start *after* the actual, because "all imperishable [*aphthártōn*] things are actual": actuality is eternal. The alternative – which is not really an alternative – to actuality, to the *eternal* prior access to being (*ousia*), is an *economy* of the (im)potentiality of being, of "that which is capable both of being and of not being" (*dunatòn eînai éndékhetai kai eînai kaì mè eînai*). Aristotle writes, "that which is capable of *being possible* (*eînai éndékhetai*) of being and of not being", and the apparent choice between being and not being remains a choice, a pure possibility *of* being, as Parmenides had argued long ago.[20]

THE COLOUR OF POTENTIALITY

"Before passing to the determination of this 'face' of potentiality", Agamben remarks, "I would like to pause on a figure of potentiality that seems to me be particularly significant and that appears in *De Anima*. I refer to darkness, to shadows." He goes on to write:

Here Aristotle is concerned with the problem of vision (418b–419e). The object of sight, he says, is colour; in addition, it is something for which we have no word but which is usually translated as "transparency," *diaphanes*. Diaphanes refers here not to transparent bodies (such as air and water) but to a "nature" as Aristotle writes, which is in every body and is what is truly visible in every body. Aristotle does not tell us what "nature" is; he says only "there is *diaphanes*," *esti ti diaphanes*. But he does tell us that the actuality (*energeia*) of this nature is light, and that darkness (*skotos*) is its potentiality. Light, he adds, is so to speak the colour of *diaphanes* in act; darkness, we may therefore say, is in some way the colour of potentiality. What is sometimes darkness and some-times light is one in nature (*hē autē physis hote men skotos hote de phōs estin*). (*OP*, 180)

"To pause on a figure of potentiality", Agamben turns first to Aristotle's evocation of the diaphanous and then to darkness "as the colour of potentiality". He goes on to argue that "when our vision is potential", "*we see darkness*". He then immediately qualifies this absolute seeing of darkness. If potentiality, he notes, were "only the potentiality for vision . . . we could never experience darkness". "But human beings", he adds, "can instead, see shadows (*to skotos*), they can experience darkness: they have the *potential* not to see, the *possibility of privation*" (*OP*, 180–1).

For Aristotle, as "the cause or source of sensation", the soul is nothing less than matter working with form, the outside working with the inside, and potentiality always in need of an external agent (*S* 415b–17a). It is from this framework that Aristotle, like Agamben, begins to talk about non-visible origins. Light and colour are the origin of the visible and, as Derrida had noted in his reading of Husserl, Aristotle illustrates this through the diaphanous: "By diaph-anous [*diaphanès*] I mean what is visible [*oratón*], and not yet visible in itself [*où kath' autò dé óratòn*], but rather owing its visibility to the colour [*khrōma*] of something else" (*S*, 418b).

The diaphanous is an example of the potential needing something other than itself to avoid its own self-combustion. If light were simply the origin of light, it would blind itself. Aristotle writes: "Light is as it were the proper colour of what is transparent [*khrōmá esti tou diaphanous*], and exists wherever the transparent is excited to actual-ity by the influence of fire or something 'resembling' the uppermost body" (*S*, 418b). If Aristotle argues that light must be "excited to actuality" to exist, it does not follow – as Agamben suggests – that darkness is simply "the colour of potentiality" (*S*, 418b). Aristotle in fact writes that "light [*phos*] is the activity [*ènérgeia*] of what is trans-parent *qua* transparent; where this power is present [*dunámei dè en*], there is also darkness [*kaì skótos*]". Light arises from the work of actuality, from the relation of the transparent to "something else" (colour), which enables it at once to be seen and not to blind or burn itself. It is from this work that a power (*dunámei*) is produced, and there can also be darkness. In other words, actuality precedes potentiality – and makes both light and darkness possible.

There are at least four ways of reading the origin of light and dark in *De Anima*. First, with the introduction of the diaphanous, Aristotle gives us a psycho-ontology: the origin of light and dark conforms to the structure of the soul, of the *not x but the possibility of x*. Secondly, when Aristotle argues that *x* can never be its own possibility, he also announces the impossibility of auto-affection, as Derrida points out. Thirdly, when he argues that it is the activity of the actual that enables not only light but also darkness to be potential and actual, he suggests that it is very difficult to entirely discriminate between the potential and the actual. When it comes to the potential and the actual, we are always somewhere in between: neither in light (*phōs*) nor darkness (*skótos*), but in shadow (*skiá*). Fourthly, at the same time Aristotle forecloses these difficult genealogies by reiterating a fundamental ontology: light is not fire, but the presence (*parousia*) of fire. Darkness is the absence (*stéresis*) of fire. Presence or absence: an either-or that does not hold us back or take us beyond Aristotle.

To pause (*pausare*), to stop (*pausis*) for a moment, Agamben evokes the diaphanous and looks through it towards the darkness (an absence of light) as "the colour of potentiality," as the origin of "the *potential not to be*." He hesitates, just for a moment, over the black abyss of a darkness that is always potential, always potentially dark, at the origin: the dream of the darkness of the origin, of starting with and holding on to an absence as a pure resource of alterity. And then, he turns away and starts again: it is not darkness I am speaking of, but shadows, he insists (*OP,* 181).[21] But when Agamben turns to Derrida in his 1990 article "*Pardes*: The Writing of Potentiality", when he makes the case for describing Derrida's work in terms of a "writing *of* potentiality", it is not of shadows (*skiá*), but of darkness (*skótos*) that he speaks:

This is why Aristotle develops his theory of matter as potentiality on the basis of Timaeus's khora. Like the eye when it is confronted with darkness, the faculty of sensation, we read in De Anima, can sense its own lack of sensation, its own potentiality.[22]

THE MANY WAYS OF ARISTOTLE

In a footnote to Agamben's 1988 article "The Passion of Facticity" there is a discrepancy in the citation of Heidegger's 1931 lectures on Aristotle's *Metaphysics*. The title of the English translation of Heidegger's work is given as *Aristotle's Metaphysics Omega 1-3*, while the original German title is *Aristoteles Metaphysik Theta 1-3*.[23] This small mistake – the substitution of Omega (Ω) for Theta (Θ) – obviously has nothing to do with Agamben's original text. But it does suggest a compelling resonance with the tradition of the *alpha* and *omega*, the apocalyptic revelation of the first and last, and the assertion of an archaeology and teleology as the guiding meaning of absence as pure possibility.

In his essay, Agamben once again reiterates the connection between potentiality and impotentiality. For Heidegger, he argues, "the most radical experience of possibility at issue in *Dasein*" is "a capacity that is capable not only of potentiality (the manners of beings that are in fact possible) but also, and above all, of impotentiality" (*PF*, 201). Above all, what is important for Heidegger is the capacity of *Dasein* for impotentiality. Agamben's confidence in the centrality of impotence in Heidegger's reading of Aristotle is evident in his summary of the 1931 lectures: "All potentiality (*dynamis*), Heidegger writes in his interpretation of Aristotle, is impotentiality (*adynamia*), and all capacity (*dynamis*) is essentially passivity (*dekhesthai*)" (*PF*, 201). As an assertion, Agamben's summation – the *alpha* and *omega* – of Heidegger's reading at once reflects an essential aspect of Heidegger's lectures and invites the very critique that Heidegger discerns in the most metaphysical readings of Aristotle's text.

Heidegger begins his lectures, as one would expect, by extricating the logos from the metaphysical tradition of logic. Through a relation that moves "back and forth", the logos accounts for *"making something accessible in a unified and gathered way"*.[24] Heidegger contrasts this to the Kantian logic of the category, as a "kind of saying which says emphatically what a being properly is", and is "involved in every assertion in a pre-eminent way". For Aristotle, Heidegger argues, the relation between potentiality and actuality cannot be described in terms of a category (*katēgorein*) (*AM*, 4–5). One would have to ask whether Agamben has not conferred on Heidegger's reading of Aristotle a categorical *assertion* when he states that "all potentiality (*dynamis*) . . . is impotentiality (*adynamia*)".

In contrast to Agamben's reluctance to return to Parmenides, in his opening lectures Heidegger argues that one cannot address the many different relations of potentiality traced by Aristotle without appreciating how Aristotle reads Parmenides. Parmenides did not merely define being as one, Heidegger argues. Rather, he saw that beings as such were gathered into being. For Heidegger, this is the "first decisive philosophical truth": philosophy begins not with the assertion of the one, but with a *gathering towards* the one (*AM*, 19). Aristotle accepts that being (*einai*) is one (*én*), but he also sees that it is said in many ways (*pollakhōs*). Aristotle moves away from Parmenides by recognizing that there is not-being, that not being also *is*, and "this intrusion of notness [*dieser Einbruch des Nichaften*] into the unity signifies its folding out into multiplicity" (*AM*, 22).[25] For Aristotle, the fundamental relation is that of *én-polla*, "one is many". Not being and impotentiality are part of a wider set of relations that confirm the "twofold" and "multi structured" nature of being (*AM*, 22–4). Heidegger contrasts Aristotle's insistence that "beings are said in many ways" (*pollakhōs*), to the categorical "saying of being in the assertion [*Aussagen*] (*lógos*) of beings", or what could be called Agamben's categorical assertion of the *monakhōs* of impotentiality (*AM*, 10–11; *MT*, 15; *BT*, 154–60).

Heidegger begins his reading of *Theta* 1 by noting that there are "other meanings" of the relation between potentiality and actuality which Aristotle takes pains to exclude from his analysis. The first of these is the association of potentiality and actuality with movement (*kinēsis*), or what Heidegger calls the meaning that is commonly present (*AM*, 41). Another of these other "enigmatic" meanings that Aristotle excludes is the relation between the *dunaton* and the *adunaton*, the powerful and the powerless (*Kräftig* and *Unkräftig*). For Heidegger, this describes the relation between a necessity not to conceal (the powerful) and a necessity to conceal (the powerless). The powerless distorts and conceals "what manifestly is". While the powerful is commensurable and compatible with an assertion, the powerless "denies the saying of its commensurability to the assertion concerning it" (*AM*, 51–2, 55–6). Agamben's assertion that "all potentiality (*dynamis*) . . . is impotentiality (*adynamia*)" can be seen as an example of a powerful assertion. A powerful assertion does not deny: it asserts what manifestly is (all x *is* y). It asserts what is, and Heidegger adds, "is able to bear it" [*vermag zu ertragen*] (*AM,* 54; *MT,* 64).

THE FULL GUIDING MEANING

If Agamben's assertion overlooks the "multi structured" nature of the relation between potentiality and actuality, he nonetheless captures much of Heidegger's "guiding meaning". Agamben writes: "The *potentia* at issue here is essentially *potentia passiva*, the *dynamis tou paskein* whose secret solidarity with active potentiality (*dynamis tou poiein*) Heidegger emphasized in his 1931 lecture course on Aristotle's *Metaphysics*" (*PF,* 201). Heidegger describes both Aristotle's method of analysis and the basis of his own way of reading as a *turning backwards* that gathers and incorporates each previous form of potentiality into a single cohesive narrative. "Surpassing Aristotle", and still, nonetheless, reflecting the spirit of his inquiry, Heidegger calls for a moving "backwards in the direction of a more original unveiling" (*einer ursprünglicheren Enthüllung*). This moving backwards (*Rückwort*) takes us forwards, leading us to the more "original" and "guiding meaning" of Aristotle's text. This reading backwards-to-be-guided-forwards takes us "before the actuality that prevails tacitly in the concepts that have lost life for the tradition" (*AM,* 68–9; *MT,* 82).

As Agamben suggests, for Heidegger the "full guiding meaning" (*die erfüllte Leitbedeutung*) of potentiality lies in the relation between a tolerance to change (*pathein*) and an intolerance to change (*apathēias*), or what Heidegger calls "bearance" (*Ertragsamkeit*) and "resistance in general". Potentiality is not only a form of doing (*poiein*), but also a relation between bearing and resisting. Though Heidegger allows for potentiality as a form of resistance, it is the relation between doing and bearing that leads to the ends of potentiality, to a potentiality that gathers itself back *towards* its proper end as the single form and meaning of an impotentiality that can maintain itself as a pure possibility. Impotentiality is the "constitutional belonging of unforce to the guiding meaning of force" (*AM,* 93). Impotentiality is the "full guiding meaning" of potentiality.

When Agamben asserts "all capacity (*dynamis*) is essentially passivity (*dekhesthai*)," he is perhaps closer to Heidegger than he intends, who translates *dēkhesthai* not as passivity but "taking-to-oneself" (*AM,* 96). At the same time, he is perhaps farther away from Heidegger than he intends, because Heidegger closes his reading of *Theta* 1 with force (*dúnamis*) as a "reciprocal relation" which cannot be defined as either activity or passivity (*AM,* 98). In trying to stop, to arrest Aristotelian potentiality as the teleological certainty of a self-sustaining impotentiality, Agamben evokes the dream of the dark sovereignty of pure possibility.

CHAPTER 3

(NOT) MEETING HEIDEGGER

LA CHANCE DE LA RENCONTRE

On 27 August 2002 Derrida delivered the paper "The 'World' of the Enlightenment to Come (Exception, Calculation and Sovereignty)" at a conference held in Nice. He opened his lecture with a dedication to Dominique Janicaud, who had died suddenly on 18 August. Expressing his "extreme sorrow" at the death of Janicaud, Derrida writes: "For more than thirty-five years his friendship and support, the vigilance of his thought, has accompanied me." He adds, "I was fortunate to share [*j'ai eu la chance de partager*] so many things with him in life and in philosophy" (*WEC,* 117).[1] Derrida says that he has had the luck or good fortune to share much with Janicaud, and one can retain the more literal sense of *la chance* here: he has had the *chance* to share.

Like Jean-Luc Nancy, Janicaud favoured the French word *partage* with its double meaning of sharing and dividing. However, it is not so much the indeterminacy of what is shared or divided among friends that is of interest here, as what Derrida calls *la chance de la rencontre*, the chance of the chance meeting or duel (*rencontre*) that both shares with and divides from an academic colleague or an intellectual figure of the times. For Derrida, *la chance de la rencontre* is a possibility of meeting that cannot be reduced to either presence or absence. It is a possibility that has a chance of resisting the traps and ruses of holding on to alterity as an absolute resource or pure possibility. It confounds the good conscience of believing that one has either truly met or clearly avoided the other. *La chance de la rencontre* exposes us to the risks of (not) meeting, and it is through this difficult injunction that we can begin to approach the relation between literature and the concept of war from the perspective of Derrida's work.

One of Janicaud's last publications was *Heidegger en France* (2001), which includes a series of interviews addressing the impact of Heidegger on French philosophy.[2] There are 18 different voices in all, 18 different personal and intellectual testimonies, or rather 19, including Janicaud their interlocutor, bearing witness to meeting or not meeting Martin Heidegger and his work. Janicaud provides a brief preface in which he notes that there were two people that he wrote to who did not reply and that there was another person who withdrew from the project. From the start, Janicaud suggests, that the history of a meeting must take account of the non-response and the withdrawal (*HF,* 8). Janicaud also gives a sense of the range of these 18 different perspectives:

> The most senior of my interlocutors, Walter Biemel, was Heidegger's student from the beginning of the 1940s: becoming one of his closest friends, he remained sincerely attached to him. The youngest, Nicole Parfait, on the contrary, testifies to a distanced reading, mediated by the great French teacher-disciples: not only has she never met the Master [*rencontré le Maître*], but she has also embarked on a critical study of his political engagement, to detach herself finally from the very principles of his thought. (*HF,* 7)

From the oldest to the youngest of the 18, Janicaud presents us with two extremes: "the closest" that "remained . . . attached" to Heidegger and "a distanced reading" that is attempting "to detach . . . finally" from Heidegger. When it comes to meeting "Heidegger", we begin with two strained propositions. On the one hand, a not meeting, or more properly a never having met that not only reads, and always at a distance (and one wonders how such a reading would be possible), but also presumes a final break, an absolute detachment. How does one detach absolutely from a distanced reading that is founded on never meeting? On the other hand, how is it possible for Biemel to be so absolutely close, and to remain unambiguously attached to Heidegger? It is striking that while Janicaud notes that Parfait "had never met" Heidegger, he gives no sense of Biemel having actually met Heidegger, as if this absolute proximity beyond life and death needed no chance encounters or contingent re-encounters, no meetings or duels.

It is with these two forms of meeting as the anxiety of either absolute proximity or absolute difference that we can start. In his interview with Biemel, Janicaud begins by asking autobiographical questions. But Biemel does not begin, as one might expect, with the date or event of his first meeting with Heidegger. Rather, he starts with his leaving Heidegger, his departing from Heidegger in the midst of the war in the summer of 1944 when the University of Fribourg was closed (*HF*, 34). Before this first parting, Heidegger had brought to Biemel's attention a book on him by Alphonse de Waelhens. Biemel says, "we had not yet read it, but I remembered the name" (*HF*, 35). Is this *we* a royal and singular we (meaning that he had not read the book) or is this a collective we (meaning that neither he nor Heidegger had read the book)? This hint of the intimacy of reading together, of reading a book at the same time or tempo, gives Biemel's apparently fortuitous narrative the blessing of an assured journey. From the name of this "Belgian Professor" given to him by Heidegger at their moment of parting, Biemel finds himself by chance in Belgium, after the German territory that he is in is returned to Belgium at the end of the war. The gift of this name, which seems to resonate or redeem the departure from Heidegger, carries Biemel to de Waelhens and, ultimately, to six years of work editing Husserl's manuscripts in Louvain.

Biemel then turns back and explains that he had begun his studies in Romania and worked on a doctoral thesis with Heidegger, but once again he offers no account of his first meeting with Heidegger. Turning back without the beginning, without the origin, Biemel says that after having left both Heidegger and Fribourg, "I had a recurring dream: I arrive at the station – and the train has left. I said to myself that this must have a meaning" (*HF*, 35). This chance event is then compounded or affirmed by "truly extraordinary good fortune" when Biemel is invited to Cologne to oversee the archives of Husserl. These ostensibly chance events are overseen or curtailed by the quiet *certainty* of Heidegger's gift of the name and Biemel's dream of returning to Fribourg. Carrying a manuscript of Heidegger's when he left Germany in the midst of the war, Biemel carried the gift and burden of Heidegger's work and name (*HF*, 43).

In contrast, Nicole Parfait never met Martin Heidegger, but she describes her first encounters with his work in terms of an incremental process of proximity. Taught by François Vezin, she first began with great difficulty to read Heidegger in 1967 when she was 17 and still at school. In 1968–1970, Parfait attended a seminar given by François Fédier, the notable Heideggerian translator in France, and spent one year studying the 13 pages of §7 of *Being and Time* (*HF,* 256–7). Parfait comments: "This was a real work of exegesis and reflection; I had the feeling of participating in a true experience of thinking. It was no longer a question of working on philosophy but of attempting to think." At the same time, looking back on these days, Parfait now questions "the quasi religious atmosphere that prevailed in this seminar." In 1969–1970, Parfait went to study with Jean Beaufret, the pre-eminent Heideggerian in Paris. Beaufret's seminars were conducted in "a very meditative – but not religious atmosphere" (*HF,* 257–8). Finally, in the early 1970s Parfait began her studies with Françoise Dastur and found, "for the first time . . . an open course on Heidegger".

The teleology of this pedagogical narrative is almost Hegelian, moving from the first difficulties of the senses and self-consciousness to reason, and from religion to the transparency of absolute knowledge. For Parfait, the clarity of *truly meeting* Heidegger's work becomes the possibility of beginning the long task of *completely breaking* with his thought: it is a *not* meeting that can only begin with an absolute meeting. In her graduate work, Parfait came to believe that "Heidegger still belongs to metaphysics," and attempted to challenge the prevailing view that he was "a post-metaphysical thinker, which gave him a very special aura and permitted him, in truth, to judge the whole history of metaphysics" (*HF,* 258–9). It is by standing away from those who have read Heidegger with the blindness of faith, and positioning herself entirely outside of Heidegger's metaphysics that Parfait herself now appears "in truth" to judge "the whole history" of Heidegger and his readers.

While the interviews with Biemel and Parfait suggest two ways of meeting Heidegger – of either maintaining a proximity that precludes all chance encounters or of struggling to get close enough to get far away as possible – some of the other interviews suggest the need for a more complex notion of (not) meeting. Most of the accounts of the first meetings with Heidegger rarely escape an institutional inevitability, and more often than not are authenticated and inaugurated by meeting Jean Beaufret, the conduit in France for all things Heideggerian. As Claude Roëls says, "finally, the following year, I had my *encounter* with Jean Beaufret" (*HF*, 268). At the same time, many of the more personal anecdotes suggest how every meeting is marked by an unavoidable and unspoken sense of not meeting. For example, Walter Biemel tells the story of Heidegger being unwell and immediately leaving a conference after giving a paper, and that Heidegger's brother then "played Heidegger" in the question and answer session, replacing and doubling his brother (*HF*, 40–1). More well known is Kostas Axelos's account of the meeting between Heidegger and Lacan in Paris in 1955, where Lacan was unable to speak German and Heidegger refused to speak French and, as Axelos says, "there was no dialogue" (*HF*, 12).

In some cases, meeting Heidegger himself only complicates matters, as if one could more truly meet the work by not meeting the man. Michel Deguy recalls meeting Heidegger in 1956 with Roger Laporte: "After the café, Heidegger went down to the sea, pulling up his right trouser leg and dipped his foot and calf into the Mediterranean. [. . .] He said some words about Greece and the Mediterranean. I found this at once interesting and, fatally, a little ridiculous. We were very pleased to be there. But, obviously, there were no exchanges between us and the Master" (*HF*, 79).

In his interview with Janicaud, Philippe Lacoue-Labarthe takes quite a different approach, explaining that his own encounter with Heidegger was mediated by reading Derrida's early work. It is a question here of not meeting, but *reading*. Derrida's work, Lacoue-Labarthe remarks, "set up a certain distance with the Heidegger of presence, that is to say the one that I had also perceived through the reading and translations of Beaufret, of Fédier". For Lacoue-Labarthe, in reading Derrida there was "finally a reading that was not submissive, allied, that kept the right measure, debating with this thought" (*HF*, 200–1). While Derrida might question the ability of any reader to maintain "the right measure" in the midst of reading, Lacoue-Labarthe suggests that Derrida's "certain distance" from "the Heidegger of presence" resisted a prior allegiance, a duty or obligation that precedes and guarantees a true meeting.

Lacoue-Labarthe had written elsewhere before this 1999 interview of "the extreme importance" for his generation of Derrida's "*Auseinandersetzung* with Heidegger", adding that it was "the only one to have taken place in France".[3] From the mid-1960s, this call for a "certain distance" informed not only Lacoue-Labarthe's approach to the works of Heidegger, but also to meeting those who were closest

Figure 3 Towards the Alexander Column, St. Petersburg, 2007 © Jane Brown 2009.

to him, to Heidegger's representatives, his translators and "doubles" in France, such as Jean Beaufret and François Fédier. Lacoue-Labarthe recalls that "I must have met Fédier once very briefly, with Deguy, in 1965-1966," and sees this chance encounter as a confirmation of a "certain climate of sacralization or devotion", of "piety" towards Heidegger and his works. For Lacoue-Labarthe, this quasi-religious veneration, this asymmetrical meeting, that is always determined and disenabled by the infinite desire to get closer *and* the infinite desire to maintain a respectful distance, embodies "the thematic of presence" that Derrida had first brought to his attention (*HF,* 200). There can be no assumption of meeting Lacoue-Labarthe argues, rather there must be a reticence, a reluctance, a refusal to meet, when it comes to this presence of the meeting, this presence *as* meeting.

One must resist meeting, and there is always the profound temptation and the respectful desire to meet. For Lacoue-Labarthe, this resistance and temptation is always political. It is "the political mistrust" that marks his chance encounter with Fédier. "I did not want this meeting [*rencontre*]" Lacoue-Labarthe says to Janicaud. But this desire not to meet can never entirely be separated from the temptation to meet, and Janicaud goes on to ask him if he had "been tempted, despite these reservations, to meet the great man"? (*HF,* 208–9). Lacoue-Labarthe goes on to explain how Derrida, Nancy, Lucien Braun and himself had almost gone to Germany in 1973 to meet Heidegger, but each time the prearranged meeting (*rendezvous*) had been cancelled at the last minute by Heidegger's wife, due to his ill health.[4] Attentive to *la chance de la rencontre*, and the impossible temptation of the *rendezvous*, Lacoue-Labarthe ends his discussion with Janicaud with an account of visiting Heidegger's home after he had died to collect some of Heidegger's French books that he had left in his will for the Institute of Philosophy in Strasbourg. In the end, standing in "the room where he died", and finding the works of Hölderlin, Goethe and Celan on his night table, Lacoue-Labarthe met Martin Heidegger (*HF,* 209).[5]

THE VOICE OF HEIDEGGER

Lacoue-Labarthe's temptation to meet and his desire not to meet Heidegger and his call to resist "the Heidegger of presence" are part of the institutional and political history of the reception of Heidegger in France after the war. As Derrida suggests in "Shibboleth" (1986), resistance – and perhaps also his earlier evocation of *la restance*, the resistance of that which remains and remains to come – cannot be separated from the events of World War II, and from "all wars".[6] Resisting the meeting as presence, taking account of the politics of (not) meeting, one cannot avoid the wars of our times.

The politics of this (not) meeting should not be confused with what Derrida calls "the non-encounter [*non-rencontre*]," or "a certain blindness to the other" (*IJD*, 118).[7] Lacoue-Labarthe's wish to have not met François Fédier is reinforced by Fédier's refusal to meet Janicaud and to participate in his interviews (*HF*, 8). One of the many histories behind these wishes not to have met and these refusals to respond is the so-called L'affair Beaufret in 1968. Before turning to this, we need to follow Derrida's own account of (not) meeting Heidegger.

In contrast to Gérard Granel, who when asked by Janicaud when did he first hear the name of Heidegger replies "I believe I remember it exactly," Derrida offers a number of "hypotheses" to account for his probable or possible first encounter with the name of Heidegger in 1947–1948 (*HF*, 172; *IJD*, 89). Derrida's first encounters with the works of Heidegger were tied to the dominance in France of Sartre and Merleau-Ponty in the late 1940s, and he acknowledges that he went through an existentialist phase: "I resonate with the pathos that one felt at this time, just after the war" (*HF*, 90). Derrida began reading Heidegger in earnest in 1953, though he dates the start of his own "interminable *Auseinandersetzung*" with Heidegger from 1964 (*IJD*, 93, 101). He did not attend the 1955 conference on Heidegger at Cerisy, and dates his first encounter with Heidegger's work to 1956, when he was invited to Maurice de Gandillac's home and "met Axelos, Wahl, Goldman". But he also recalls that in the winter of 1955 he was invited to a gathering where a recording of Heidegger's talk at Cerisy was played. Derrida's first encounter with Martin Heidegger was with "the voice of Heidegger" (*IJD*, 94). Derrida remarks:

I was a student at the Ecole Normale and I heard the voice of Heidegger for the first time in a living room of the sixteenth arrondissement. I particularly remember one sequence: we were all in the living room, listening to this voice. At that time tapes [*les bandes*] were not as advanced as today; I especially remember the moment of the discussion that followed Heidegger's lecture:

Marcel and Goldman's questions. One of them made the following objection, more or less, to Heidegger: "But don't you think
that this method of lecturing or this way of reading or questioning
is dangerous?" – a methodological, epistemological question. And
I can still hear [*j'ai encore dans l'oreille*] – there was a silence – the
response of Heidegger: "*Yes!* It is dangerous. [Ja! *C'est dangereux.*]
This is a student memory. (*IJD,* 94–5)

In this memory of the 25-year-old Derrida there are so many resonances here with his later work. The author of *Speech and Phenomena*
(1967), who will argue that the ideality of autonomous interiority in
metaphysics has been registered and retained in the voice, first
encounters Heidegger through his voice alone.[8] This is also the author
of "Heidegger's Ear" (1989), who will argue that Heidegger "clearly
intends to return to a pre-Aristotelian, indeed pre-Platonic, hearing
of *lógos*" (*HE,* 190–3). One can also hear an echo of later preoccupa-
tions in Derrida's emphasis on the faultiness of the tape recording,
on the unreliability of "*les bandes*", of the *tekhnē* or prosthetic that
both enables the voice of Heidegger to be heard in the absence of
Martin Heidegger and makes this voice jump away from itself and,
finally, in the affirmation (*Ja!*) in Heidegger's dangerous way of
reading.

In Derrida's memory of listening to this recording of Heidegger's
voice one can hear the title of Derrida's 1975 interview "Ja, or the
faux-bond", a title which literally means "yes, or the missed meeting".[9]
In this 1975 interview, perhaps in part as a distant reverberation of
hearing the voice of Heidegger 19 years before, Derrida seems
fascinated and disturbed by the tape machine that is recording the
interview. "What happens", he asks,

when 'here-now' is put in quotation marks? And when one
says that one is using quotation marks even though no one can
read them here and now, and when a tape recorder [*un magnéto-
phone*] records that which – such is the implicit contract of this
interview – I will certainly reread, which I may even transform
here and there, perhaps even from beginning to end, before
publication?[10]

How, Derrida asks, does one mark and re-mark, transform and
redirect a recording, how does one find the chances of the chance

meeting (*la chance de la rencontre*) in this moment, already in quotation marks, here and now?

At the beginning of the second part of the interview, Derrida notes that the "magnetophonic band" itself is jumping – keeping back and pulling along at once – and he does this by starting with the affirmation and urgency of a yes, a *oui* or a *Ja!*: "Yes. Well, the tape does not wait for us [*la bande n'attend pas*]. I mean the recording tape, the second one. It's making a little noise [*grésille*], no time to look for the right words."[11] Recalling perhaps that first encounter with Heidegger's voice through the tape recorder, Derrida suggests that in the recording of one's voice it is the machine that is pushing along, forcing the "right words" to already run ahead of themselves, to give themselves to the other, beyond any claim to good conscience:

> The effect of the band, I mean the tape recorder band, in its *impatience*, is no doubt to *hasten* [presser]: one is afraid of the loss – the virgin tape, force expended for nothing, unproductive time.
>
> But it/id hastens, it/id prevents one from looking for the right words, up to a certain point, as soon as the other is there.
>
> And as soon as some other is there, there is a band.
>
> And one must learn to make it wait, and as far as possible, *just what it takes*. (*JA,* 33; *JO,* 40)

For Derrida, keeping back and pushing ahead, "the magnetophonic band" marks at once "a differentiated apparatus or system interposed between an emission and a reception", and a hounding urgency that forces the speaker "to expose himself without any defences, in his naked voice [*à voix nue*]" (*JA,* 33–4; *JO,* 40–1). This recording of the voice (and the first encounter with the voice of Heidegger) is inseparable from the (mis)chance of *la chance de la rencontre*. One cannot avoid, Derrida stresses, "the skip of a missed encounter [*la volte d'un faux-bond*]. One always responds off the beat and off to one side, off balance, even over the head [*à contretemps et à côté et à côté, en porte à faux, voire plus haut*]."The only chance for *la chance de la rencontre* is the risk of the *faux-bond*, of lacking the truth, of leaving the "truth behind" while showing up exactly at the right time for the *rendezvous* (*JA,* 34–5; *JO,* 41–2). "*Ja!* C'est dangereux", Derrida the student recalled from the voice of Heidegger, and some 20 years later, he finds in Zarathustra's "vast and boundless Yes" (*oui prodigieux et sans limites, ungeheuren unbegrentzten Ja*), a yes that can no longer be confined to "any logic of the *rendezvous*": the remorseless affirmation of (not) meeting that always remains to be met (*JA*, 65; *JO*, 69).

To return to Janicaud's 1999 interview with Derrida. In 1964 and 1965 Derrida ran two seminars at the École normale supérieure devoted to Heidegger and published "Violence and Metaphysics" (1964) and the article "Of Grammatology" (1965), both of which marked the distinctive reading of Heidegger that inspired Lacoue-Labarthe to question "the Heidegger of presence." In 1967, François Fédier prepared a collection of essays on Heidegger in honour of Beaufret, *L'endurance de la pensée: pour saluer Jean Beaufret*, which would include contributions from Heidegger, Blanchot, Char and others, and invited Derrida to join the project. Derrida hesitated. As he says to Janicaud:

> At first I hesitated because, really, I didn't feel particularly close to Beaufret, with whom I had a good personal rapport; but I did not feel Beaufretian nor Heideggerian in Beaufret's way and, as there are some uneasy questions in *Ousia* and *Grammē* [the text that Derrida offered for the book] about Heidegger, I decided to say no. (*IJD*, 97)

Derrida makes some important distinctions here. Having a "good personal rapport" with Beaufret, he is at the same time not intellectually "close" to him or to his reading of Heidegger. One can meet another intellectual, have "a good rapport" with them and not meet them, not be close to their work or viewpoint. Derrida was eventually persuaded to include "*Ousia* and *Grammē*: Note on a note from *Being and Time*", his reading of Heidegger, Hegel and Aristotle, in Fédier's collection of essays.

It was at this point, after the book had gone to press, that Derrida heard from Roger Laporte that Jean Beaufret had not only made some anti-Semitic remarks about Emmanuel Lévinas, but also cast doubt on the magnitude of the *Shoah*. Derrida's immediate response was to write to Fédier and ask that his essay be withdrawn (and one can perhaps also catch an echo of this event in Derrida's later emphasis on withdrawal (*retirer*) in his retranslation of Heidegger's notion of *Entziehung*).[12] Eventually, a meeting (*une rencontre*) was held in Derrida's office at the ENS, where Beaufret denied everything and Laporte repeated his charges.[13] It was, Derrida remarks, a "contradictory encounter", a meeting without meeting and a duel without resolution (*IJD*, 98). However, this meeting also led to another far more significant meeting for Derrida.

At this point in early 1968, Derrida had not yet met Maurice Blanchot. "We had exchanged some letters", he notes, "but I had never met him [*rencontré*]" (*IJD*, 98).[14] Having had the *rencontre* between Beaufret and Laporte brought to his attention, Blanchot contacted Derrida and they soon had their own *rencontre*, meeting during the events of May 1968. Blanchot and Derrida discussed the best strategy to respond and whether "to withdraw or not to withdraw the texts", and decided, confronted by the "contradictory encounter" between Beaufret and Laporte, they would allow their essays to be published (*IJD*, 98).

Derrida and Blanchot also decided to write a joint letter to the other participants in the collection explaining their actions. While Derrida was away in America in September 1968, Blanchot mailed these letters to the press on the day that the book was published, but the letters were never delivered to the other participants, and it is possible that Fédier intercepted and suppressed them (*IJD*, 99). Needless to say, the theme of letters being sent out and the risk of not arriving at their destination dominates Derrida's later work *The Post Card* (1980), which is also a critical reading of Heidegger's emphasis on *Geschick* or a destiny (without chance or accident) as the historical gathering of the epochs of being (*IJD*, 117–18).[15] Heidegger was also a contributor to this collection, publishing "Time and Being" in a translation by Fédier, and one wonders if Blanchot and Derrida also sent a letter that never arrived to Heidegger.[16]

Janicaud goes on to ask Derrida why he was not invited to the 1968 and 1969 seminars which Heidegger held at Le Thor in Provence. Derrida responds, "by 1969, my cover was already blown! [*j'étais déjà grillé!*]." In other words, Derrida "read Heidegger", but he was not considered "as someone who was linked [*lié*] to Heidegger in a privileged way" (*IJD*, 100). Janicaud responds to this strategy of reading by asking Derrida about a note that he added to "*Ousia* and *Grammē*" when it was published in 1972 in *Margins of Philosophy*. But Derrida corrects him: the note was already included in the 1967 text. This note concerns how Derrida approaches the "reading of the entire Heideggerian text itself", and raises the question, to which we will come in a moment, of reading as a (not) meeting. Derrida had written:

Only such a reading [*lecture*], on the condition that it does not give authority to the security or structural closing off [*fermeture*] of questions, appears to us capable of undoing *today, in France*, a profound complicity: the complicity which gathers together [*rassemble*], in the same refusal to read [*refus de lire*], in the same denegation of the question, of the text, and of the question of the text, in the same reeditions, or in the same blind silence, the camp of Heideggerian devotion and the camp of anti-Heideggerianism. Here, political "resistance" often serves as a highly moral alibi for a "resistance" of an other order: *philosophical* resistance, for example, but there are other resistances whose political implications, although more distant, are no less determined. (*OU,* 62 n. 37)[17]

It is here, already, in 1967 that Derrida sees a "complicity" between the presumption of an absolute meeting and an absolute not meeting, and resists a reading of Heidegger that is either devotional or anti-Heideggerian. Derrida's reading is ironic, ambivalent, admiring, disturbed, at once patient and impatient, and always a little violent (*IJD*, 100, 103–6).

Heidegger hated to travel, and for Derrida reading Heidegger is a kind of travelling that is haunted by what refuses to travel. As he says to Janicaud:

I keep disobeying the Heideggerian injunction that, nonetheless, I feel in me. And therefore, he is there; it amuses me [*m'amuse*, diverts, distracts me] to imagine him reproaching me for travelling: one cannot think while travelling, it is distracting. And this from someone who never travels! I do the contrary all the time – but under his gaze. He is a kind of spectre. (*IJD,* 115)

Derrida travels and he reads, and while he travels he does not directly counter (*Gegen*) Heidegger's notions of the region (*Gegend*) or of the encounter (*Begegnen*), but retranslates them as *parages* (vicinities) and the (mis)chances of the chance meeting. "In a way", Derrida says, "I have tried not to protest against what he says about the *Gegend*, of the *Begegnen*, but to draw out towards me or towards another configuration the thought of travelling as the encounter [*la pensée du voyage comme rencontre*]" (*IJD,* 115–16).

For Derrida, in all these histories of (not) meeting Heidegger, there is a constant injunction to resist a gathering or re-collecting, to assume or to yearn for an impossible unity. The *rencontre* can never gather or re-collect itself into an assured or pure resource: this is its unavoidable distress, its dislocation, and its only chance to have a chance – an imperative that is always a question of politics. As Derrida says to his friend Janicaud:

> Resisting gathering can be experienced as distress, misfortune, loss – dislocation, dissemination, the-not-being-at-home [*chez-soi*, in one's self], etc. – but this is also a chance. The chance of the encounter [*la chance de la rencontre*], of justice, of the relation to absolute alterity. While, on the contrary, where this risk and this chance are not found, the worst can happen: under the authority of the *Versammlung*, of the logos and of being, the worst can advance in its political forms. (*IJD*, 118)

READING-THINKING

That everyone is allowed to learn to read ruins not only writing in the long run, but thinking too.[18]

Nietzsche

In "Désistance", his 1987 essay on Lacoue-Labarthe and his reading of Heidegger, Derrida appears to make a remarkable assumption: it is only by *reading* Lacoue-Labarthe that one can register his *thinking*. He writes: "Lacoue-Labarthe's work, his oeuvre, resembles, for me, the very *trial* of the ineluctable: insistent, patient, thinking – the experience of a very *singular* thought of the ineluctable."[19] Whatever thinking does, or has done to it, it only happens, it only takes place, or has its place taken, in reading. "In short", as Derrida says in his interview with Janicaud, "it is necessary to begin with *reading*" (*IJD*, 112).

On 16 August 2004, in his last interview in *Le Monde* before his death, Derrida says, "from the start, and well before my current experiences of surviving, I marked that survival is an original concept, that constitutes the very structure of what we call existence, *Da-sein*, if you like."[20] Derrida begins again, leaving us with the future possibilities of *la survivance* as the immense re-translation of Heidegger's *Dasein*. To mark this labour, which occupied much of his work in the 1970s and the 1980s, he goes on to single out one essay, "Pas". First published in 1976, the year that Heidegger died, "Pas" appeared in a special issue of *Gramma* entitled *Lire Blanchot*.

How does one *lire* Blanchot? How does one read? Among its definitions of *lire*, *Le Robert* offers this remarkable platitude: to read means "being capable of reading a writing" (*être capable de lire une écriture*). There is something very compelling about this simple statement: reading is being capable of reading a writing. Being capable, from *capabilis*, takes one back to *capere*, to take. To read, I must capture and take hold of writing: of letters, words, content, meaning. And it is only by being capable, by taking, that one can become *capacious* and, like a leviathan, take in, swallow, what Plato called the "ocean of words".[21] I am large, I contain multitudes. By taking and taking in, my language, my thoughts become spacious, roomy, expansive, expanding. I have room, I have space: I can invite in others, and welcome the other. Welcome to the roomy room of my own! I am reading.

This notion of reading would of course fail Hillis Miller's ethics of reading, because it assumes, from the start, not only the impossibility of misreading, of mis-taking, but also the terrible good conscience of hospitality, of graciously inviting the others in, of making room for the other and feeling very moral about one's own morality.[22] As Derrida suggested, hospitality begins with an *unavoidable* hospitality. Turn around, they are already there: already there wasn't enough time for good conscience.

In the opening pages of "Pas", Derrida refers to an "incapability" (*incapacité*) in Blanchot's work that cannot be described merely as the absolute other of capability. He also links this incapability not only to a reading again, a rereading, but also to an other thinking of thought (*PA*, 31).[23] Echoing the well-known opening words of *Specters of Marx*, "someone, you or me, comes forward and says: I would like to learn to live [*apprendre à vivre*] finally,"; in "Pas" Derrida warns that in reading Blanchot we will need "to learn to read" (*apprendre à lire*) (*PA*, 38–9).[24] Learning to read *in the midst* of reading, the possibility of reading can only be found – already – in reading: there is no "Idea in the Kantian sense", no pure possibility or *not x but the possibility of x* for reading. There is rather a finitude, an indefinite finitude in reading. We are always waiting to learn to read, while we are reading.

It is through the steps and negations of the *pas*, a moving and movable negative, that Derrida gestures to a relation between reading and thinking:

More than thirty years after *Thomas the Obscure* we could still have reread [*relire*] all the steps of distancing [*les pas d'éloignement*] (for example, but return these fragments without totality to their *récit* and remember that he himself never underlines): "... as I was only real under the name of death, I let shine through, *blood mixed with my blood*, the deadly spirit of shadows, and the mirror of each of my days will reflect the confused images of death and life. [. . .] This Thomas forced me to appear [. . .] body *without* life, insensible sensibility, *thought without thought*. At the highest point of contradiction, I was this *illegitimate* death. Represented in my feelings by a double for whom each feeling meant as much an absurdity as a death, I suffered, at the height of *passion*, the height of strangeness and I seemed abducted from the human condition for having truly fulfilled it. Being, in each human act, the dead one who at once makes it possible and impossible and, if I walked, if I thought, the one whose complete absence allowed only the *step* and the *thought*, faced with beasts, beings who did not carry within them their double death, I lost my last reason for being. There was between us a magical *interval*." This interval has the form of an absence that allows "the *step* and the *thought*," but it first intervenes as the relation of step to step or of thought to thought, step without step [*pas sans pas*] or "thought *without* thought." This play (*without* play) of the *sans* in his texts, you will come to see that it disarticulates all the logic of identity or contradiction and that he starts from "the name of death" or the non-identity of the double in the name. This is a reading that it is still necessary to keep patiently in reserve. (*PA,* 41–2)

Derrida frames this passage on the interval of the *pas* of the *sans*, the step/not of the without, as the possibility of the "relation . . . of thought to thought", with two suspended readings. We start with a rereading, a reading again that evokes a still unread future of the past: "we could have reread the *pas*." We end with a reading that is held back, still reserved, put to one side, for a future that has yet to come. In the interval that marks the relation of thinking to thinking, no reading takes place. In other words, there is no reading as a present event, as an event of the present. Reading does not take place, does not take the place, in the interval that makes thinking possible.

Later in "Pas" Derrida quotes from Blanchot's "Literature and the Right to Death" (1949). Blanchot is touching on the strange resistance of things in literature, and for Derrida, "this singular materiality of the step [*pas*] goes beyond any 'materialist thesis'" (*PA,* 80). Blanchot writes:

> Where in a work lies the beginning of the moment when the words become stronger than their meaning and the meaning more physical than the word? [. . .] At what moment, in this labyrinth of order, in this maze of clarity did meaning stray from the path, at what turning did reason become aware that it had stopped "following," that something else was continuing, progressing, concluding in its place, something like it in every way, something reason thought it recognized itself as itself, until the moment it woke up and discovered this other that had taken its place [*pris sa place*]? But if reason now retraces its steps [*revient-il sur ses pas*] in order to denounce the intruder, the illusion immediately vanishes into thin air, reason finds only itself there, the prose is prose again, so that reason starts off again and loses its way again, allowing a sickening physical substance to replace it, something like a walking staircase, a corridor that unfolds ahead.[25]

At what moment in reading do we become aware that we have lost our place, that we have lost the place, that the other has "taken its place"? Reading: the other always taking the place of the reader. As Blanchot suggests, this losing the place, this twisting and turning of the place, cannot be registered, recovered or retraced. We always have to start reading again, to read on – and lose our place.

Reading is the labyrinth *of* order, the maze *of* clarity. Order and clarity, so indispensable and necessary to reading, cannot posit a place, a position beyond the labyrinth or the maze. There are only the ingenious bends and curves, the twists and turns, of order and clarity within the labyrinth. Between philosophy and literature, there is always the *between* of reading.

READING: *THE COGITO*

In "Pas," Derrida suggests that the interval of *pas*, as the possibility of the "relation . . . of thought to thought", also precedes and exceeds the *Cogito* and its other. Derrida writes, within the citations and re-citations, the cuts and re-cuts, of reading:

> I have cut out this passage from the middle of the one that displaces the step (the not-step [*ne-pas*] rather, because the step of a not-step is not in itself negative) between the *I am* and the *I think* [. . .] until the alternation of the not-step affecting the *I am* or the *I think* lets itself be described as not-walking without step [*dé-marche sans pas*], certainly counting its steps, but steps carried beyond themselves. (*PA*, 42–3)

For Descartes, when it comes to *Meditations on First Philosophy*, reading is always at once before and after the *Cogito*: the problem of rereading never stops. The presentation of the *Cogito* can be seen as the re-invention of reading. In stating that the reader must have "a mind which is completely free from preconceived opinions and which can easily detach itself from involvement with the senses", Descartes anticipates the very conditions for announcing the possibility of the *Cogito* (*MF*, 5). Without a certain kind of reading there can be no *Cogito*.

Descartes can only repeat and extend this precarious reliance on "a very attentive reader" in the "Preface to the Reader":

> I would not urge anyone to read this book except those who are able and willing to mediate seriously with me, and to withdraw their minds from the senses and from all preconceived opinions. Such readers, as I well know, are few and far between. (*MF*, 8)

Descartes cannot extricate the *Cogito* from a conflict of reading.[26] On the one hand, he requires "an attentive reader" (*un esprit tout entier*) that is free of "preconceived opinions" and the influence of the senses (*MF*, 5).[27] Without any prior opinions or senses, this newly born and blind reader becomes the ideal other, a diaphanous other, who is always "willing to mediate seriously with" Descartes. Always *with* Descartes, this ghostly other can only reflect the ideal objectivity of the mind. On the other hand, this reader cannot avoid being read by a still prejudiced, stubbornly resistant reader, as the never ending "Objections and Replies" suggest.

The sheer scale of the demands of these other readers is extraordinary: while some 60 pages are devoted to the *Meditations*, some 330

pages are given to the "Objections and Replies". Descartes can never
stop replying to his objecting readers and can never stop losing hold
of the ideal objectivity of the reader. "I would have done better to
avoid writing on matters which a large number of people ought to
avoid reading about," he complains in the midst of these objections
(*MF,* 172). All he can do is evoke an endless injunction to be read
again, to call for "a careful and repeated re-reading [*sérieuse et
fréquente lecture*]" (*MF,* 300; *MPP,* 890). The *Cogito*: an interminable
re-reading that never reads *with* Descartes. As he later observes, to
read the *Cogito* "we should need more time for reading . . . than our
present life allows (*MF,* 401).[28] Reading the *Cogito*: *la survivance*.

READING AS GATHERING

In § 35 of *Being and Time* Heidegger argues that idle talk (*Gerede*), a
communicating and being with another without primary understanding, "spreads [*breitet*] to what we write" and "feeds upon superficial
reading [*dem Angelesenen*]" (*BT,* 168–9).[29] Talking spreads – perhaps
even like a Cartesian *extensio* – into writing, it moves into writing, it
takes up room in writing, like a capacious parasite. Beguiled by this
"superficial reading", Heidegger adds, "the average understanding
of the reader will *never be able* to decide what has been drawn from
primordial sources with a struggle and how much is just gossip".
This is the mis-reading of *Dasein*: reading as presence.

On the one hand, for Heidegger reading as idle talk is "a positive
phenomenon" because it defines "the kind of Being of everyday
Dasein's understanding and interpreting" and indicates what exceeds
the everyday "understanding and interpreting" of *Dasein* (*BT,* 167).
On the other hand, how are we, we readers – who may or may not
have an "average understanding"– to keep reading *Being and Time*
after this? Heidegger leaves his readers with the possibility that they
too are not immune to the force of idle talk, to its power to take up
the space of writing and make reading, always, undecidable.

But if this was the case in 1926, by 1935 Heidegger had made a
decision. In *Introduction to Metaphysics*, he takes a position. He gives
reading its place, or at least the teleology of its proper place. In the
fourth chapter, which is concerned with the "restriction [*Beschrän-
kung*] of Being through an Other", he identifies four distinctions or
divisions "between Being and its Other": Being and becoming; Being
and seeming; Being and thinking; Being and the ought.[30] He goes on

to challenge the apparent opposition between each of these four meetings or duels. In each case there is a "belonging-together [*Zusammengehörigkeit*]", a "concealed unity [*verborgene Einheit*]," a prearranged *rendezvous*.

Despite the Platonic associations of seeming with multiplicity and distortion, Heidegger argues that thinking, or the thinking of the difference between Being and thinking, begins when seeming becomes at once self-aware and self-conscious, when "seeming covers itself over as seeming" and, at last, "shows itself as Being". Thinking starts when we can read the tracks and traces of the "path into unconcealment" (*IM*, 114–15). For Heidegger, this is the *polemos* before the difference of Being and thinking, a simultaneous risk and overview of not two but three paths: of being, of not-being and of seeming, or what Heidegger calls the way of the *doxa* (*IM*, 117–20). The way of the *doxa* is a sliding back and forth on the path, a blind mixing of being and seeming in which they both lose their place. One could, with all the precautions for the gathering that is to come, call this the advent of reading. Reading as the logos losing its way. Reading as the loss of the place, of the temple, and the advent of the book that moves and moves away with what Lévinas called "an oceanic rhythm".[31]

Everything changes with thinking. Everything takes on a "definite form" and belongs to another level. Being is represented (*Vorstellung*), and it is now that we freely choose, at our own disposal, to represent Being as an object before us, as a universal and within the grid of logic. Even more than on the way of the *doxa*, today we have lost our way Heidegger intones, and it all began by confusing the original unity between Being and *phusis*, and *phusis* and *logos*. It is time for the harvest, for the gleaning, for reading as a re-gathering.

Heidegger must re-invent reading, he must call on "reading a book" to bypass language and find its way back to what gathers towards itself. *Logos* and *legein*, he argues, did not "originally and authentically mean thinking, understanding and reason":

> *Logos* does not originally mean discourse, saying [*Rede, Sagen*]. What the word means has no immediate relation to language. *Legō, legein*, Latin *legere*, is the same word as our *lesen* [to collect]: gleaning, collecting wood, harvesting grapes, making a selection; "reading [*lesen*] a book" is just a variant of "gathering" in the authentic sense [*'ein Buch lesen' ist nur ein Abort des 'Lesens'*

in eigentlichen Sinne]. This means laying one thing next to another, bringing them together as one [*in eines Zusammenbringen*] – in short, gathering [*Sammeln*]; but at the same time, the one is contrasted to the other (*IM*, 131; *EidM*, 118).[32]

For Heidegger, reading is "just a variant of 'gathering' in the authentic sense". Reading is just a variation on a theme of *Versammlung*, but its task is immense and serious: reading saves the logos for Being.

Timothy Clark has characterized Heidegger's definition of reading as the preservation or holding open of a singular force of defamiliarization.[33] Heidegger's reading of Hölderlin, he argues, brings to light "an action whose effect is to open and to hold open a space – that of the absence of gods – in which the poem will unfold".[34] Can one *hold open* a space, and most of all when reading? As we have seen with Agamben holding on to potentiality, such a holding open already assumes a profound calculation on absence, whether it be in the name of the poetic, singular creativity or a perfect ethics. And while Heidegger does not begin with reading as the already-gathered into one, as in his reading of Aristotle's *Metaphysics*, the many ways of authentic reading still give way to a gathering towards a single guiding meaning. One may have lost one's place, but only in order to be guided back to the proper place of reading.

In his readings of Heidegger, Derrida characterizes Heidegger's emphasis on *die Versammlung des Denkens*, the gathering or re-collection of thought, as a return to the *logos*. As he writes in "Heidegger's Ear": "At bottom logocentricism is perhaps not so much the gesture that consists in placing the *lógos* at the center as the interpretation of *lógos* as *Versammlung*, that is the gathering [*le rassemblement*] that precisely concenters what it configures" (*HE*, 187).[35] One could say that from Descartes to Heidegger, philosophy has assumed that it already knows how to read. For Derrida, on the contrary, one never stops learning how to read.

ONE MUST LEARN TO READ

Recalling what he had written in "Pas", in "Désistance" Derrida argues that not only thinking, but the singularity of the thought of the other, can only be approached through learning how to read: "One must learn to read [*il faut apprendre à lire*] Lacoue-Labarthe, to listen to him, and to do so at his rhythm. [. . .] One must learn the necessity of a scansion that comes to fold and unfold a thought" (*DE*, 198).[36] Reading the thought of Lacoue-Labarthe, Derrida suggests, begins with the oscillating *impasse* of a double bind that opens every closure without giving itself to a hyperbolic opening that would break free of all constraint: "the double bind leaves no way out, nor does the hyperbologic – one has to know this in order to begin to think" (*DE*, 203). Derrida insists on this oscillating impasse when reading Lacoue-Labarthe's description of Heidegger's project as "a thinking concerned with thinking [. . .] the *unthought* itself (l'impensé *même*)" (*DE*, 205; *Des* 210). In Heidegger's work, Derrida argues, this impasse of the double bind is *passed over*, "the *un*-thought is un-*thought*" (l'*im*-pensé est im-*pensé*). Heidegger thinks of the unthinkable as that which "gathers each time in the unity of a single site, as if there were only *one* unthought in which each 'great' thought – and herein would lie its greatness – would find its secret law" (*DE*, 205; *Des*, 210). As one of the narrators suggests in Derrida's "Telepathy" (1981), the "unique encounter [*rencontre*] with the unique" is the site, the place *par excellence* for the attempt to claim the "unthinkable", to put it to work for thinking one and for one thinking.[37]

If one *reads* this pull towards unity in Heidegger's work as always a pull towards unity, one has already passed over the impasse of the oscillating impasse, the hovering at the threshold that loses its place, that gives itself to another place. For Derrida, Lacoue-Labarthe himself is in danger of confirming the possibility "the very site [*le lieu*] out of which a thought gives – or gives itself – to think". He writes:

> What if Heidegger's unthought (for example) was not one, but plural? What if his *un*thought was believing in the unicity or the unity of the un*thought*? I will not turn my uneasiness into a critique, because I do not believe that this gesture of gathering is avoidable. It is always productive, and philosophically necessary. (*DE*, 212; *Des*, 219)

Derrida contrasts this necessity to think as and of the gathering back into unity, the untouchable "secret law" of the uniquely unthinkable, to what he calls a "thoughtful reading" [*lecture pensante*] of both Lacoue-Labarthe and Heidegger (*DE*, 206, 208; *Des*, 211).

At the very least, a "thoughtful reading" is an interminable demand to "work at reading and rereading", of always learning to read in the *midst* of reading (*DE,* 209). Of reading as losing the place that is taken by the unique place of re-collection.

(NOT) MEETING AGAIN

Reading, and always risking *la chance de la rencontre*, I have already lost my place; I have already given myself to the other reading, to another reading.[38] For Derrida, this question of taking place as taking away the place is also always institutional and political. In his 1987 essay "Fifty-two Aphorisms for a Foreword", Derrida notes, "the Collège International de Philosophie [which he helped to found in 1983] owed it to itself to make space for and give rise to an *encounter* [*une* rencontre], a thinking *encounter* [*une* rencontre *pensante*]."[39] This countering institution, Derrida suggests, can give the place, give away the place, can risk *losing* its place, for a *rencontre pensante*, a thinking of the *chance* of the chance meetings between philosophy and literature. Derrida's essay is also a preface, and he argues that in giving (away) the place for this "thinking encounter" the International College of Philosophy should also be seen as a prefatory institution, an institution that gives up the place to take its place at the front, as the *precedant* of a meeting that has yet to take place. The prefatory institution is instituted and held in reserve for the chances of another meeting, for the risks of (not) meeting, for a calculating *from* absence without rest (*FT,* 120; *CD,* 124).

Reading-thinking begins in "the risk or chance" of losing one's place (*ATV,* 147). As Derrida remarks in *Signsponge*, his reading of the names and texts of Francis Ponge, "that which interests, or interests us, and engages us in reading, is inevitably what happens in the middle."[40] Reading, reading-thinking of a relation between philosophy and literature, between literature and war, I am always interested, I am always *in the middle*, in the midst of the chances of the chance encounter, of (not) meeting, of the words and spaces, of the gaps that move and move *you*, you whom I still don't know how to read (*ATV,* 171). "We can meet them after having begun to read them."[41] "It would be necessary to think (what does this mean here, you, do *you* know?)" (*TEL,* 227).

PART TWO

LA CHANCE DE LA RENCONTRE

CHAPTER 4

(MIS)CHANCES

Philosophy itself could not begin without *la chance de la rencontre*. As Socrates tells us at the opening of the *Lysis*, "I was going from the Academy straight to the Lyceum . . . when . . . I fell in with Hippothales," or at the start of the *Republic*, "I went down yesterday to the Piraeus with Glaucon . . . at that instant Polemarchus the son of Cephalus chanced to catch sight of us."[1] One could spend much time with the title and subtitle of Derrida's 1982 essay "My Chances/*Mes Chances*: Rendezvous with some Epicurean Stereophonies": my chances of mischance, of a bad and even evil business (*mes chances*), at a prearranged meeting (*au rendezvous*).[2] Derrida asks at the opening of his essay,

> what are my chances of reaching my addressees if, on the one hand, I calculate and prepare a place of *encounter* [*un lieu de* rencontre] (and I underscore the word) or if, on the other hand, I hope as we say in French *to fall upon* [tomber] them by chance? (*MC,* 345).[3]

Derrida presents us with a risky alternative, a swerve from the out-set: in making his address, either he can fall upon his audience by chance or he can try to "prepare a place of *encounter*" – a *meeting place* – in advance. However, as we have seen, this meeting place is itself as much, if not more, a risk because it is not a *rendezvous*, but a *rencontre*, a chance encounter. In French, *rencontre* has retained two quite different meanings: to meet, to come upon, to encounter by chance *and* to meet in conflict, to collide, to fight a *duel*.[4] The *rencontre* registers at once the chance of a chance meeting and the mis-chance of conflict, of a fight to the death, of the outbreak of hostilities that could lead to war. It is with the unavoidable (mis)chances of *la chance de la rencontre* that we can begin to think about a relation between war and literature.

In "My Chances/*Mes Chances*", Derrida allows himself to be detained by what Kant called at the end of the *Critique of Pure Reason* "the deep well of Democritus".[5] Derrida had made a few passing comments in *Of Grammatology* on Democritus, the father of the *a-tom* (of that which cannot be cut). The *grammē* (both a line and a trace) indicates an "element without simplicity", a non-simple element that prevents the concept of "the irreducible atom" being defined as a resource for metaphysics. *Sans simplicité*, the atom is always already cut and cutting (*OG,* 9; *Dlg,* 19–20). In the wake of Democritus, Epicurus was credited with the variation of atoms that bend and swerve.[6] As Lucretius noted, in falling an atom can also make a "tiny swerve" (*exiguum clinamen*), a swerve "in no determined direction of place and at no determined time" (*nec regione loci certa nec tempore certo*).[7] In *De Fato*, Cicero suggested that this "very small swerve" (*declinent uno minimo*) opens or is opened by an interval, as "the atom swerves sideways a minimal space" (*declinant atmos intervallo minimo*).[8] The *interval* of a smallest swerve becomes the "origin" of (mis)chance.

In "My Chances/*Mes Chances*", Derrida argues that before and after the element would be the mark (*stoikheion*): divisible, different, and dividing (*MC,* 354). These marks (*stoikheia*), which extend beyond "the verbal sign and even beyond human language", are the possibility – and the ruin – of an assured deviation, of the *programmed* swerve, of the Epicurean *clinamen* or a chance bias that begins only with *a vertical or straight fall* from the high to the low (*MC,* 360).[9] These marks can only mark themselves with another swerve, with a re-mark that deviates and doubles as it identifies itself. These re-marks are the swerving bias (*epikarsios*) that precedes and exceeds the *etymon*, the truth of the proper name, of a proper name such as *Epicurus*. For Derrida, these swerving marks never stop re-marking the possibility of a (mis)chance: they give chance its *chance*.[10]

Long before Kant had stared into the deep well of Democritus, Montaigne had suggested that one cannot avoid the terrible laughter of Democritus. In his essay "Democritus and Heraclitus", Montaigne describes the method of the *essai*, of starting a narrative: "I take the first subject Fortune offers: all are equally good for me.

I never plan to expound them in full for I do not see the whole of anything: neither do those who promise to help us do so!"[11] Writing "with no plan and no promises", Montaigne addresses the traditional difference between Democritus and Heraclitus. Democritus, he writes:

> finding our human circumstances so vain and ridiculous, never went out without a laughing and mocking look on his face: Heraclitus, feeling pity and compassion for these same circumstances of ours, wore an expression which was always sad, his eyes full of tears.

Montaigne prefers the attitude of Democritus, "because it is more disdainful and condemns us men more than the other". One of the qualities of man, he concludes, "is to be equally laughable and able to laugh."

This vision of Democritus as the philosopher who laughs (when he could also be weeping) with disdain and condemnation at the absurdity of "human circumstances" – at the irreducible chances, the chances that cannot be cut and that never stop cutting – is perhaps one of the causes for Plato's exclusion of Democritus from his works. As Derrida notes, Plato effaces the name of Democritus, a near contemporary of Socrates, from his work. This repression of Democritus is indicative of Plato's need to exclude the swerve and bias of the divisible and dividing marks that resist the call of the vertical (*MC,* 371, 370).

Perhaps one can hear the exclusion of Democritus in the irrepressible reverberating swerves of the laughter of Socrates, in the gravity of his mimicking disdain. The bias of Democritus has been cut out of Platonism. Why this inaugural cutting of what cannot be cut? This was not even the first cut. Archelaus, considered to be the first philosopher who was born in Athens, was the teacher of Socrates. Diogenes reports that Archelaus was best known for his belief that "things are just or ignoble not by nature but by convention" (*F,* 240). Needless to say, Socrates reacted against this nascent sophism by never ceasing to talk about it, by having to refute it over and over again, right to the end, as if he never quite managed to outmanoeuvre this absent father, to calculate on the absence of the father. Like Democritus, Archelaus is never mentioned in the Platonic dialogues, and he becomes another father to-be-cut-out: like Plato himself, the

Figure 4 The National Archaeological Museum of Athens, 2007 © Jane Brown 2009.

philosopher who never appears.[12] Democritus is one of the unrepresented and unrepresentable fathers of Platonism – and there are so many of them.

In "My Chances/*Mes Chances*", Derrida addresses the question of what he calls in a later essay "the crossing of chance and of program, of *the aleatory* and necessity".[13] This junction of hazard and necessity, he argues, cannot be reduced to an opposition. Language is a system of marks or traces that has at once chances and controls: "these effects of chance appear at once produced, multiplied *and* limited by language" (*MC,* 345). This unity of rule and chance in a system indicates an unavoidable "law of destabilization". Derrida writes:

> Language, however, is but one among those systems of *marks* that all have as a proper feature this curious tendency: to increase *simultaneously* the reserves of random indetermination *and* the powers of coding or overcoding, in other words of control and self-regulation. This competition between randomness and code disturbs the very systematicity of the system, even though it regulates that system's play in its instability. (*MC,* 345–6)[14]

As he had noted a decade earlier in "Outwork, Prefacing" (1972), "the game here is the unity of chance and rule, of the program and its leftovers or extras" (*OWP,* 54).[15]

In "My Chances/*Mes Chances*", Derrida also questions the bias in Heidegger's association of chance with the assumption of a vertical fall (*Verfallen*), and a decline or decay (*Verfallenheit*) (*MC,* 252–3). In his two essays in the following years on Heidegger, "*Geschlecht* I: Sexual Difference, Ontological Difference" (1983) and "Heidegger's Hand (*Geschlecht* II)" (1985), Derrida marks a frail fault line between Heidegger's emphasis on decay and decomposition, as the inauthenticity of dispersion, and an oppositional or duelling sexuality, as the dispersing multiplicity of a sexual difference that "would still not be sexual duality, difference as duel" (*GSD,* 24–6). For Heidegger, Derrida argues, this duel of the sexes cannot avoid falling into open warfare:

> And as for the word *das Zwiefache*, the double, the dual [*le duel*], the duplicitous, it carries the whole enigma of the text that plays itself out between, on the one hand, *das Zwiefache*, a certain duplicity, a certain fold of sexual difference or *Geschlecht*, and, on

the other hand, *die Zwietracht der Geschlechter*, the duality of sexes as dissension, war, disagreement, opposition, the duel of violence and of declared hostilities. (*HH,* 54; *MH,* 60)

Derrida points out that for Heidegger the *decline* of thought – after the pure thinking of Socrates, who does not write – is registered by its fall, its dispersion, into writing and literature (*HH,* 48; *WCT,* 11).

From the Greeks, *la chance de la rencontre* has been tied to the spatial–theological concepts of the high and the low, to the good and the bad and a polyphony of Falls. In his travelling letters dispersed throughout Catherine Malabou's *Counterpath* (1999), Derrida links the Heideggerian determination of spatiality and a distancing-towards-proximity in §23 of *Being and Time* to a very determined notion of the encounter (*Begegnen*):

I think I remember that soon after, in *Sein und Zeit*, as he often does he critiques the meager evidence of the inside, of being-in: space isn't *in* the subject nor the world *in* space. That, for him, is the underivable, what can't drift. For every drift or derivation has its place or takes place there. Spacing itself, the spatiality of spacing, distancing, does not drift or derive, and what is *a priori*, originary, absolutely prior, is the "encounter (*Begegnen*)," the encounter with space as region (*Gegend*).[16]

Derrida responds to this unmovable encounter that has no (mis)chance, by retranslating the Heideggerian link between *Begegnen* and *Gegend* to the unstable relation and "undecided precipitation" between *rencontre* and *contra* (which means both in the way *and* out in front):

We should stop to think travel on the edge of the encounter. Not everything comes down to the encounter, but can you imagine a traverse without encounter? Should we cultivate the virtualities of this lexicon, between "with" (*apud hoc, cum*) and "contra." In Latin, therefore contra Heidegger [. . .] contradictions, contre-temps, and contracts would be there to point out the way, referring us to what, in the idea of the encounter or meeting sends us back out *en voyage*, and therefore sends us back. [. . .] But there you have it, if one travels *in view of* the meeting, there is no more encounter, nothing happens. The encounter is the undecided precipitation, without the least preparation, at the mercy of the other who decides, the irruption of what one has, above all, not seen coming – and that can arrive or happen, yes indeed, "at home".[17]

Before and after this travelling letter from 1997, first in 1984 and then again in 2002, Derrida turned to Paul Celan's phrase "*Geheimnis der Begegnung*", from his 1960 address "The Meridian", which Derrida translates as "*le secret de la rencontre*" (*SB,* 9).[18] In "Shibboleth" (1986), a work marking the "indiscernible discernment between alliance and war", Derrida explores "the secret of the encounter" in Celan's poetry, a poetry ravaged by the "experience of the date". For Derrida, the date is the date of a *rencontre* that gives itself to "the date of an other". This is an encounter that both reserves the secret of its singularity and *exceeds* this "absolute singularity", transgresses this absolute secrecy, and gives itself over to the (mis)chance of another secret, of the another date, of another meeting or duel. As Derrida writes:

> Encounter [*rencontre*] – in this [French] word two values without which a date would never take place encounter one another: the encounter as random occurrence, as chance, as luck or coincidence, as the conjuncture that comes to seal one or more than one event *once*, at a particular hour, on a particular day, in a particular month, year, and region; and then the encounter with the other [*la rencontre de l'autre*], the ineluctable singularity from which and destined to which a poem speaks. In its otherness and its solitude (which is also that of the poem, "alone," "solitary"), it may inhabit the conjuncture of one and the same date. This is what happens. (*SB,* 9; *Sch,* 23)

For Derrida, this "particular day" – here and now – retains its transgressed secrets because it is also itself always more than one:

> Several singular events may be conjoined, allied, *concentrated* in the same date, which therefore becomes both the same and an other, wholly other as the same, capable of speaking to the other of the other, wholly other as the same, to the one who cannot decipher such an absolutely closed date, a tomb, closed over the event that it marks. (*SB,* 10)

In his paper "No Apocalypse, Not Now: Full Speed Ahead, Seven Missiles, Seven Missives" (1984), published in the same year as this first reading of Celan was written, Derrida argues that war always makes us "think the *today*".[19] This is perhaps a first gesture towards the problem of the relation of literature to the wars of "our times", to a writing where the "one and the 'same' date commemorates heterogeneous events".[20] In literary works, we have the *chance* of thinking of one war *in the midst* of another: in literature there is always the possibility of more than one war, of many wars.

The caveat that Derrida adds in "Shibboleth" is found in Celan's "terrible" emphasis on the word "*concentrated*". The great reader of Heidegger that he was, and marked by his (not) meeting the philosopher, Celan echoes the Heideggerian tradition of a re-collecting or gathering (*Versammlung*), of a "gathering of the soul" (*SB,* 10). Eighteen years later in his 2002 seminar, Derrida again reiterates this "Heideggarian motif" in Celan's work. In the context of the question of the poem, Derrida notes that Celan describes the poem as "a speaking of two", as "a speech of more than one" (*Gespräch*). But this "speaking of two" also "*maintains* more than one in it" (my emphasis). It is "a speaking that *gathers* more than one in it". As a chance of "being-together", this is "a chance of gathering" that has few (mis)chances.[21] As Derrida had argued elsewhere, such an assured "speaking of two" already cannot avoid "that the verbal structure maintain[s] a relation to what was aleatory in the encounter [*l'aléa de la rencontre*] such that no semantic order could stop the play, or totalise it from a centre, an origin, or a principle" (*WH,* 108).[22]

At the same time, Celan suggests this *Gespräch* is "often" a "despairing dialogue," which prompts Derrida to argue that the poem is

> a speaking of two ... even if it fails, even if the address is not received or does not arrive at its destination, even if the despair of the other, or about the other, is always waiting, and even if it must always be waiting, as its very possibility, the possibility of the poem.

The hope of "being-together", the prearranged meeting or duel must always contend with the despairing possibility of not meeting, of waiting for the meeting or duel that never arrives (*MAJ,* 119). Celan's notion of the "secret of the poem" as the "secret of the encounter" (*im Geheimnis der Begegnung*) is at once the despairing attempt *to make* (to present) *and* the chance encounter with that which "does not present itself", with the *unmakeable*, with what cannot be made self-evident, with what remained, for the poet of a war without end, the absurd showing of nothing. "Nothing shows itself," Celan wrote, "the nothing, the absurd shows itself in manifesting nothing" (*MAJ,* 114). We will come back to this question of war and making and unmaking in the next chapter.

In his 2003 lecture on the archives of Hélène Cixous, Derrida gestured to what may be an alternative translation of the chance encounter to the *Begegnen* of Heidegger and the *Geheimnis der Begegnung* of Celan. In his warm tribute to Cixous, Derrida follows the two paths of the phrase *se trouver*:

> The "*se trouver*" can consist of finding, of discovering oneself, of encountering oneself [*se rencontrer*] reflexively, speculatively and transitively oneself (finding oneself), but also to be passively and unconsciously localised, situated, placed [*à avoir lieu*], to be posed, thrown, placed here or there rather than elsewhere, in a contingent, indeed miraculous, in any case fateful way.

Finding oneself *finding* (*se trouver trouver*), Derrida suggests, there is an interlacing oscillation between these two turns. Between these findings that are always finding again, one can retranslate *la rencontre* as *das treffen*.[23] If *Begegnen* is to meet, to come upon, *zugfällig begegnen*, chance or stumble upon, *treffen* is to fall in with, encounter, find. But it is also to hit or to strike, from *treff*, blow, knock. *Treffen* is an encounter that cannot be separated from the (mis)chance of the blow that *never stops reverberating*: a *rencontre* for "our times".

It is perhaps the frail hope of avoiding this blow, of a falling into a fatal collision, that Celan evokes in his poem "The bright stones" (*Die hellen Steine*), from his 1963 collection *Die Niemandrose*:

> THE BRIGHT
> STONES ride through the air, bright
> White, the light-
> bringers.
>
> They want to
> Not sink, not fall,
> Not collide [*nicht treffen*].[24]

However, in the opening of another poem from the same collection, "Radix, Matrix", Celan suggests that there are also stones of the night, stones that cannot avoid the blows that linger on and on and last for what seems a lifetime – and more (*SB*, 55–6).[25] Here, Celan cuts like a mason into the Heideggerian concept of *Begegnen*:

> As one speaks to stone, as
> you,
> to me from the abyss, from
> a homeland con-
> Sanguined, up-
> Hurled, you,
> You of old to me,
> You in the Nix of a night to me,
> You in Yet-Night en-
> Countered, you
> Yet-You —:

> [du in der Aber-Nacht Be-
> *gegnete, du*
> *Aber-Du* —:][26]

Speaking to a stone. As Derrida pointed out in *Of Spirit: Heidegger and the Question* (1987), according to Heidegger, one cannot talk to stones because in contrast to the "world-forming" powers of man and the privation of the world for animals, "the stone is without world (*weltlos*)." Starting from a "pure and simple absence", from a clear-cut difference – "the stone has no access to entities, it has no experience" – Heidegger defines the complex differences of and between animals and man. The silence of the stone, its inaugural and pure difference, is the possibility of "animals," of "man", of *Dasein*.[27] But for Celan, one never stops speaking to stones.

As Celan's poem suggests, in speaking to stones, one is already enmeshed both in the difference and mischance of an absence that one cannot count on, and a swerve that is never simple or pure. From the opening words, "As one speaks to stone, as / you" (*Wie man zum Stein spricht, wie / du*), one expects that it is the I of the poem that is speaking to stone – to the absent and dead "you", to the tombstones, to the statues, to the ruins, or to the small stones (*even*) placed on a Jewish tombstone as an act of remembrance, of loss and mourning.

But it is not *you*, whom I still do not know how to read, the *du* from the abyss, which is figured as the stone. When *you* speak from the abyss (*vom Abgrund*), from the homeland (*Heimat*), from the homeland as the abyss, it is *me* who is the stone:

> As one speaks to stone, as
> you,
> to me from the abyss

When you speak to me, in times of war without end, as "one speaks to stone", from the homeland-as-the-abyss, a proximity – that was so close it made us like brothers and sisters – has been lost, removed, stopped (*Ver-schwisterte*), and the meeting, the *en-counter*, has been surrounded and sundered (*Be-gegnete*), exposed to the (mis)chances and impossible duels with "you / Yet-you" (*du / Aber-Du*) in the "Yet-Night" (*Aber-Nacht*), a night always marked by the enemy that can never be met.

CHAPTER 5

WAR AND ITS OTHER

– Well, then, is any war in Homer's time remembered
that was won because of his generalship?
– None.

The Republic[1]

NARRATIVE AND WAR

From the sixteenth to at least the end of the nineteenth century, *la chance de la rencontre* played a notable role in British literature and philosophy as the *rencounter*. A rencounter was a chance encounter between two armies or two individuals that led to a clash of arms. It was the necessary accident before an apparently necessary act of private or public violence. Without this accidental meeting, there could be no conflict, no duel – and no war. And in many cases, without such chance encounters, there could also be no narratives, no stories – no literature. The epistolary madness of *Clarissa* (1747–1748), and the duel to the death between Clarissa Harlowe and Richard Lovelace, begins with "the rencounter" between Lovelace and James Harlowe.[2] Some 50 years later, in William Godwin's *Things as They Are; or, The Adventures of Caleb Williams* (1794) – a wartime novel written when "terror was the order of the day" – the plot can only advance with a series of "unexpected" and "accidental" rencounters. These fortuitous meetings are never far from the relentless duel between Caleb Williams and Mr. Falkland that dominates the novel.[3]

From at least Richardson to Hardy, the (mis)chance of the rencounter is an integral aspect of literature and literary narrative. In Hardy's case, these chances events are the remorseless evidence of necessity. In *Tess of the D'Urbervilles* (1891), it is the "heavy moment" of "the rencounter" between Tess and Alec D'Urberville that begins the inexorable narrative.[4] As overwrought as the chance meetings may seem in Hardy's work, as a writer he is obsessed with "the result" of these "casual rencounters" (*CA*, 235).[5] On at least one occasion, he recognizes that there are "rencounters accidental and contrived" (*WD*, 223). One can both choose and cannot choose these chance encounters: the rencounter is the possibility of the subject-that-can-choose and the objective forces of destiny, fate or necessity. For Hardy, these rencounters are a testament to the apparent limitations of the late nineteenth-century novel, which he would abandon after *Jude the Obscure* (1895). They are also a testament to his relentless search for the pure possibility of chance or necessity.

As a strategy and constraint of literary narrative, the rencounter was also a key motif in representing the conflict of the duel, of violence and war. As Hume had acknowledged in *An Enquiry Concerning the Principles of Morals* (1751)

the rage and violence of public war; what is it but a suspension of justice among the warring parties, who perceive, that this virtue is now no longer of any *use* or advantage to them? The laws of war, which then succeed to those of equity and justice, are rules calculated for the *advantage* and *utility* of that particular state, in which men are now placed. And were a civilized nation engaged with barbarians, who observed no rules even of war, the former must also suspend their observance of them, where they no longer serve to any purpose; and must render every action or rencounter as bloody and pernicious as possible to the first aggressors.[6]

In the "rage and violence of public war", Hume argues, equity and justice give way to the utility of state-sponsored "laws of war". However, when "a civilized nation" is at war with "barbarians", even these laws of state, which civilized states at war can ostensibly share, are abandoned. In warfare, after or below the laws of war, are the rencounters: the chance meetings, the violent actions that have no other directive than to be "as bloody and pernicious as possible": the rencounter as a theory of total war.

The rencounter plays a more complex role in Hume's later *History of England* (1754–1762). He argues that in the medieval period it was the lack of civilization that prevented rival kingdoms from fighting wars. In its encounters with France, England could not avoid rencounters:

> The general want of industry, commerce, and police, in that age, had rendered all the European nations, and France and England no less than the others, unfit for bearing the burthens of war, when it was prolonged beyond one season; and the continuance of hostilities had, long ere this time, exhausted the force and patience of both kingdoms. Scarcely could the appearance of an army be brought into the field on either side; and all the operations consisted in the surprisal of places, in the rencounter of detached parties, and in incursions upon the open country; which were performed by small bodies, assembled on a sudden from the neighbouring garrisons.[7]

Writing of the earliest period of English history, Hume implies that in the age of rencounters war was not yet possible: "The whole amount of the exploits on both sides is, the taking of a castle, the surprise of a straggling party, a rencounter of horse, which resembles more a rout than a battle" (*HOE* I: 400). At the same time, in this period if a rencounter (a chance encounter with the enemy) precluded the formality of a battle, a rencounter (an arranged duel, "the image of war" rather than "the thing itself") could also lead to a wider and more general battle. Hume writes:

> In his passage by Chalons in Burgundy, he was challenged by the prince of the country to a tournament which he was preparing; and as Edward excelled in those martial and dangerous exercises, the true image of war, he declined not the opportunity of acquiring honour in that great assembly of the neighbouring nobles. But the image of war was here unfortunately turned into the thing itself. Edward and his retinue were so successful in the jousts, that the French knights, provoked at their superiority, made a serious attack upon them, which was repulsed, and much blood was idly shed in the quarrel. This rencounter received the name of the petty battle of Chalons. (*HOE* II: 74–5)

Charting the history of England, Hume suggests that the rencounter is not so much the common barbarism of total warfare, but something that both resists *and* produces the battles of war. The rencounter is a concept of war and it is also the possibility, the chance, of a clash or collision that may or may not break out into open warfare.

"Though in itself of small importance", Hume recognizes that the narrative of the rencounter has a distinctive place in the history of England (*HOE* V: 395). An ambassador is sent by the Dutch with "the narrative . . . of the late rencounter" between English and Dutch ships in a vain attempt to prevent the First Anglo-Dutch War (1652–1653) (*HOE* VI: 48). In his account of the Third Anglo-Dutch War (1672–1674), the "casual rencounter" is used as a pretext by the English to start the war (*HOE* VI: 256). The rencounter is the violent and destructive meeting that could lead to war. As the contrived or accidental possibility of war, the rencounter can be the manufactured pretext for war, but when given a *narrative* it can also be the chance of preventing war.

Hume had first addressed the question of chance in *A Treatise of Human Nature* (1739–1740), and his later historical work can be seen as an ongoing attempt to come to terms with the limitations of what he calls a "more or less perfect" rencounter. In the midst of his discussion of the passions, Hume turns to the variations in the relation between contrary passions:

> Upon this head there may be started a very curious question concerning that contrariety of passions which is our present subject. It is observable, that where the objects of contrary passions are presented at once, beside the encrease of the predominant passion (which has been already explained, and commonly arises at their first shock or rencounter), it sometimes happens that both the passions exist successively, and by short intervals; sometimes that they destroy each other, and neither of them takes place; and sometimes that both of them remain united in the mind. It may therefore be asked, by what theory we can explain these variations, and to what general principle we can reduce them.[8]

Hume uses rencounter here in the sense of meeting, though the conflict of the duel and problem of chance are never far away. The "first shock or rencounter" of an object that generates contrary passions usually allows one passion to dominate the other: it is a chance encounter with an object that leads to the briefest of duels between the passions, until there is a clear victor. Hume's problem is with a rencounter that has no clear winner or even a clear and absolute difference between the combatants.

There are times, Hume goes on to suggest, when there is such a clear difference between objects that contrary passions "take place alternately". There are also times when the difference between contrary passions is such that "both passions, mingling with each other by means of the relation, become mutually destructive" (*T,* 441–2). Hume then offers a third possibility beyond either a clear difference or a self-cancelling difference. This is a difference founded on probability. "Probability is of two kinds," he writes, "either when the object is really in itself uncertain, and to be determin'd by chance; or when, tho' the object be already certain, yet 'tis uncertain to our judgment, which finds a number of proofs on each side of the question' (*T,* 444). It is from an unavoidable probability of both the object and the subject, from a difference determined by chance and uncertainty, that two contrary passions can coexist at the same time:

> But suppose, in the third place, that the object is not a compound of good or evil, but is considered as probable or improbable in any degree; in that case, I assert that the contrary passions will both of them be present at once in the soul, and, instead of destroying and tempering each other, will subsist together, and produce a third impression or affection by their union. (*T,* 442)

Whilst one could call this a difference of the rencounter, for the chance meeting or duel in which difference is neither destroyed nor tempered, Hume treats this third relation of the passions as a union or synthesis: in the difference of their meeting or duel the combatants become one. He also contrasts the imperfection of this probability of coexisting contrary passions to what he calls the perfection of an "exact rencounter" (*T,* 442). For Hume, there can be a "more or less perfect" chance meeting, a "more or less perfect" duel.

THE CHANCE OF THE DUEL

The duel is commonly understood as a premeditated single combat between two living men.[9] But from the start, there will always be more than two, there will be seconds and witnesses. Though a witness to a duel is not always a second. In Turgenev's *Fathers and Sons* (1862), Bazarov suggests before his duel with Pavel Petrovich, "we shall have no seconds, but we could have a witness."[10] The presence of a witness is the formal possibility of the duel, distinguishing it from a murder and giving it the status of an affair of honour. As Kleist writes in his story "The Duel" (*Der Zweikampf*) (1811) – a work referring to more than one date, as it was written *in the midst* of the Napoleonic wars and set in the medieval period – "the code of honour required" that Lady Littegarde be a witness to the "armed encounter" between Friedrich von Trota and Count Jakob Rotbart.[11] Yet it is also the absence of a witness to the whereabouts of Lady Littegarde that has precipitated this duel (*K,* 303).[12] As a "life and death ordeal by combat", this duel stands as representative of "God's judgement". It is "the sacred verdict" of the duel that will "infallibly bring the truth to light" (*K,* 301, 303).

However, as Kleist suggests, this notion of the duel as a God-like revelation of the truth, as a clear-cut act of violence, is disturbed by the chance "mishap" of von Trota tripping during the duel and then, unexpectedly, surviving his wounds, of living beyond the decisive "life and death ordeal" (*K,* 301, 303). Von Trota wants to fight again, to continue the duel. To which his mother responds, "do you not know that according to the law a duel which has been declared by the judges to be concluded cannot be resumed in order to invoke the divine verdict a second time in one and the same case?" There cannot be a repetition, a second chance in the sacred duel: the duel as a sign of "God's judgement" can only take place once. But for Trota, the chance (*Zufall*) "mishap" of his tripping and his unexpected survival should overturn the law of the divinely ordained encounter as a one-off and instant verdict. Von Trota wants to fight his second duel with the law itself, fighting for the rational possibility of a duel without end. As he says to his mother: "What do I care for these arbitrary human laws? Can a fight that has not been continued until the death of one of the two opponents be held to have been concluded, if one considers the matter at all rationally?" (*K,* 307–8). Writing in the midst of the interminable Napoleonic wars, Kleist gestures to the ordeal of a secularized duel, or at least to the duel as a chance encounter, of the narrative of the duel *as* a (mis)chance without end.[13] We will come back to this in the next chapter in Conrad's extraordinary story "The Duel" (1908).

As Derrida suggested, we should question both the inevitable fraternity of the encounter, this would-be war of brothers, and the assumption that it is only the living who can duel. One can already begin to see this in *Romeo and Juliet* (1595), which Derrida described as "the *mise-en-scène* of all duels", of missed *rendezvous* and all the *contretemps* of the *rencontre*.[14] Benvolio warns Mercutio, "the Capels are abroad / And if we meet we shall not scape a brawl."[15] Benvolio and Mercutio are prepared, and yet the duel remains an event that cannot be planned. The private duel between two is always before the law, it cannot avoid becoming public and a duel of always more than two. Benvolio warns: "We talk here in the public haunt of men. / Either withdraw into some private place ... or depart. Here all eyes gaze upon us." Mercutio replies: "Men's eyes were made to look, and let them gaze" (*RJ,* 3. 1. 45–9).

Some 19 years after *Romeo and Juliet*, Bacon would address the problem of "private duels" in *The Charge Touching Duels* (1614). As the Attorney General, he is acting "by his Majesty's direction" to make the case against private duels.[16] For Bacon, it is a question not only of duels, but of a private violence, of the violence of the private: when "private men begin once to presume to give law to themselves, and to right their own wrongs, no man can foresee the dangers and inconveniencies that may arise and multiply thereupon" (*CTD,* 305).[17] This is the hyperbole of an untamed and unreclaimed private violence that Hobbes will later evoke to launch what Derrida called the phantasm of an indivisible sovereignty.[18] The private duel becomes the justification for founding the sovereign authority of the state. For Bacon, the private duel has the power to threaten the king himself: "it may grow from quarrels to banding, and from banding to trooping, and so to tumult and commotion". From *one* chance encounter, the public space, the sovereign power and the state could collapse. At stake is the law itself. The private duel "expressly gives the law an affront, as if there were two laws" (*CTD,* 305).

Nearly two hundred years later, Kant accorded a similar power to the duel in *The Metaphysics of Morals* (1797). A duel, he argues, is a public return to a state of nature governed by a sense of honour, which is valued more than life itself.[19] At the same time, the duel remains a problem for Kant. It creates a gap between the people's subjective sense of justice and the state's objective claim to public justice. The state can neither execute the duellist (and deny honour) nor can it condone an unlawful killing. The *aporia* of the duel suspends the right of the sovereign power to punish crimes with the death penalty. One kind of honour suspends another since, as Derrida notes, it is precisely the propriety of a sacrifice above and beyond life that gives the death penalty its sovereign right.[20] The duel confronts Kant with the *aporia* of the sovereignty of sacrifice as the transcendental possibility of the law (*FWT,* 133).[21]

One can contrast the unresolved dilemma of the duel in *The Meta physics of Morals* to Kant's earlier analysis of war in "Toward Perpetual Peace" (1795) as "the regrettable expedient for asserting one's right by force in a state of nature".[22] As Derrida points out in *Adieu,* for Kant everything starts with war: war is natural, and peace follows as an instituted convention (*AD,* 154).[23] At the same time, Derrida suggested in his reading of Lévinas, Kant's notion of an instituted peace as "the end of all hostilities" lends itself to an unforeseen complicity between holding on to a perpetual concept of peace and generating a self-evident concept of war *as* the natural other of peace, as the possibility of this peace without end (TPP, 320; *AD,* 88–91). This concept of peace would retain and rely on a natural concept of war and invite Clausewitz's well-known observation that war is only the continuation of peace by other means (*AD,* 95). We will come back to Clausewitz and his treatise on war. Derrida argues that Kant is unable to maintain this natural concept of war (*AD,* 88). A perpetual peace can be menaced by the threat of a virtual or non-natural concept of war, by a concept that is neither simply natural nor conventional: a concept of war that cannot forbid the (mis)chances of non-natural or fictional narratives.[24]

It is precisely in beginning to read and think of the chances of the encounter or duel, of the narratives of duels in the midst of war, that we need to take care to avoid the "recourse to literature as [a] reappropriation of presence" (*OG,* 144). As Derrida argued in his readings of Lacan and Freud, the *uses* of literature must always alert us to what literature cannot be used to support or illustrate, to the resistances of literature.[25] In "My Chances/*Mes Chances*", Derrida addresses the chances of the literary work while always being attentive to the temptation and presumption to comprehend or understand as self-evident the (mis)chances of the work:

> I come back to literature, to the work of art, *l'oeuvre d'art,* to the oeuvre in general, to what is so named in the tradition of our culture. No oeuvre without mark, of course. Yet each oeuvre, each work being absolutely singular in some way, it can bear and contain [*porter et comporter*] only proper names. And this in its very iterability. Whence, perhaps, the general form of the privilege that

it retains for us, in our experience, as the place of chance and luck. The work provokes us to think the event. It challenges us to *understand* chance and luck, to take sight of them or take them in hand, to inscribe them within a horizon of anticipation. It is at least in this way that they are works, oeuvres, and, in defiance of any program of reception, they make for an event. Works befall us; they say or unveil what befalls us *by* befalling us. (*MC,* 360–1)

As Derrida goes on to argue, literature should not be seen as an "infinite" or absolute *resource* of chance. There are always margins, borders and rules of reappropriation in the very "large margin" afforded to the shifting contexts and chances of the literary work (*MC,* 374).[26] At the same time, it is these shifting contexts – of taking on *more than one* side or battlefront or war – that gives the literary work its distinctive chances.

OUR PLACE IS WITH THE NON-COMBATANTS

Thackeray remains a distinctive voice in the first half of the nineteenth century for the rencounters in literary texts that are caught up within war, but which cannot be *reduced* to a concept of war. In contrast to Hume, for Thackeray the rencounter can never be "more or less perfect". The rencounter, as both the chance and the rule of the chance meeting, is part of how literature responds to the so-called totality of war. As he writes in *Vanity Fair: A Novel without a Hero* (1847–1848), in the midst of the events leading up to the Battle of Waterloo:

> We do not claim to rank among the military novelists. Our place is with the non-combatants. When the decks are cleared for action we go below and wait meekly. We should only be in the way of the maneuvers that the gallant fellows are performing overhead.[27]

Thackeray suggests that the place and the work of literature "is with the non-combatants", and one can trace this distinguished literary tradition to Primo Levi and beyond.

Having stated that "our place" – the place of both the writer and the reader – is with the non-combatants, Thackeray closes his narrative of war with Captain Dobbin witnessing the "speechless misery" of the non-combatant Amelia Osborne saying goodbye to her husband George Osborne as he leaves for the battle. Thackeray writes:

> "Thank Heaven that is over," George thought, bounding down the stair, his sword under his arm, as he ran swiftly to the alarm ground, where the regiment was mustered, and whither trooped men and officers hurrying from their billets; his pulse was throbbing and his cheeks flushed: the great game of war was going to be played, and he one of the players. What a fierce excitement of doubt, hope, and pleasure! What tremendous hazards of loss or gain! What were all the games of chance he had ever played compared to this one? (*VF*, 355)

For the combatant, war would be the absolute or pure encounter, the absolute test of life and death, a meeting where chance has no chance. However, as we shall see, one can challenge this definition of war. For the non-combatant, on the other hand, these chances are relative and, as Thackeray had already suggested in *The Luck of Barry Lyndon* (1844–1856), can be described as a *series* of encounters, of (mis)chances, of chance meetings and duels. There is no absolute encounter: the duel always invites other duels, other narratives *en abyme*.[28] Thackeray ends his account of George Osborne, in his last appearance before he is killed in battle, with a critique of the limitations of a literature without rencounters. In other words, of a literature with heroes:

> Time out of mind strength and courage have been the theme of bards and romances; and from the story of Troy down to to-day, poetry has always chosen a soldier for a hero. I wonder it is because men are cowards in heart that they admire bravery so much, and place military valour so far beyond every other quality for reward and worship? (*VF*, 356)

Some 20 years after Thackeray, in *War and Peace* (1865–1869) Tolstoy suggested that even for the combatant it is only the *story* of war, the already fictionalized narrative, that can be told: the truth of war, war itself, cannot be told. After his first experience of battle at Schöngraben, and before the more traumatic events at Austerlitz, the young Nikolai Rostov sits down to tell his war stories to his friends. Tolstoy writes:

He told them about his Schöngraben action in just the way that
those who take part in battles usually tell about them, that is, in the
way that they would like it to have been, the way they have heard
others tell it, the way it could be told more beautifully, but not at
all the way it had been. Rostov was a truthful young man, not for
anything would he have deliberately told an untruth. He began telling his story with the intention of telling it exactly as it had been,
but imperceptibly, involuntarily, and inevitably for himself, he went
over into untruth. If he had told the truth to those listeners, who,
like himself, had already heard accounts of attacks numerous times
and had formed for themselves a definite notion of what an attack
was, and were expecting exactly the same sort of account – they
either would not have believed him or, worse still, would have
thought it was Rostov's own fault that what usually happens in
stories of cavalry attacks had not happened with him. (*WP*, 242)

ON WAR: IN A KIND OF TWILIGHT

"Yes, they say war has been declared," said the guest.
"They've been saying that for a long time," said the count.
War and Peace (41)

In 1799, responding to the wars without end that dominated his
times, Schiller turned back to the Thirty Years War in his trilogy
Wallenstein. Schiller writes of one war without end in the midst of
another war without end. He opens his work with what appears to be
a confirmation of the Hegelian harnessing of the negative. It is war
alone that enables us to confront death, and it is only by looking at
"death in the face" that one can be free. As a dragoon says in *Wallenstein's Camp*,

> The soldier alone, of the whole human race,
> Is free, for he can look death in the face.[29]

At the close of *Wallenstein's Camp*, the first part of the trilogy, a
trooper restates this unique privilege of the soldier, but also introduces a slight equivocation:

> Let your breasts rise and swell for the fight!
> Let us follow where youth's rushing torrent leads,

Figure 5 Kronberg Castle, Elsinore, 2007 © Jane Brown 2009.

Come, away! while the spirit is bright.
For if your own life you're not willing to stake,
That life will never be yours to make. (*W*, 214)[30]

In the short delay, the briefest of detours, between marching out and arriving at the battle, the soldier is only half alive and risks, through the possibility of not fighting, a life that "will never be yours to make" (*gewonnen*, win, earn, secure). This frail *chance* of an unmade life, before the absolute risk of death or of a life that has been absolutely won, is the possibility of the *other* of war.

Max Piccolomini later gestures to this chance when he asks, "For if not war in war already ceases / When then shall peace be found?" (*W*, 238).[31] How or when are we to decide when "war in war" (*der Krieg im Kriege*) ceases, when the warlike ceasing of war shall allow us to find peace, to find the other of war, if there is one?[32] Foucault addressed this question in his 1975 seminar, "*Society Must be Defended*". War, he argued, never ends. Even during times without large-scale military operations, "a battlefront runs through the whole of society, continuously and permanently."[33] War itself is "force-relations laid bare", while peace is never itself, or at least never alone, since war is the "ineradicable basis of all the relations and the all institutions of power" that constitute civil society (*SMD*, 46, 49). Peace is just the beginning of a "silent war" (*SMD*, 16). War is the other of peace, Foucault suggests, but war itself has *no other*. The forces of war operate "in and through war" (*SMD*, 15). In the name of the exercise of political power, Foucault gives war and its other no chance. There are no chances, only the "struggles" of war (*SMD*, 16).

In contrast to Foucault, in *A Thousand Plateaus: Capitalism and Schizophrenia* (1980), Deleuze and Guattari argue that the concept of war precedes and exceeds its appropriations by the state. Nomadic in origin, fluid in practice, the force of war is always more than its history of state-orchestrated conflict.[34] But the nomadic fluidity of this concept of war is only made possible by the assumption of the static rigidity of the state. In this case, war is the other *of* the state. Both Foucault and Deleuze and Guattari position their writing on war in relation to Clausewitz's famous saying that "*war is nothing but the continuation of policy with other means*" (daß der Kriege nichts ist als die fortgesetzte Staatspolitik mit anderen Mitteln) (*OW*, 69).[35] Clausewitz informs his reader at the start of *On War* (1832) that "if this [dictum] is firmly kept in mind throughout it will greatly facilitate the study of the subject and the whole will be easier to analyze" (*OW,* 69). In other words, if we read Clausewitz as he wished to be read we would take this dictum as our guiding thread, not least because it should make the whole easier to analyze and allow us to "fill in various gaps, large and small" in the work (*OW,* 69).

But if anything, *On War* is a work with gaps, not least because while Clausewitz insists that "war is nothing but the continuation of policy with other means," he also opens his work by saying that "war is nothing but a duel on a larger scale" (*der Krieg ist nicht als ein erweiterter Zweikampf*) (*OW,* 75; *VK,* 89). As we shall see in the following chapter, at the very least, Conrad's story "The Duel" challenges this assertion. What weight can the assertion "war is nothing but . . ." (*der Krieg ist nicht als*) carry when it gives itself with seemingly equal force to more than one assertion? How can we formulate a concept of war, how can we write *on* war, how can we calculate on war, when it is both "nothing but the continuation of policy with other means" and "nothing but a duel on a larger scale"?

Carl von Clausewitz died on 16 November 1831, two days after Hegel and on the day of Hegel's funeral in Berlin. Death surprised both men, and Clausewitz left an unfinished work, which his widow published in 1832 under the title *On War* (*Vom Kriege*) (*OW,* 66–7). It was not only Clausewitz's death that made it impossible to read *On War* as a complete work; it was also the history of its composition and its very subject matter. Clausewitz began his work in 1804, and 25 years later when he died in 1831 it was still not finished. *On War* begins with no less than five inadvertent and posthumous prefaces: a preface by Clausewitz to an unpublished manuscript from 1816–1818; a note from 1818 on his work in progress; a preface from 1832 by his widow, Marie von Clausewitz; a note from 1827; and, finally, another note from 1830.[36]

Clausewitz served in the Russian army during the 1812 campaign, and makes a brief, and somewhat negative, appearance in *War and Peace*, as the embodiment of the German theoretician of war (*WP,* 774).[37] It is also possible that Tolstoy had *On War* in mind in his descriptions of General Pfuel in *War and Peace*: "Pfuel was one of those theorists who so love their theory that they forget the purpose of the theory – its application in practice; in his love for theory, he hated everything practical and did not want to know about it" (*WP,* 640). In his many prefaces, Clausewitz is in fact preoccupied with the problem of the grave differences between a theory of war and the actual experiences of war (*OW,* 61).[38] A theory of war always takes itself to the extreme: "in the field of abstract thought the inquiring mind can never rest until it reaches the extreme [*dem Äußersten*], for here it is dealing with an extreme: a clash of forces freely operating and obedient to no law but their own" (*OW,* 78: *VK,* 93). Thinking about war "purely in absolute terms", Clausewitz argues, can only go to the extremity or ideal of war as a force without limit. A theory of war can only lead to total war, to the absolute violence of what Clausewitz calls "logical fantasy". This would be war as "nothing but the play of the imagination," a solipsistic abyss.

Clausewitz attempts to moderate or check this theoretical force by insisting on three empirical truths: "war is never an isolated act"; "war does not consist of a single short blow"; and "in war the result is never final" (*OW,* 78–80). In other words, he can only counter the absolute assertions of thinking theoretically about war with three practical assertions. Writing on war, one cannot avoid making assertions about the truth of war. However, Clausewitz goes on to acknowledge that experience shows "the very nature of war impedes the *simultaneous concentration of all forces*" (*OW,* 80). Between these two modes or rules of writing on war – of a force without any limits (the theoretical) and of forces that can never be concentrated into one force (the empirical) – Clausewitz concludes that "the *laws of probability*" will be the only inconstant constant in defining a concept of war (*OW,* 80). If anything, as he notes, when "material calculations take the place of hypothetical extremes," these empirical contingences do not so much counteract the violent ideal of war without limit as reinforce that there can be no limit to a concept of war. A concept of war, writing *on* war, would be interminable (*OW,* 79).[39]

This gap between logic and experience in presenting the concept of war, which has contributed to Clausewitz's project remaining unfinished and unpublished, is complemented by a formal gap in the style and arrangement of the text. As Clausewitz writes in his second chance preface: "My original intention was to set down my conclusions on the principal elements of this topic in short, precise, compact statements, without concern for system or formal connection. [. . .] I thought that such concise, aphoristic chapters, which at the outset I simply wanted to call kernels [*Körner*], would attract the intelligent reader by what they suggested as much as by what they expressed" (*OW,* 63; *VK,* 73). For Clausewitz, these aphoristic kernels are indispensable in attempting to address his initial question, "What is war?"

Nonetheless, he starts this induction as a series-of-kernels by stating that when it comes to war, one must begin with a deduction: "But in war more than any other subject we must begin by looking at the nature of the whole [*das Wesen des Ganzen*]; for here more than elsewhere the part and the whole must always be thought together" (*OW,* 75; *VK,* 89).

While he intended these kernels for a reader "who was already familiar with the subject", as if this is the most appropriate style in which to address fellow soldiers and combatants, Clausewitz soon found himself exhaustively elaborating and expanding these kernels into systematic chapters for "a reader who was not acquainted with the subject" (*OW,* 63). Caught between addressing both combatants and non-combatants, between compact gnomic kernels and inexhaustible explanations that run away from him, Clausewitz was never able to finish writing *On War*.

He closes his prefatory note from 1818 with a task that still remains to be done:

> In the end I intended to revise it all again, strengthen the causal connections in the earlier essays, perhaps in later ones draw together several analyses into a single conclusion, and thus produce a reasonable whole [*eine erträgliches Ganze*], which would form a small volume in *octavo.* (*OW,* 63; *VK,* 73)

Nine years later in 1827, with this "reasonable whole" still eluding him, Clausewitz directs his would be reader to take the dictum "war is nothing but the continuation of policy with other means" to close the gaps of *On War*. It is by taking this dictum as both aphoristic kernel *and* systematic demonstration, as the moderating connection between the theoretical and the empirical, that Clausewitz's quasi-Hegelian gesture is realized: the becoming of the concept of war is an initial theoretical absolute which is then tempered by empirical contingency until the political becomes the *Aufhebung* of the concept of war. The judgements of policy will then minimize and reduce the mischances of a concept of war (*OW,* 80–1, 87).

At the same time, one cannot forget that Clausewitz had also insisted that, "war is nothing but a duel on a larger scale." The duel (*Zweikampf*), the conflict, the battle, the encounter of two, of the more than one, can never entirely be removed from a certain ambiguity (*zweideutig*), equivocation (*Zweideutigkeit*) and uncertainty

(*Zweifel*).[40] Clausewitz's progressive dialectical gesture, which he describes at the end of his first chapter as the "three tendencies" – "blind natural force", "the play of chance and probability" and the rational submission to "an instrument of policy" – is haunted by the profound acknowledgment that "no other human activity is so continuously or universally bound up with chance [*Zufall*]" than war (*OW*, 85; *VK*, 105).

A work that remains unfinished and unmade, *On War* recognizes that the chances of the other of war are unavoidable in defining a concept of war. "In short", Clausewitz writes:

> so-called mathematic factors never find a firm basis in military calculations. From the very start there is an interplay of possibilities [*ein Spiel von Möglichkeiten*], probabilities, good luck and bad that weaves its way throughout the length and breadth of the tapestry. In the whole range of human activities war most closely resembles a game of cards [*dem Kartenspiel*] (*OW*, 86; *VK*, 106).[41]

Clausewitz later writes:

> all action takes place, so to speak, in a kind of twilight [*Dämmerlichte*]. . . whatever is hidden from full view in this feeble light has to be guessed at by talent, or simply left to chance [*muß dem Glück überlassen bleiben*]. So once again for lack of objective knowledge one has to trust to talent or to luck [*die Gunst des Zufalls*]. (*OW*, 140; *VK*, 187)

After having guided his readers to the rational submission of the concept of war in his chance preface of 1827, Clausewitz seemed once again compelled to admit the interminable incommensurability of his work: "I regard the first six books . . . merely as a rather formless mass [*unförmliche Masse*] that must be thoroughly reworked once more" (*OW*, 69). As a chronicle of writing on war as a death foretold, he ends again with this metaphor, this representation of the work as a shapeless, formless mass: "If an early death should terminate my work, what I have written so far would, of course only deserve to be called a shapeless mass of ideas [*eine unförmliche Gedankenmasse*]" (*OW*, 70; *VK*, 78–9). Three years later, and a year before his death, Clausewitz seemed already to be describing his work in the strained future of the past tense, of a work that will have always remained incomplete:

> The manuscript on the conduct of major operations that will be found after my death can, in its present state, be regarded as nothing but a collection of materials [*eine Sammlung von Werkestücken*] from which a theory of war was to have been distilled. (*OW*, 70; *VK*, 79)

What is writing *On War*? Perhaps nothing but "a collection of materials" that cannot be collected into "a theory of war".

In *War and Peace*, having heard General Pfuel's insistence that his theoretical plan for the defence of Russia against Napoleon had foreseen "not only everything that had happened, but everything that could happen", Prince Andrei asks,

> What science can there be in a matter in which, as in any practical matter, nothing can be determined and everything depends on countless circumstances, the significance of which is determined at a certain moment, and no one knows when that moment will come? (*WP*, 644)[42]

Though in the epilogue to *War and Peace* Tolstoy debunks the association of "*chance* and *genius*" as an explanation for Napoleon's greatness, and counters this with the cosmic geographical historical necessity of global forces moving from west to east and back again (*WP*, 1132–8), in his analysis of the unintended actions that led to Napoleon's destruction of his own army in the retreat from Moscow he also observes:

> The facts say the obvious thing, that Napoleon did not foresee the danger of moving on Moscow, nor did Alexander and the Russian commanders think then about luring Napoleon, but both thought the opposite. The drawing of Napoleon into the depths of the country occurred not according to someone's plan (no one even believed in such a possibility), but occurred as a result of the most complex interplay of intrigues, aims, and desires of the people participating in the war, who did not perceive what was to happen and what would be the only salvation of Russia. It all occurs by chance. (*WP*, 684)

As Clausewitz said, when it comes to writing on war, we are always "in a kind of twilight."

THOUGHTS FOR THE TIMES

Armed with what Schiller calls in *Wallenstein* the "empty toys" of "service and arms", Max Piccolomini will die caught in the duel between two fathers, two deceptions and two visions of peace. Trapped between his own father, Octavio Piccolomini, who incites the assassination of Wallenstein, and Wallenstein, the father that he has made, Max Piccolomini has no chance. As he makes his long way towards this battle, and struggles with a life that has not yet been made, he is tortured by the *cul-de-sac* of how free he has been not to be free. Fate, the external, the supersensible, the objective, has taken on the insurmountable force of an inner prompting, a call of the heart that has the pitiless certainty of a categorical imperative. "Our own heart's prompting is the voice of fate" (*der Zug des Herzens ist des Schicksals Stimme*), Thekla says (*W,* 285; *Wa,* 121). Wallenstein, commander of the Imperial forces, can only agree:

> Fate always wins, for our own heart within us
> Imperiously furthers its design. (*W,* 346)[43]

It is Wallenstein – self-deceiver, betrayer and peace visionary – who believes that war can only be a duel, the fateful demand to end all chance meetings, and the need to take a side:

> Duty with duty clashes.
> You must take sides, for war is breaking out
> Between your friend and Emperor. (*W,* 348)[44]

In his elegant translation F. J. Lamport captures Max Piccolomini's horrified disbelief at Wallenstein's news with the simple words, "What, war?" Schiller writes, "*Krieg! Ist das der Name?*" War! Is this you? Is this what you are called? Is this your proper name? Vainly hoping for the chance meeting that will liberate him, and make him free from his freedom to be fated to follow his inner promptings, Max Piccolomini can only ask if this duel without chance between his friend and his emperor is really the proper name of war. At the same time, the only alternative he can offer to this duel between his own side is a war against another side, a clear-cut enemy, which has been sanctioned and determined by heaven:

> What, War?
> War is a terror, like the scourge of heaven,
> Yet it is good, our heaven-sent destiny.
> Is this war good, that you wage upon
> The Emperor with his imperial army? (*W,* 349)[45]

In *Wallenstein's Death*, the title as the inevitable end of a death foretold, there are only the voices of the murdered (Wallenstein) and murderer (Butler), mirror images of the inner abyss and outer necessity that leaves us, in times of war, with no chance:

> The thoughts and deeds of men, I tell you this,
> Do not roll blindly like the waves of ocean.
> The inner world, the microcosm, is
> The deep eternal fountain of their motion. (*W,* 356)[46]

> Man thinks that he is free to do his deeds,
> But no! he is the plaything of a blind
> Unheeding force, that fashions what was choice
> Swiftly into grim necessity. (*W,* 432)[47]

Some time in late 1800 or early 1801, Hegel wrote a short piece on *Wallenstein* that begins, as ever, with the "immediate impression" that is waiting-to-be-refuted. "The immediate impression after the reading of *Wallenstein*", he writes, "is to fall silent in sadness over the downfall of a powerful man before a deaf and mute, dead fate [*toten Schicksal*]". For Hegel, the immediate impression is a falling silent before a silence, of falling in behind a fate that can neither hear, nor speak, a fate that is "dead". In the end, this "dead fate" can only take us to "the kingdom of nothingness [*das Reich des Nichts*]", to a death without reconciliation: "When the play ends, then all is finished, the kingdom of nothingness, of death has carried the day; it ends not as a theodicy."[48] Long before Brecht, Schiller leaves us with no relief, no onto-theological closure, against the evil of the Thirty Years Wars or, indeed, of the Napoleonic Wars, and of all wars without end.

Hegel recognizes, with some anxiety, that despite its conclusion that war produces an unavoidable and fateful complicity between the inner abyss and outer necessity, *Wallenstein* ends with a far graver risk or chance. As Derrida suggests in a postscript to his late essay on Freud, "Psychoanalysis Searches the States of its Soul" (2000), echoing "My Chances/*Mes Chances*", the meeting – the meeting to be moral, the meeting with morality – can never exclude, never avoid, "the insignificant bad luck [*méchance*] of evil" in "the aleatory nature of the encounter [*à l'aléa de rencontre*]".[49] Today, Derrida will argue, there is an urgent task to think, once again, about the (mis)chance of meetings and duels in times of war.

Taking the prompts of command and decision, Hegel attempts to enmesh *Wallenstein* into the *Aufhebung* machine of indetermination and determination but, in the end, he cannot overcome "the kingdom of nothingness":

> "Life against life; but only death rises up opposite life, and incredibly! abominably! death triumphs over life! This is not tragic, but terrible! This rips . . . [the heart] to pieces, from this one cannot emerge with a lightened breast!" (*Wall,* 197)[50]

Not tragic but terrible, Schiller's play leaves us with a heart torn to pieces by war; a heart that can no longer provide a perfect reflection for the sovereignty of heaven and the grim necessity of fate.

LITERATURE AND THE FIGURE OF WAR

For Freud, Schiller was a writer who knew his parapraxes. In the second of his *Introductory Lectures on Psychoanalysis*, also delivered in the midst of war, in October 1915, Freud singled out *Wallenstein* as an example – the unique and singular that somehow demonstrates the common and general – of a "creative writer" who has "made use of the slip of the tongue" and "intends to bring something to our notice".[51] Freud goes on to quote from the second part of the trilogy, *The Piccolomini*, when Octavio Piccolomini mistakenly refers to Wallenstein as "her", after realizing that his son Max has gone over to the Duke's side because he is in love with Thekla, Wallenstein's daughter (*W,* 239). It could be said that Wallenstein's equivocal call for peace, which can never be untangled from his self-deception and betrayal, has also "feminized" the commander-in-chief in the eyes of his lieutenant general, who will soon plot his murder. To put it in Freud's terms, what is Schiller trying to bring to our notice, and to the notice of his audience of soldiers past and future, with Octavio Piccolomini's losing control of both his son and his language?

In "Psychoanalysis Searches the States of its Soul", and thinking very much of the resistances of psychoanalysis and of the aftermath of the French Revolution that so troubled Schiller, Derrida called, urgently, to readers of Freud:

> If there is still war, and for a long time yet, or in any case war's cruelty, warlike, torturing, massively or subtilely cruel aggression, it is no longer certain that the figure of war [*la figure de la guerre*], and especially the difference between individual wars, civil wars, and national wars, still corresponds to concepts whose rigor is assured [*à des concepts assurés de leur rigueur*]. A new discourse on war is necessary. We await today new "Thoughts for the Times on War and Death" . . . and a new "Why War?" . . . or at least new readings of texts of this sort (*PSS,* 246; *EAD,* 24).[52]

Writing in 2000, before the start of the so-called wars *of* and *on* terror, Derrida argued that *today* the "figure" of war may no longer correspond to the assurance of a rigorous concept. Today, it is unlikely that we can still follow Clausewitz's already tortured attempts to assert that "war is nothing but . . . ." Today, there is a good chance that *la figure de la guerre*, the picture, the illustration, the representation or diagram of war will not match the concept (the signified even) of war. What sounds and images (signifiers) would there then be for a new discourse or reading of war that exceeds or remains disproportionate to its concept?

Nietzsche had argued in "On Truth and Lie in an Extra Moral Sense" (1873), that "every concept originates through our equating what is unequal," of giving a general and universal quality to particular and contingent instances.[53] In "Thoughts for the Times on War and Death" (*Zeitgemässes über Krieg und Tod*), written in March–April 1915, one can see Freud both repeating the tradition of the concept that Nietzsche warns against *and* gesturing towards what is at once less and more than a concept of war.

In the first part of his essay, "The Disillusionment of the War", Freud begins with "the confusion of wartime [*dem Wirbel dieser Kriegszeit*]". In wartime, we are "too close" to "great changes", and can only rely on "one-sided information". But then, like Thackeray before him, Freud suggests that psychoanalysis can *only* devote itself to "non-combatants [*der Nichtkämpfer*]. In times of war, psychoanalysis can only address the profound "disillusionment [*Enttäuschung*]" of the non-combatants and their "altered attitude towards death".[54] How are we to understand this psychoanalytical protest, this single combat, this duel (*der Zweikampf*), which from the outset insists that it cannot speak to or speak for the combatants (*der Kämpfer*)? From the start, Freud will not speak to war, but only of war *from afar*, from a distance. The war of the combatants, war itself, is absent. This reticence allows Freud to argue that psychoanalysis can reveal a truth about this war from afar. But it also opens the space for the other of war.

According to Freud, this war from afar causes confusion and bewilderment *and* it presents the occasion for a psychoanalytic truth that can make it easier in a "one-sided" world for the non-combatant "to find his bearings within himself" (*TT,* 275). Freud ends the first part of his essay, begun in the confusion of the "one-sided information" of wartime, by calling for "a little more truthfulness and honesty on all sides", as if psychoanalysis – like the Kantian interest of reason – can look at itself taking sides from a vantage point that is beyond all sides, beyond all combatants. The truth that psychoanalysis brings to this war from afar is that the unavoidable disillusionment of the non-combatant at the cruelty and barbarity of civilized white European men in civilized white European nations is itself an illusion. War, or the "disappointment" that it brings to those at home, leads to "the destruction of an illusion", and forces us to accept that we are driven by primitive, egotistical and cruel instincts (*TT,* 280–1). In other words, war enables psychoanalysis to reveal the truth of the self-deception of civility. This is the *truth* of the concept of war, according to Freud.

As Nietzsche had suggested, Freud's use of the concept of war here also reveals the deception of revealing a deception. While Freud had gleaned from Nietzsche that "truths are illusions about which one has forgotten," he had forgotten that "only through forgetfulness can man ever achieve the illusion of possessing a 'truth'" (*OTL,* 43, 45). At one point, Freud seems almost surprised by what he calls the "want of insight shown by the best intellects, their obduracy, their inaccessibility to the most forcible arguments and their uncritical credulity towards the most disputable assertions" in times of war (*TT,* 287). Evidently, he had also forgotten Nietzsche's warning that the first "effect of the intellect" is the deceptive "evaluation of knowledge itself" (*OTL,* 42).

While Freud uses the concept of war to uncover a deception that can only reveal psychoanalysis as the truth, and suggests that the chances of the concept of war can be situated and contained within the psychoanalytical project, he also follows Nietzsche in placing the primitive – the illusion of civilization – beyond good and evil, beyond truth and deception (*MC,* 375). These primitive instincts, he insists, are "in themselves are neither good nor bad" (*TT,* 281). Freud gestures here to something more than psychoanalysis as the truth of war. The war of the "non-combatants", war from afar, is already set at a distance from war *itself*, from the concept of war. This other of war is a deception that can only reveal another deception. This other of war is founded on the practice of "deliberate lying and deception" (*TT,* 279).

The other of war is always vulnerable to the practices of the state. The state not only encourages "the practice of lying and deception" in its citizens, but also "treats them like children by an excess of secrecy and a censorship upon news and expressions of opinion which leaves the spirits of those whose intellects it thus suppresses defenceless against every unfavourable turn of events and every sinister rumour" (*TT,* 276, 279). This double deception of the state, making its citizens both deceivers and deceiving them, leaves "the citizen of the civilized world . . . helpless in a world that has grown strange" (*TT,* 280). The other of war leaves us deceiving and deceived "in a world that has grown strange", a world that is no longer itself, no longer at home with itself.

While it is necessary to keep in mind that Freud associates this state engineered deception with a vigilant call to all non-combatants to resist the force that "disregards all the restrictions known as International Law", "ignores the prerogatives of the wounded and the medical service", and "tramples in blind fury on all that comes in its way, as though there were to be no future and no peace among men after it is over", he also suggests that this other of war, this deception which reveals another deception, exceeds the strategies and manipulations of the state (*TT,* 278–9). In the second part of his 1915 essay, "Our Attitudes towards Death", Freud turns to the question of literature, to a non-state run deception that reveals another deception. In times of war-from-afar, when death is everywhere and nowhere, and we cannot "imagine our own death", we are drawn towards literature, *where death still has a chance* (*TT,* 289).

In war, Freud argues that

death is no longer a chance event [*ist auch kein Zufall mehr*]. To be sure, it still seems a matter of chance whether a bullet hits this man or that; but a second bullet may well hit the survivor; and the accumulation of deaths puts an end to the impression of chance [*dem Eindruck des Zufälligen ein Ende*]. (*TT,* 291; *ZUK,* 203–4)

In literature, on the contrary, as a deception that reveals another deception, death remains "a chance event". Freud writes:

It is an inevitable result of all this that we should seek in the world of fiction [*der welt der Fiktion*], in literature and in the theatre compensation [*Ersatz*] for all that has been lost in life. There we still find people who know how to die – who, indeed, even manage to kill someone else. There alone too the condition can be fulfilled which makes it possible for us to reconcile ourselves with death: namely, that behind all the vicissitudes of life we should still be able to preserve a life intact. (*TT,* 291; *ZUK,* 204)[55]

As Derrida argued in *Of Grammatology*, since at least Rousseau "the world of fiction" has been treated as the *Ersatz*, the compensation, substitute, the replacement, the restitution, the shifting supplement that leaves us with neither presence nor absence. For Derrida, as for Freud, the *Ersatz* is unavoidable. As Derrida observes in *Glas* (1974): "The text treats of *ersatz* . . . of what is posed and added instead. The thesis (the position, the proposition, *Satz*) protects what it replaces, however" (*G,* 216b). Derrida returned to this link between *Erstaz* and "the question of the position (*Setzung*)" in his later essay "To Specu-late – on 'Freud' " (1975–1980). The "question of positionality in general, of positional (oppositional or juxtapositional) logic", he noted, is founded on "the theme or the thesis", and he examines the possibility of an "athesis" that precedes and exceeds the assertion of starting with a position (*Setzung*) (*TS,* 259).[56] In times of war, litera-ture can be treated as the (mis)chance of the *Erstaz*, of an apositionality that is set at a distance from the apparent figure – the position and thesis – of war.

LITERATURE AND WAR

As Alan Bass has noted, Derrida's retranslation in the late 1960s of the Hegelian *Aufhebung* as *relevé*, as a raising up that also re-places and dis-places, has a military resonance, of a replacement that relieves, "as when one soldier on duty relieves another" (*DF,* 20 n. 23).[57] According to Freud, literature only functions as compensation and relief (*Ersatz*) from the death that we cannot face in times of peace. "It is evident," he writes, "that war is bound to sweep away this conventional treatment of death" (*TT,* 291). One can both challenge Freud's clear distinction between literature and war and, at the same time, take it very seriously.

Freud's attempt to describe the relation between literature and death in times of peace is already involved in a kind of warfare. Not least because *Ersatz* has unavoidable military associations: *Ersatzmann* (replacement, reserve soldier); *Ersatzbataillon* (depot battery); *Ersatzbehörde* (recruiting authority); *Ersatztruppen* (reserve, depot troops). In times of peace, as the *Ersatz* of death, literature is already a kind of war-like replacement, a war-like reserve, a military stand-in, or extra for death. Literature is a reserve soldier for death, at once a quasi-combatant and a quasi-non-combatant. In avoiding death, in making mortality more bearable – if this is indeed what literature does – it creates the *chance* for recruiting reserves that replace, for the replacement that will take my place, that has *already* taken my place (LRD). While Freud advocates a literature of heroes in which "we die with the hero with whom we have identified ourselves; yet we survive him, and are ready to die again just as safely with another hero," a literature which promises an illusory immortality, he also suggests that literature belongs to a time before and after war, to a time when death – and life – still seems to have a chance (*TT,* 291). Literature as *la chance de rencontre*.

In "Encountering the Imaginary", from *The Book To Come* (1959), Blanchot argues that "*la rencontre de l'imaginaire*" takes the literary work beyond itself, exposing it to an interminable temporality that is as "limitless" as the ocean:

It is indeed true that it is only in Melville's book that Ahab encounters [*rencontre*] Moby Dick; but it is also true that this encounter alone allows Melville to write the book, such an overwhelming, immoderate, and unique encounter that it goes beyond all levels in which it occurs, all the moments one wants to place it in; it seems to take place [*avoir lieu*] well before the book begins, but it is such that it also can take place only once, in the future of the work, in that sea that the work will have become, a limitless ocean.

For Blanchot, "*la rencontre de l'imaginaire*" takes characters, authors and readers beyond an overburdened presence. The *rencontres* of literature are a taking place that is always *taking away* the place, a taking away that "does not belong to any present, and even destroys the present into which it seems to introduce itself." When it comes to *la rencontre de l'imaginaire*", we cannot avoid the meeting as a gap that moves: "opening of this infinite movement that is the encounter itself [*la rencontre*], an encounter that is always apart from the place [*à l'écart du lieu*] and the moment in which it is spoken, for it is this very apartness [*écart*], this imaginary distance, in which absence is realized."[58]

As one would expect, in his later "War and Literature" (1971), Blanchot offers neither compensation nor reconciliation in his treatment of the relation between literature and war. Asked by a Polish journal, "In your opinion, what is the influence that the war has had on literature after 1945?" Blanchot responds, "I would like to answer briefly."[59] What is the relation between war and literature? First and foremost, it is one of brevity, of urgency, of speeds that literature can hardly tolerate. In the fictions after 1945, and most of all after the *Shoah*, Blanchot argues, one finds "the accelerated confirmation of the fundamental crisis in the war." When it comes to war, literature *follows* (*ATT,* 392–3). As Blanchot writes – and the works of both Schiller and Freud attest – "in the crisis that keeps getting deeper and that literature also conveys according to its mode war is always present and, in some ways, pursued." (*WL,* 109). Literature runs after war, harrying and chasing it, without rest. Literature cannot avoid what Derrida called "the *impossibility of waiting*".[60] Literature, the dead man running, can never stop (DMR). It is the chance for the other of war.

CHAPTER 6

CONRAD AND THE ASYMMETRICAL DUEL

NAPOLEON AND THE DUEL AGAINST THE
WHOLE OF EUROPE

In the early months of 1907, while Joseph Conrad was revising *The Secret Agent*, he wrote the story "The Duel", which was published in 1908 in a collection of shorter fiction, *A Set of Six*. From the opening sentence, Conrad suggests that the duel stands for far more than a premeditated or unpremeditated single combat between two living men: "Napoleon I., whose career had the quality of a duel against the whole of Europe, disliked duelling between the officers of his army."[1] Napoleon does not stand at ten paces facing one man in an affair of honour: he stands alone "against the whole of Europe." This duel of one, this duel against an entire continent, is a break with the tradition of the duel itself. Conrad notes that the Emperor "disliked duelling between the officers of his army", and adds: "the great military emperor was not a swashbuckler, and had little respect for tradition" (*TD*, 165). It is difficult, at the very least, to separate Napoleon from ostentatious daring, if not swaggering and bullying. Conrad perhaps wanted to stress that Napoleon was sufficiently in control of himself and his army to avoid fighting duels so that he could fight a new kind of duel, a duel without swaggering or blustering or boasting: a duel without noise, a silent duel, a duel to the death with the *whole* of Europe. This is apparent in "Autocracy and War", an article from 1905 on the Russo-Japanese War, in which Conrad had written: "The subtle and manifold influences for evil of these Napoleonic episodes as a school of violence, as a sower of national hatreds, as the direct provocateur of obscurantism and reaction, of political tyranny and injustice, can not well be exaggerated."[2]

117

In his 1920 "Author's Note" to *A Set of Six,* Conrad describes the starting point of "The Duel". "It springs", he writes, "from a ten-line paragraph in a small provincial paper published in the South of France". Whether one accepts this as the true and single source of "The Duel", Conrad's emphasis, some 14 years after the event, on "a ten-line paragraph" is certainly redolent of the ten paces of the traditional duel. He goes on to say that this ten-line paragraph "referred for some reason or other to the 'well-known fact' of two officers in Napoleon's Grand Army having fought a series of duels in the midst of great wars and on some futile pretext. The pretext was never disclosed".[3] In "The Duel", D'Hubert and Feraud fight at least five, perhaps more, duels over a 15-year period from 1801–1816. How does one fight a 15-year duel *in the midst* of a war that has been described as a duel against the whole of Europe?

Conrad's story is as much a story about the literature and narratives of post-Napoleonic duels, of duels after the long wars without end that shaped the first half of the nineteenth century, in Kleist, Pushkin, Stendhal, Lermontov, Turgenev, Dostoyevsky, Tolstoy and Chekhov, to only name the most well known. As Irina Reyfman has noted in her study of the duel (*poyedinok*) in Russian culture and literature, almost all of the literary narratives of the duel break the formal rules and traditions of the duel.[4] Less than twenty years before Conrad's "The Duel", Chekhov's story "The Duel" (1890) highlighted the importance of this literary tradition or genealogy. Chekhov writes:

> It turned out that not one of the whole assembled company had ever attended a duel before and no one knew precisely how they should stand, or what the seconds should say or do. But then Boyko remembered and he smiled as he began to explain. 'Gentlemen, who remembers Lermontov's description?' von Koren asked, laughing. 'And in Turgenev, Bazarov had a duel with someone or other . . .' 'Why bring all that up now?' Ustimovich asked impatiently as he halted. 'Just measure out your distances, that's all.[5]

We first meet D'Hubert and Feraud as hussars in 1801, and it is at the end of things, in 1815, that we meet the young hussar Fabrizio del Dongo in Stendhal's *The Charterhouse of Parma* (1839). Before he leaves for France, Fabrizio tells the Contessa Pietranera of his reasons for deciding to join the Emperor, reasons which the narrator comments, "we take the liberty of finding rather comical." Fabrizio describes how he first heard of Napoleon's return:

> Yesterday evening, it was just seven minutes to six, we were strolling, as you know, by the shore of the lake along the plane-tree avenue, below the Casa Sommariva, and we were walking in a southerly direction. It was there that I first noticed, in the distance, the boat that was coming from Como, bearing such great news. As I gazed at this boat without thinking of the Emperor, and only envying the lot of those who are free to travel, all at once I felt myself seized with a feeling of deep emotion. The boat touched ground, the agent said something in a low tone to my father, who changed colour, and took us aside to announce the *terrible news*. I turned towards the lake with no other object but to hide the tears of joy that were flooding my eyes. Suddenly, at an immense height in the sky and to my right, I saw an eagle, Napoleon's bird. He was flying majestically past on his way to Switzerland and consequently towards Paris. (*CP*, 43)

Fabrizio's chance sighting of "Napoleon's bird", and his certainty about its flight plan to Paris, also describes the unique status of Napoleon in these narratives: he is never close – he is at an "immense height" – but he is also never absent.[6] After 1799, Napoleon stands above France – and Europe. As the youthful Pierre Bezukhov says in *War and Peace*, "Napoleon is great, because he stood above the revolution" (*WP*, 20). This elevation becomes unassailable after Napoleon became Emperor in 1804. As Tolstoy has a French soldier remark in front of Prince Andrei before the battle at Hollabrunn, "There is no Bonaparte. There is the Emperor!" (*WP*, 177). Tolstoy also conveys a sense of the "rather comical" blinding adoration for the sovereign when, while standing on a review before the Tsar Alexander I, the young Nikolai Rostov notices the sovereign hesitating for a moment. Tolstoy writes: "'How can a sovereign be undecided?' thought Rostov, and then even this indecision seemed majestic and enchanting to Rostov, like everything the sovereign did" (*WP*, 246).

Stendhal reinforces the quasi-theological sovereignty of Napoleon when, again comically, in the midst of the battle of Waterloo the disorientated and slightly drunk Fabrizio just misses seeing the Emperor:

> Suddenly the sergeant called out to his men: "Can't you see the Emperor, you blasted fools?" Whereupon the escort shouted, "Long live the Emperor!" at the top of their voices. It can well be imagined that our hero stared till his eyes started out of his head, but all he saw was some generals galloping, also followed by an escort. The long floating plumes of horsehair which the dragoons of the bodyguard wore on their helmets prevented him from distinguishing their faces. "So I have missed seeing the Emperor on a field of battle, all because of those cursed glasses of brandy!" This reflection quite roused him out of his stupor. (*CP*, 62)[7]

As the late W. G. Sebald noted, the 53-year-old Henri Marie Beyle looking back on his own experiences of crossing the Alps as a 17-year old with Napoleon's army in 1800, finds that "images appear of such extraordinary clarity he feels he can scarce credit them". Beyle is particularly interested in his possible sighting of General Marmont at Martigny. Sebald suggests that Beyle recognizes that one can neither trust nor avoid the "extraordinary clarity" of these improbable and long past chance sightings.[8] In the *Charterhouse of Parma*, either misdirected from a great height as the idealized projection of "Napoleon's bird" on its way to Paris or missed altogether in the drunken disorientation, the young Fabrizio never really sees the Emperor.[9] What is "Napoleon"? For Stendhal, he is always there, but one never actually gets close enough to meet him.[10] One can never "meet" him even by chance: as a duellist he holds a position of absolute asymmetry.[11] After 1815, one must confront Napoleon as, precisely, the one that cannot be confronted.

In Conrad's story, Napoleon's duel with the *whole* of Europe is predicated on discouraging duelling between his officers, but "The Duel" is about two men who, for some reason, resist or disobey the Emperor: their 15-year "private contest" runs "through the years of universal carnage". Conrad writes: "Nevertheless, a story of duelling, which became a legend in the army, runs through the epic of imperial wars. To the surprise and admiration of their fellows, two officers, like insane artists trying to gild refined gold or paint the lily, pursued a private contest through the years of universal carnage" (*TD*, 165). How much we can read Conrad's description of both of these officers (whom he later takes great pains to distinguish) as "insane artists", as his own possibly half sceptical yearning for the apparently more honourable world of the early nineteenth century, or how much this reflects his conscious description of two outdated and "romantic" figures who are hopelessly resisting the imperial *realpolitik* of the day, is difficult to say.

What does it mean to fight a duel, to pursue a "private contest" as *insane artists* in the midst of a war? How are we to understand this war within a war, this private war that runs "through" a war of "universal carnage"? On the one hand, this duel creates a symmetrical immunity that seems to pass untouched through the years of warfare. On the other hand, the duel not only begins in the relative peace of 1801, but "ends" in the more emphatic peace after the battle of Waterloo: it is a war that precedes and exceeds the wars of Napoleon and his duel with the whole of Europe.

The first duel, in Strasbourg, takes place when both D'Hubert and Feraud "were enjoying greatly a short interval of peace". It begins in the strange time and space of a "short interval" in a global war. At the same time, this peace is not as much a cessation, as a preparation of hostilities: "They were enjoying it, though both intensely warlike, because it was a sword sharpening, firelock-cleaning peace, dear to a military heart and undamaging to military prestige, inasmuch that no one believed in its sincerity or duration" (*TD*, 166).

D'Hubert and Feraud, who will later seem so different, are both "intensely warlike". In 1907 Conrad could still take a kind of comfort – an always sceptical comfort – in the shared "warlike" intensity of his duellists, a comfort that would be impossible after the First World War, as Joseph Roth suggests in *The Radetzky March* (1932). In Roth's novel, the collective failure of the Austro-Hungarian Empire to be "warlike" is seen in the duel between the regimental surgeon Dr. Demant and Captain Count Tattenbach. For the regiment's commanding officer, Colonel Kovacs, Dr. Max Demant is a Jew and a good man, but "unmilitary". He smiles like a civilian.[12] Having learnt that his beloved wife does not love him (and there are echoes here of the duel of Pierre Bezukhov in *War and Peace*), the drunken Dr. Demant challenges Captain Tatttenbach over rumours about his wife that he knows are groundless.

For Dr. Demant, the duel cannot be separated from the anguish of tradition, from the dead: "'There are so many graves,' said the regimental surgeon. 'Don't you feel as I do the way we live off the dead?'"

Demant is thinking of his grandfather, "an old tall Jew with a silver beard", and in the middle of the night a few hours before the duel it is his grandfather who becomes his ghostly second, his spectral witness:

> Tomorrow I'm going to die like a hero, a so-called hero, completely against my grain, and against the grain of my forebears and my tribe and against my grandfather's will. One of the huge old tomes he used to read says, "He who raiseth his hand against his neighbour is a murderer." Tomorrow someone is going to raise a pistol against me, and I'm going to raise a pistol against him. And I will be a murderer. (*RM,* 102)

Both Captain Count Tattenbach and Dr. Demant are killed in the duel.

In Conrad's "The Duel", the extraordinary 15-year duel within a war is almost always based on a kind of self-perpetuating symmetry. The equally "warlike" duellists fight twice as lieutenants, and twice as captains and finally as generals. When D'Hubert is made a captain, Feraud is furious because "now that D'Hubert was an officer of superior rank there could be no question of a duel." It is only after the battle of Austerlitz, when Feraud is made a captain that the next duels can take place in Silesia and Lübeck (*TD,* 203, 204–6). The only stage in their military promotions when the men do not fight is when they are both colonels, and it is in the extremity of 1812, during the retreat from Moscow that Colonel D'Hubert and Colonel Feraud have what might be called a warlike non-duel, which at once suggests that their "private contest" protects them from the "universal carnage" and exposes them to a terrible and debilitating absent and yet always present third: Napoleon.

"The retreat from Moscow submerged all private feelings in a sea of disaster and misery," Conrad writes (*TD,* 211). In the catastrophe, all energy is put into "preserving some semblance of order and formation" as the "bonds of discipline and duty" undergo a "general destruction". In these exceptional circumstances, Colonel D'Hubert and Colonel Feraud fight a "private contest", a non-duel to preserve the army. This private duel is conducted in almost total silence or, even more strangely, in a world where each phrase and gesture, used with such economy, can only be rephrased and echoed by the other.

In this silence, where the two duellists only seem to have enough language for one person, the non-duel takes place.

In the retreat from Moscow, Napoleon's army has lost its ability to make a noise, to impinge upon and dominate the "mortal silence" of the natural world. The army, Conrad writes, "plodded on, and their passage did not disturb the mortal silence of the plains, shining with the livid light of snows under a sky the colour of ashes". The army, as a whole, seems to have become speechless and blind. In the "mortal silence" of the "white immensity of the snows", which is the only source of any sound, touch becomes the strongest sense, but it is almost the touch of the dead, of the walking dead:

> It struggled onwards, the men exchanging neither words nor looks; the whole ranks marched touching elbow, day after day and never raising their eyes from the ground, as if lost in despairing reflections. In the dumb, black forests of pines the cracking of over-loaded branches was the only sound they heard. Often from daybreak to dusk no one spoke in the whole column. It was like a macabre march of struggling corpses towards a distant grave. (*TD*, 211–12)

It is in this half-living half-dead army that Colonel D'Hubert and Colonel Feraud become not only heroic, almost monolithic, but also tied together, doubles mirroring their speech and gestures with the impossible proximity of a non-duelling duel:

> During that afternoon they had leaned upon each other more than once, and towards the end, Colonel D'Hubert, whose long legs gave him an advantage in walking through soft snow, peremptorily took the musket of Colonel Feraud from him and carried it on his shoulder, using his own as a staff. (*TD*, 213)

Having become almost one person, carrying the whole army, they are no longer capable of single combat between two living men. Touching one another, they are too close to fight.

Marching and fighting side by side, the two men take on an indifference to each other, and as the difference between them diminishes they both acquire vitality, a life force that sustains the whole battalion. Conrad writes: "Though often marching in the ranks, or skirmishing in the woods side by side, the two officers ignored each other; this not so much from inimical intention as from a very real indifference … to the last they counted among the most active, the least demoralized of the battalion; their vigorous vitality invested them both with the appearance of an heroic pair in the eyes of their comrades" (*TD*, 212). Conrad is careful here: D'Hubert and Feraud *appear* as "an heroic pair" to the other soldiers. It is the others who see them as a "a pair", who not only link them together, as twins, as two-in-one, but also who misinterpret the source of their heroic vitality, having no access to the "private feelings" that exist between the two duellists.

The twenty words spoken by Feraud and the ten words spoken by D'Hubert on the retreat from Moscow, all of which perfectly echo and interlock, are the public face of their duel: two counterbalancing assertions of natural superiority that are acknowledged by a nod. This public *rencontre* gives the "appearance" of a perfectly symmetrical duel of words and gestures, of a militant and military sympathy. But Conrad immediately tempers this heroic public story, with the very different private experiences of the two men. "Colonel Feraud's taciturnity", he writes, "was the outcome of concentrated rage" (*TD*, 214). Feraud, who will become a kind of Colonel Chabert in the post-Napoleonic dispensation (the central character in Balzac's remarkable 1832 story of a returning solider who has been declared dead and can only remain a ghost in the new Royalist France), identifies himself entirely with the fortunes of Napoleon and thinks of what has happened to himself and the army only in terms of the duel of this one man with the whole of Europe: "he accused fate of unparalleled perfidy towards the sublime Man of Destiny." Napoleon will always remain a "father" to him (*TD*, 213, 242).

From this moment on, Feraud will justify and perhaps rationalize his duel with D'Hubert purely in terms of the "Man of Destiny": from 1812, or in fact from 1801, Napoleon and his duel, has always stood in between Feraud and D'Hubert, an indivisible but fallible sovereignty that could be treated as the very possibility of this private duel. Learning, some time later in Paris, that D'Hubert has become a general and, once again, that they cannot fight, as they are no longer equal, Feraud says publicly, "'I can't believe that that man ever loved the Emperor.'" This charge will be repeated again and again in the rest of the story: D'Hubert "*never* loved the Emperor" (*TD*, 218, 224, 238, 265). This is the most unpardonable crime: to have fought as a soldier in Napoleon's army all these years, and to have never loved the Emperor. I have fought for the Emperor, for the President or Prime Minister even, but I have never loved him.

Conrad's analysis of this charge is brief and unadorned and illustrates, with pages on the motives and feelings of D'Hubert, his increasing inability to maintain any kind of equality or symmetry in his treatment of the two protagonists in "The Duel". Of Feraud, Conrad simply writes: "the strain of unhappiness caused by military reverses had spoiled Colonel Feraud's character. Like many other men, he was rendered wicked by misfortune" (*TD*, 218). Conrad's own duel with his story becomes markedly lopsided: Feraud is externalized, impermeable, taciturn, while D'Hubert is internalized, transparent and vocal. It is worth pointing out that that this neat, if lopsided, opposition of externalization and internalization can itself also be taken as an implicit hope for a meta-symmetry, and it is important not to underestimate the force of this hope in Conrad's work.

While Feraud solders himself to the fate of the Emperor, D'Hubert takes "a more thoughtful view of events". If Feraud stops thinking after 1812, D'Hubert starts thinking; and this process will culminate in a restoration that cannot be separated from the return of the sovereign, Louis XVIII. Like Balzac's Colonel Chabert, Feraud will soon become one of the ghosts of the old regime, the living dead "who cherished dingy but glorious old tricolour cockades in their breast pockets" (*TD*, 214, 220). D'Hubert will bypass and transcend this fate, somehow becoming more and more alive till finally, in a perfect symmetry, he is both loved by and loving to his young bride to be at the end of the story.

This process begins in the retreat, where D'Hubert starts thinking. His trousers almost torn to shreds, he refuses the "ghastly intimacy of a wrestling match with the frozen dead" to find a pair of pants, and ends up wearing "a bell shaped nether garment, a sort of stiff petticoat" (*TD*, 215). Rather than wrestling with the dead, D'Hubert acquires masculine-feminine potency, a self-protecting, self-regenerating clothing. It is from this extraordinary sartorial transformation, that D'Hubert is able to avoid "the unreasoning indignation" of Feraud, and to temper his "patriotic sadness". He is "surprised to discover within himself a love of repose", and his "returning vigour" seems "strangely pacific in its aspirations". D'Hubert is losing his warlike passions, and seems to be undergoing a revitalizing pacification that Conrad encapsulates in this image of the "stiff petticoat", an androgynous bell-like encircling erection, a-mother-and-father-in-one-garment.

While D'Hubert's outlandish clothes of necessity precede a profound shift in his outlook, Feraud remains with those who, after Waterloo, "buttoned with forbidden eagle buttons their shabby uniforms". Conrad hints that this "bizarre change in mood", this inexplicable intervention or loss of the warrior's self-knowledge, begins to alter D'Hubert's attitude towards Napoleon (*TD*, 215, 220). It is not that D'Hubert never loved the emperor, but that he will begin to love other things than the Emperor. Writing a letter to his sister, who is arranging for him to marry, D'Hubert acknowledges that the Emperor, the "mythological demi-god" is, in truth, "but a man": an almost democratic stance. On the very next page, Conrad tells us that D'Hubert has "come under the imperial eye" and has been seen by Napoleon himself, and is soon promoted to a general, while remaining silent about his private "misgivings" (*TD*, 220, 217). Seeing, but not seen, Napoleon arrests, temporarily, this transformation.

D'Hubert's sister has become a monarchist, but the reluctant duellist is not replacing one sovereign power for another: he is beginning the painful process of separating himself from the quasi-theological sovereignty, the absolute asymmetry of the Emperor. And this process is painful, ending with the wounded D'Hubert on crutches trying to get on his horse to ride to the battle of Waterloo: "such were the effects of imperial magic upon a calm temperament and a pondered mind," Conrad comments (*TD*, 220).

Even while it is tempting to draw a clear distinction in the relation to the sovereign power between these two private duellists, between the believer and the agnostic or atheist, Conrad constantly suggests that they are still leaning on one another, as they had done in Russia, and can in fact still replace one another. Wounded in battle, General D'Hubert hears that Feraud has been made a general and "sent to replace him at the head of the battle" (*TD*, 219). Replaceable and interchangeable in the public theatre of war, it is only in their "private contest" that the duellists diverge into if not a warrior and a pacifist, at least between one who can never stop the war – the war against the whole of Europe – and one who has chosen to end the "special relationship".

But things are perhaps not so straightforward. D'Hubert's return to life without war is full of all the compromises, settlements and secrets of "regime change", and Feraud's refusal of a final reconciliation has a certain integrity or mad resistance that comes in part from his spectral inability to draw an absolute separation between international wars and private duels. Riding on his way to his last duel with D'Hubert, Conrad writes of Feraud: "A mere fighter all his life, a cavalry man, a *sabreur*, he conceived war with the utmost simplicity, as, in the main, a massed lot of personal contests, a sort of gregarious duelling." As D'Hubert says at the end of Feraud, "he *won't* be reconciled" (*TD*, 235, 265). For Feraud, the duel will always be for the Emperor, for the sovereign, and that is why it can never end.

THE DUEL +N: ABSURDITY

As we have seen, in his "Author's Note" from 1920 Conrad says that his story was prompted by an article in a French newspaper, and that in the absence of a "pretext" for a long duel he had to "invent" his own. How does one invent the reasons for going to war, one might ask? The French newspaper in question has been identified as an 1858 issue of the periodical *L'audience*.[13] Nonetheless, Conrad scholars have also felt the need to "invent" their own pretexts for "The Duel". Conrad's grandfather and great uncle both served in Napoleon's army and this personal family history has also been linked to Conrad's later works set in the Napoleonic era, "The Warrior's Soul" (1916) and the unfinished *Suspense*.[14] Two further possible sources for the story have also been identified: a tale Conrad heard from an artillery officer that he had met in France, and from an article that appeared also in 1858, but in an American newspaper.[15] It has also been suggested that Conrad was inspired by another work of fiction: Pushkin's 1831 story, "The Shot", in which the same duel is fought twice after a lapse of many years.[16] The tradition of the duel as always more than a one-off, as a *series*, can also be seen in Dostoyevsky's *The Devils* (1871) in the duel between Gaganov and Stavrogin. Dostoyevsky writes: "All the conditions of the encounter proposed by Stavrogin were at once accepted without the slightest objection. Only one addition, and a ferocious one at that, was made. If after the first shots nothing decisive happened, they were to have another encounter, and if that, too, was inconclusive, a third one. Kirilov frowned, objected to this third encounter, but, having got nothing for his pains, agreed on one condition, namely: "Three times – yes, but a fourth time – no!"[17]

These different possible sources – a chance sighting of a newspaper article that was either French or American, a chance meeting with an old soldier, an autobiographical imperative, or a literary inspiration – are also matched by the three different possible titles of the story: "The Duel" in *A Set of Six* in 1908, "The Point of Honour" as it was called when published as a work on its own, also in 1908, and "The Masters of War", Conrad's first idea for the title.[18] One can only wonder what Bob Dylan would have made of Conrad's first title "The Masters of War", with its more emphatic and perhaps ironic suggestion that the duellists' "private contest" makes them, uniquely, masters of war. "The Point of Honour" is the least compelling title, and Conrad alludes to this in his "Author's Note" when he remarks that the story, with its original title "The Duel", has now been "reinstated in its proper place" (AN viii). This title is taken from D'Hubert's stumbling reply to the Duke of Otranto to explain why he is intervening to save Feraud from the post-Napoleonic cull. Otranto asks him if Feraud was an "intimate friend", and D'Hubert replies, "'Intimate . . . yes. There is between us an intimate connection of a nature which makes it a point of honour with me to try . . .'" (*TD*, 228). While using this phrase as the title emphasizes the "intimate connection" between the adversaries, it also suggests that the duel is about honour, something that Conrad seems, for the most part, to be at pains to deny: whatever is happening in these endless duels, it is not really about honour.

The first duel, and perhaps the most asymmetrical duel of all, takes place before the narrative begins: Feraud has gone out and fought a duel with a civilian. This leads to the second duel, the first non-duel, between D'Hubert and the "young maid" in the "private house" where Feraud is staying. D'Hubert questions the maid at the door, and slowly pushes his way into the house, as she obliquely tries to avoid telling him where Feraud has gone. Using all his charm and masculine wiles, D'Hubert eventually finds out where Feraud has gone (*TD*, 166–71). These first two unconventional duels set the pattern for the duel *without end*, the duel +n, that becomes no longer the formality of a single event of (un)premeditated combat, but the structure for *all the encounters* within the story. In such a world, it is not an equal "meeting" of minds, but an asymmetrical relationship of power, an almost absurd and unavoidable imbalance, that dominates all interactions and contact.

As Conrad said in 1920, he had to "invent" a "pretext" for the duel, and concludes: "I think that . . . I have made it sufficiently convincing by the mere force of its absurdity" (*AN* viii). For Conrad, the duel without end begins in absurdity. *Absurditas* denotes that which is out of harmony, out of tune, ridiculous, inappropriate, incongruous and, most of all, without or taken away from (*ab*) a symmetrical relationship to reason: the asymmetrical *par excellence*. The duel without end becomes a force of absurdity. Conrad's emphasis on absurdity echoes a distinctive tradition in the narratives of the post-Napoleonic duel. In Lermontov's *A Hero of Our Time* (1841), Pechorin muses during a sleepless night before a duel that he has provoked, "one just goes on living out of curiosity, waiting for something new. It's absurd and annoying."[19] In *Fathers and Sons* (1862), before being challenged by Pavel Petrovich, Bazarov remarks, "from the theoretical standpoint, duelling is absurd" (*TUR,* 235). Tolstoy carries on this tradition of absurdity in *War and Peace*, when Pierre challenges Dolokhov to a duel. After inadvertently wounding Dolokhov and exposing himself to his opponent's misfired shot, he is overcome by the absurdity of the event: "Pierre clutched his head and, turning round, walked off towards the woods, treading on the untouched snow and mouthing incoherent words aloud. 'Stupid . . . Stupid! Death . . . lies . . .,' he repeated, wincing" (*WP,* 316).[20]

Dostoyevsky also touches on this unavoidable absurdity in *The Devils* in a scene that may have influenced Conrad. He suggests an absurdity in the encounter which borders on the impossibility of the duel itself, of the duel as a *series* of fights sliding into a non-duel. After the first round of shots, in which Gaganov grazes Stavrogin's little finger and Stavrogin fires in the air, against all protocol an argument breaks out:

> "I declare," Gaganov croaked (his throat was parched), addressing himself again to Drozdov, "that this man" – he pointed again at Stavrogin – "fired in the air on purpose – deliberately. That's another insult! He wants to make the duel impossible!"
>
> "I have the right to fire as I like so long as I keep to the rules," Stavrogin declared firmly.
>
> "No, he hasn't!" Gaganov shouted. "Explain it to him, please!"
>
> "I'm entirely of the same opinion as Mr. Stavrogin," Kirilov announced.

"Why does he spare me?" Gaganov raged, without listening. "I despise his clemency! I refuse to accept it – I –"

"I give you my word that I had no intention of insulting you," Stavrogin declared impatiently. "I fired in the air because I don't want to kill any more people, either you or anyone else. It's nothing to do with you personally". (*DEV*, 292–3)[21]

In the second round of shots, Gaganov once again misses, and Stavrogin once again fires into the air. In the third and final round, Gaganov puts a bullet through Stavrogin's hat, missing his head by "a quarter of an inch" – much as he had earlier grazed his little finger. Stavrogin has to be prompted to fire by one of the seconds, turns his back on Gaganov, and this time fires into the ground.

While D'Hubert is unable to avoid the absurdity of the duel without end, Conrad places all the weight of this force that stands apart from reason in the underdeveloped character of Feraud. Feraud's character cannot be developed, cannot be given equal time, because it is absurd. From the first moment, it is apparent to D'Hubert that "Feraud took a view of his duel [with the civilian] in which neither remorse not yet a rational apprehension of consequences had any place." It is this lack of reasonable relation to reason that precipitates the beginning of the duel without end: "'Oh, do be reasonable!' remonstrated Lieut. D'Hubert. 'I am reasonable! I am perfectly reasonable!' retorted the other with ominous restraint" (*TD*, 172, 175).

Like Conrad, the other third in this duel-of-two, D'Hubert will come to see the origin of the duel without end as absurd, while Feraud appears oblivious to this reasonable analysis of the lack of rational causation: Feraud is blind to both reason *and* its other. The witnesses to the first meeting of the two men can only see it in these terms: "the affair was so absurd from the worldly, the military, the honourable, or prudential point of view." D'Hubert, in contrast, sees the duel as a "deadly absurdity", but he cannot speak of it to anyone, he feels he must keep the absurdity a secret. Before the fourth duel at Lübeck, D'Hubert recognizes that "this affair had hopelessly and unreasonably complicated his existence," and that even though "all absurdity was distasteful to him [. . .] one absurdity more or less in the development did not matter" (*TD*, 191, 198, 206).

After the fall of Napoleon, D'Hubert no longer simply accepts this absurdity with a stoic fortitude, he also comes to yearn for it, to feel for it, to have "an irrational tenderness" for this secret and dormant irrationality in his life: "He felt an irrational tenderness towards his old adversary and appreciated emotionally the murderous absurdity their encounter had introduced into his life." What is most striking here is D'Hubert's process as he moves to the other side of reason: he has not left reason, he is still attached to rationality, but he is now part of the irrationality that he has fought against for nearly fifteen years: the "intimate connection" that he has with "his life-long adversary," as Feraud calls him (*TD*, 223, 228, 217). The "point of honour" has become the secret of a duel without cause, an absurdity without beginning and without end that has become part of D'Hubert's very existence. One might be pressed to find a better definition of war, and perhaps for a global war *on* terror or a global war *of* terror most of all. War: the duel +n.

"He will never believe the story," D'Hubert thinks when talking to his future father-in-law the Chevalier the night before his final duel, the true beginning of the duel without end (*TD*, 242). There is something inherently unbelievable about this story of a duel without end in the midst of Napoleon's global war, a war "against the whole" that aspires to the phantasm of an absolute asymmetry. How can one have a relation of absolute asymmetry "against the whole"? What vantage point, what transcendental reach could avoid the *absurditas* of an asymmetrical relation to *the whole*? Where else could a global war *on* or *of* terror stand than in the absurdity of being *against* – and first and foremost above and outside – the whole? The duel +n becomes an impossible story, a story that cannot be believed, and D'Hubert's irrational longing for the irrationality of the duel without cause or without end remains irreconcilable, it leaves him disgusted, nauseous and doubtful about his own existence. D'Hubert is overcome by a "nauseating disgust at the absurdity of the situation, doubt of his own fitness to conduct his existence, and mistrust of his best sentiments" (*TD*, 247).

But Conrad does not end with disgust and nausea, he ends with a Pyrrhic victory: D'Hubert outwits Feraud in this last duel, he has the chance to kill him and he decides to let his adversary live. At first, D'Hubert is prompted by the "atrocious absurdity" that he has endured to kill Feraud, but he then finds a way – at last – of transferring this absurdity, of giving it to his enemy. "By every rule of single combat your life belongs to me," he tells the defeated Feraud. He goes on to say:

"You've forced me on a point of honour to keep my life at your disposal, as it were, for fifteen years. Very well. Now that the matter is decided to my advantage, I am going to do what I like with your life on the same principle. You shall keep it at my disposal as long as I choose. Neither more nor less. You are on your honour till I say the word."

"I am! But, *sacrebleu*! This is an absurd position for a General of the Empire to be placed in!" cried General Feraud, in accents of profound and dismayed conviction. "It amounts to sitting all the rest of my life with a loaded pistol in a drawer waiting for your word. It's – it's idiotic; I shall be an object of – of – derision."

"Absurd?—idiotic? Do you think so?" queried General D'Hubert with sly gravity. (*TD,* 257–8)

D'Hubert takes this victorious gift of absurdity to his rival as a denial of Feraud's existence: "I can't really discuss this question with a man who, as far as I am concerned, does not exist." This is not so much death by absurdity as an absurd negation of existence, of a living-death sentence, an indefinite suspension. When asked by Feraud's seconds if there has been a reconciliation, D'Hubert responds, "Reconciliation? Not that exactly. It is something much more binding" (*TD,* 258). The absurd duel remains a duel without end, a duel without reconciliation, a duel that binds the duellists beyond life and death, beyond the Napoleonic transformation of the duel as a war-like duel against the whole of Europe.

This absurd binding of the living to the living without existence exceeds both D'Hubert's experience of the *negativity* of the duel as the encounter with death that makes life all the sweeter ("Thus to this man, sobered by the victorious issue of a duel, life appeared robbed of its charm, simply because it was no longer menaced."), and the *affirmation* of his recognizing in the aftermath of the duel that he loves and is loved by Mademoiselle de Valmassigue ("'I owe it all to this stupid brute,' he thought. 'He has made plain in a morning what might have taken me years to find out—for I am a timid fool.'") (*TD,* 259, 264). Later, happily married and with a son, the now General Baron D'Hubert writes to General Feraud and declares that he will "give you back in all form your forfeited life". But Feraud, the half-living half-dead asymmetrical ghost, refuses this full return to life. "I keep a loaded pistol in my drawer," he replies. D'Hubert then secretly ensures that he can keep his unreconciled duellist and

interminable antagonist alive, as the precarious guarantor of his own
vitality and happiness (*TD,* 265–6).

DE ANIMOSITAS AND HEBETUDE

*"Gentlemen!" a voice said. At that instant, Regimental Surgeon
Dr. Demant took off his glasses as fussily as ever and placed them
carefully upon the wide tree stump. Oddly enough, he could still
clearly see his path, the designated place, the distance between himself and Count Tattenbach, and he saw the count himself. He waited.
Until the final moment, he waited for the fog. But everything
remained clear, as if the regimental surgeon had never been near-
sighted. A voice counted, "One!"*

*(*RM, *109)*

Joseph Roth's remarkable description of Dr Demant's sudden loss of
a terrible near-sightedness moments before he is killed in a duel
already looks back to a tradition of heightened senses in the post-
Napoleonic narratives of the duel. The night before his duel in
Lermontov's *A Hero of Our Time*, Pechorin cannot sleep and stays
awake reading Scott's *The Tale of Old Mortality*, itself an extraordinary meditation on the violence of religious enthusiasm and political
insurrection.[22] As he walks to the duel the next morning, Pechorin
remarks, "I can't remember a bluer, fresher morning. . . . With what
fascination I studied each trembling dewdrop on the broad vine leaves
that reflected a million multicoloured rays" (*HOT,* 133).

Tolstoy echoes this narrative of vivid and acutely heightened senses
in Pierre's duel in *War and Peace*. In the deep snow of winter, there is
a heavy fog and, standing "some forty paces from each other,"
neither Pierre nor Dolokhov can see each other. Almost blind in the
fog, surrounded by "the untouched snow" and profound silence,
Pierre advances towards Dolokhov and finds he can neither hold on
to his pistol nor keep on the beaten path:

At the word three, Pierre walked forward with quick steps, getting
off the beaten track and stepping into the untouched snow. Pierre
stretched his arm out and held the pistol as if he was afraid of
killing himself with it. He carefully put his left hand behind him,
because he would have liked to support his right hand with it, and
knew that he was not allowed. Having gone some six paces and

veered off the track into the snow, Pierre looked down at his feet, again gave a quick glance at Dolokhov, and, pulling his finger as he had been taught, fired. Never expecting such a loud noise, Pierre gave a start, then smiled at his own impression and stood still. The smoke, especially thick because of the fog, at first prevented him from seeing anything; but the other shot he was expecting did not follow. (*WP*, 315–6)

Beyond the cliché of a keener awareness of life at a possible moment of death or, indeed, of the Hegelian "labour of the negative" that always returns to and is put to work by the life of spirit on its way to absolute knowledge, Tolstoy alludes to a disruption or dysfunction *between* the senses.[23] The post-Napoleonic narratives of the duel puts a strain on Aristotle's confident assumption that there can only be five senses and that the relation between the five senses is always mediated and unified, always held in a perfect ratio, by the untouchable work of the soul (*S*, 426b).

This strained disruption or dysfunction between the senses is perhaps the most distinctive aspect of Conrad's attempts to narrate a 15-year duel without end, and it also plays a significant role in *The Secret Agent*, which he was revising at the time. In his "Author's Note" from 1920 Conrad notes that while his story "Gaspar Ruiz" was written at the same time that he was finishing *Nostromo*, they have "nothing in common" (*AN* vi). Despite Conrad's confidence, there are many crossings between "The Duel" and *The Secret Agent*, not least the repetition of the word *hebetude* which has its origins in *hebetare*, to make or become dull: "The leaden weight of an irremediable idleness descended upon General Feraud, who having no resources within himself sank into a state of awe-inspiring hebetude" (*TD*, 230); "In the doorway Stevie, calmed, seemed sunk in hebetude."[24]

To cite only a few of these crossings beyond the shared hebetudes of Stevie and Feraud, like Feraud and D'Hubert, who spend 15 years duelling, the revolutionary Michaelis has spent 15 years in prison (*SA*, 31–3); both the bomb carrying perfect detonator Professor and Feraud are described as having an "owlish" look (*SA*, 62; *TD*, 233); while Feraud threatens to cut off D'Hubert's ears, Stevie reads the story of "a German solider officer tearing half-off the ear of a recruit" (*TD*, 44); the absurdity of the duel without origin or end echoes the general "absurd ferocity" of the terrorist attack in Greenwich (*SA*, 25, 68); with the notable exception of the extraordinary duels between the Professor and Chief Inspector Heat and the final duel between Verloc and Winnie, most of the encounters are highly asymmetrical (Verloc and Mr. Vladimir, Heat and the Assistant Commissioner) (*SA*, 70–1, 90–1, 169–94); from the dangers of losing "all sight and touch" of an anarchist, to the disconnection of motion, touch, sound and sight in the duel between Verloc and Winnie, *The Secret Agent* shares with "The Duel" a narrative where the senses are always losing their sense with each other; a loss which is, not necessarily, to be defined as either the cause or product of a general hebetude (*SA*, 63, 36, 43, 169–94).

Marking the centenary of these works on duelling in the midst of a global war and the political and social (if not religious) complexities of a terrorist attack in London, it is perhaps worth taking great care with Conrad's transhistorical analysis of both the France of 1801–1816 and the England of 1894 as worlds burdened by a general lethargy, dullness and indifference, by a general loss of sensation, as if this is at once the inevitable cause and product of all war and terrorism. Such moralism on the bluntness of society, not only invites a highly romantic critique of the artifices of society (in his preface to the *Lyrical Ballads*, Wordsworth had warned that the "present state of the public taste in this country" was blunting "the discriminating powers of the mind"), but also returns us back to Aristotle, who had defined touch as the "exactness of discrimination": when we are out of touch with the soul (the untouchable *par excellence*), we sink into hebetude.[25]

One of the more obvious examples in "The Duel" of this disorder of the senses, as the assurance of the five-in-one and one-in-five, is apparent in the first meeting between Feraud and D'Hubert.

"I can't listen to this nonsense," murmured Lieut. D'Hubert, making a slightly contemptuous grimace.

"You call this nonsense? It seems to me a perfectly plain statement. Unless you don't understand French."

"What on earth do you mean?"

"I mean," screamed suddenly Lieut. Feraud, "to cut off your ears to teach you to disturb me with the general's orders when I am talking to a Lady!"

A profound silence followed this mad declaration; and through the open window Lieut. D'Hubert heard the little birds singing sanely in the garden. He said, preserving his calm, "Why! If you take that tone, of course I shall hold myself at your disposition whenever you are at liberty to attend to this affair; but I don't think you will cut my ears off". (*TD*, 175–6)

I love the phrase "the little birds singing sanely in the garden". From D'Hubert saying "I can't listen," to Feraud threatening to cut off his ears, to the "profound silence" that follows, to the sudden sanity of the singing little birds, Conrad brings hearing, the duels *of* hearing and *between* hearing and the other senses, to the centre of this first duel.

Under the mad threat of losing his ears, D'Hubert makes use of his ears: "Hearing, however, the unmistakable sound behind his back of a sword drawn from the scabbard, he had no option but to stop" – and so the 15-year duel, the duel without end, begins. Feraud then invites D'Hubert to fight in the garden where the birds are singing sanely. D'Hubert refuses to fight without the propriety of seconds, and Feraud dismisses this basic structure of the duel, of the secret encounter that is always in need of witnesses: "We don't want any seconds." He then settles on the only available witness: "Stay! There's the gardener. He'll do. He's as deaf as a post, but he has two eyes in his head" (*TD*, 176–7). It is with this *deaf* witness to a fight to protect a pair of ears in the profound silence of birds sanely singing, that Conrad brings in the other disturbed and dysfunctional senses.

The two men touch for the first time – Feraud "lowering the point of the sword, brushed past the perplexed D'Hubert, exclaiming, 'Follow me!'" – and this leads directly to another witness, a third, receiving a blow on the ears that temporally blinds her, until it is only the blind and the deaf who can witness this first duel: "Directly he had flung open the door a faint shriek was heard and the pretty maid, who had been listening at the keyhole, staggered away, putting the backs of her hands over her eyes." This clash between touch and hearing leads directly to a stand-off between the (still) rational gaze of D'Hubert and the increasingly irrational and animal-like gestures of Feraud: "'This enraged animal will have me against the wall directly,' thought Lieut. D'Hubert . . . it seemed to him that he was keeping his adversary off with his eyes rather more than with his

Figure 6 Royal Museum of Central Africa, Tervuren, 2007 © Jane Brown 2009.

point" (*TD*, 177–8, 180). If Conrad still retains a certain privileged immunity for sight at this point, it is only to contrast it to the metamorphosing animalization of Feraud, or the loss of all ratio and mediation between the senses which is nothing less than the unimaginable loss of the Aristotelian soul.

Holding off his adversary with the power of his gaze, D'Hubert at once recognizes his mortal danger and loses sight of Feraud as either simply a man, a human being, or merely an animal: "he meant to kill – nothing less. He meant it with an intensity of a will utterly beyond the inferior faculties of a tiger" (*TD*, 180). After the fourth duel, Conrad writes of Feraud, "more than ever he resembled an irritable and staring bird – something like a cross between a parrot and an owl" (*TD*, 210). D'Hubert will later compare him to a dog (*TD*, 245). D'Hubert's ability to fend off this shape-shifting animalization with the eye of reason falters after the first duel when he himself becomes deaf and blind: "Owning to the gravity of the incident, he was forbidden to see any one. He did not know what had happened, what was being said, or what was being thought" (*TD*, 186).[26] We will come back to the question of the animal in the next chapter.

D'Hubert himself cannot explain the absurdity of this asymmetrical and unending duel, this war of the senses that leaves him not senseless but without any order between the senses; he must remain silent, but nor can he ever escape that which refuses reconciliation (*TD*, 187, 189, 194–5, 202, 211, 231). As D'Hubert's wife will later say of the 15-year duel, "*c'est insensé* [insane, crazy] – to think what men are capable of." Her father, an old royalist, extends this description – much as Napoleon had done – to the whole army of the Emperor and his global war, "that Bonaparte's soldiers were savages. It is *insensé*" (*TD*, 264–5).

D'Hubert's only response, and perhaps Conrad's – beyond his highly moral social critique of a general hebetude – to this duel without end, is a quasi-deafness and quasi-blindness that forbids the ease, the deafening blindness, of any good conscience. Contrary to Clausewitz's dictum that "war is nothing but a duel on a larger scale" Conrad suggests that in times of war, literature is a kind of insane artistry, an asymmetrical duel with the asymmetric war, a duel that is always more and less than the representation of war itself (*OW*, 75). As Derrida observed in his interview soon after the attacks on the World

Trade Centre in 2001, whatever the war to come will be, it can no longer be described as a finely balanced duel (*AU*, 98).

An Iraqi vice-president has proposed that Saddam Hussein and George W. Bush should fight a duel to settle their differences. Taha Yassin Ramadan, who is not noted for a sense of humour but occasionally resorts to sarcasm, made the proposal in an interview with the Associated Press. Mr Bush's spokesman Ari Fleischer rejected the idea saying, "there can be no serious response to an irresponsible statement like that." His remarks came as the UN Security Council discussed the Iraqi offer for arms inspectors to return to Baghdad – the more straightforward route to avert war. "Bush wants to attack the whole [of] Iraq, the army and the infrastructure," the Iraqi vice-president said. "The American president should specify a group, and we will specify a group and choose neutral ground with Kofi Annan as referee and use one weapon with a president against a president, a vice-president against a vice-president, and a minister against a minister in a duel." Mr Fleischer poured scorn on the proposal saying: "In the past when Iraq had disputes, it invaded its neighbours. There were no duels; there were invasions. There was use of weapons of mass destruction and military. That's how Iraq settles its disputes.[27]

CHAPTER 7

(NOT) MEETING WITHOUT NAME

As if it were not true that when we name the cat, we retain nothing of it but its absence, what it is not.

Blanchot *(*LRD, *375)[1]*

SANS NOM

In 1976 Emmanuel Lévinas published *Noms propres*, a short collection of essays devoted to individual philosophers and writers, including Buber, Celan, Derrida and Proust. The French press describes *Noms propres* as "*le livre des rencontres.*"[2] In *Noms propres*, there are 15 essays each with a proper name in the title, but there is also a sixteenth and final essay in this book of meetings and duels, which is entitled "Nameless" (*Sans nom*). It is with those who do not choose to be without name that Lévinas ends his work.[3] He is concerned with a war without end, and the countless, nameless victims: "Since the end of the war, bloodshed has not ceased. Racism, imperialism and exploitation remain ruthless. Nations and individuals expose one another to hatred and contempt, fearing destitution and destruction."[4] "Sans nom" confronts us with anonymity as catastrophe, as deprivation, as the loss of the singularity of the name, of names upon names erased without end.[5]

There is an echo of this injunction to resist and to protest against the worst anonymity, the state's violent imposition of namelessness, in Derrida's 1996 intervention in support of the *sans-papiers*, the undocumented aliens in France, "Dereliction of the Right to Justice (But what are the 'sans-papiers' lacking?)." Derrida was responding to the introduction of a law in France to permit "the prosecution, and even the imprisonment, of those who take in and help foreigners whose status is held to be illegal". Any hospitality towards the *sans-papiers* is a crime, a breaking of the law.[6] What, Derrida asks are these so-called *sans-papiers* lacking? The without (*sans*) of anonymity has been claimed by the state and ostensibly put to work: *sans* papers, these foreigners are without rights and, ultimately, without the rights of human dignity (*DRJ*, 135). For Derrida, this prompts a question: "one must ask oneself what happens to society when it ascribes the source of all its ills . . . to the 'without' of others" (*DRJ*, 139–40).

In supporting the *sans-papiers*, Derrida reiterates that this does not mean a speaking "*for them*". Those whom the state has defined as *sans-papiers*, as *sans nom*, as being without a name that has been recognized and processed by the state, "have spoken": "They have spoken and they speak for themselves, we hear them, along with their representatives or advocates, their poets, and their songsters" (*DRJ*, 134). The anonymous, those without a state-name, those who have had the anonymity of an unrecorded and unrecordable name imposed upon them, are speaking. But how does one hear, or how does one stop hearing the nameless speak, the political and philosophical reverberation of the without name? This question of anonymity, of the *sans nom* – which returns to the *sans mot* and *sans date* that we began with – confronts us with the (mis)chance of (not) meeting, with the chance of literature as the other of the concept of war.

Today, one might expect that celebrity (the name known by everyone) would be the opposite of anonymity (the name known by no one). But celebrity can be characterized as a kind of anonymity, as a not knowing someone that everybody knows and, as Derrida said of the secret, anonymity needs witnesses, and relies on someone knowing that the proper name is being hidden or held in reserve (*E*, 46–7). If such a thing is possible, the profound desperation or the radical liberation of the without name would be known by no one, as if it is only no one who can know no one. Celebrity and anonymity are predicated on the assumption of meeting or not meeting, of two absolutes, of an all public and all private, that mirror and sustain each other. A globally diffused media access and a legal *cordon sanitaire* or institutional conceit of impartiality are equally haunted by an economy of perpetual insufficiency: the public is never public enough, the private is never private enough.

While the word "anonymity" apparently was coined in the early nineteenth century, according to the *OED*, the word "anonymous" belongs to the late Elizabethan period. That indefatigable translator of the age, Philemon Holland, noted in his translation of Pliny's *Natural History* (1601) that when something was found to have "no name to be called by, [it] got thereupon the name anonymos".[7] In other words, the birth of the "anonymos" does not announce what is without name as much the *naming* of the nameless. Authored by "Anonymous" becomes the proper name, the capitalization, the socially recognized form of the without name. The legacy of the emergence of a name for the without name and the invention of the concept of anonymity can be seen today in privileged social spaces and imposed social conditions.[8] At the same time, this arresting potency of the withdrawal of the name, this dark sovereignty of anonymity that has always been haunted by *la chance de la rencontre*, has its origins in antiquity.

NAMING THE UNNAMEABLE

"Now a man from the house of Levi went and took (to wife) a daughter of Levi. / The woman became pregnant and bore a son."[9] From the start, in *Exodus* neither Moses nor his parents are given any names: the future liberator of the Hebrews, of the man who will meet God and ask him for his name, begins in anonymity. It is only after the baby Moses has been found in the rushes that he is given a name. This is not just any name: it is a name that describes and preserves a chance meeting:

> Pharaoh's daughter said to her:
> Have this child go with you and nurse him for me,
> And I myself will give you your wages.
> So the woman took the child and she nursed him.
> The child grew, she brought him to Pharaoh's daughter,
> And he became her son.
> She called his name: Moshe/He-Who-Pulls-Out;
> she said: For out of the water *meshitihu*/I-pulled-him (*EX* 2. 8–10).

As Everett Fox suggests in his translation, this scene of naming operates on a number of levels. On the one hand, the Pharaoh's daughter – whose name we are never given – names the fortuitous and happy chance of a chance encounter: I pulled him out, and he was the one who was pulled out, so let's call him Moshe. "Moshe" both gives a name to this chance meeting and marks the name *as* a chance meeting.[10] On the other hand, "Moshe", this anonymous and presumably already named baby, is called "He-Who-Pulls-Out", because one day in his duel with the Pharaoh he will pull the Hebrews out of Egypt. "For out of the water *meshitihu*/I-pulled-him," the Pharaoh's daughter says, and it is Moshe who one day will pull apart the waters of the Red Sea. This naming, this loss of anonymity, is at once a chance meeting and a meeting without chance, a meeting that will take Moshe to meeting God and to ask for the name of God. A future meeting with the Unnameable already overwhelms the chances of a naming of the moment, of a contingent naming. The eschatology of an anonymity without chance is, seemingly, unavoidable.[11]

When Moshe encounters the burning bush, God says "I am the God of your father, / the God of Avraham, / the God of Yitzhak, / and the God of Yaakov" (*EX,* 3. 6). But this affiliation to the ancestors without naming is not enough for Moshe. The authority of this patriarchal anonymity is in itself insufficient and must be supplemented by the name. The wonder of the text that follows is that it at once gives a name – as the promise of a future assurance, as the assurance of the future – and withdraws the possibility of ever speaking or pronouncing the name of God:

Moshe said to God:
Here, I will come to the Children of Israel
and I will say to them:
The God of your fathers has sent me to you,
and they will say to me: What is his name? —
what shall I say to them?
God said to Moshe:
EHYEH ASHER EHYEH / I will be-there howsoever I will be-there.
And he said:
Thus shall you say to the Children of Israel:
EHYEH/ I-WILL-BE-THERE sends me to you. . . .
Go,
gather the elders of Israel
and say to them:

YHWH, the God of your fathers, has been seen by me. (*EX,* 3: 14–16)

YHWH, known later as *Hashem* (the Name), as the name for what (uniquely) cannot be named, gives the name not as a chance encounter of the moment, but as a promise of a future without end: "I-WILL-BE-THERE" – "That is my name for the ages, / that is my title (from) generation to generation (*EX,* 3. 15). At the same time, the repetition in the name of God ("I will be-there howsoever I will be-there") is the echo of God calling Moshe from the burning bush:

> God called to him out of the midst of the burning bush,
> he said:
> Moshe! Moshe!
> He said:
> Here I am. (*EX,* 3. 4)

This repetition of the unique name of Moshe can be seen as an anticipation of the promise of the future in the name of God. However, this takes place before the unameable names itself: the uniquely without name repeats the unique name of Moshe, the name *as* a chance meeting, marking the name as a singularity that can be repeated and as a *series* that relies on, and even requires, an interval.

The *Torah* gives us both the possibility of naming as chance *and* the possibility of the without name, of an exceptional anonymity that can only name itself as a promise, as a blank guarantee, as an always difficult call for trust (*ehmuna*). As Moshe says after this giving-withdrawing of the name: "But they will not trust me, and will not hearken to my voice" (*EX,* 4: 1). And even with the name of God as this assurance of the future, Moshe, with the name given in the chance encounter, still does not trust that he can speak for what is without name: "Please, my Lord, / no man of words am I, / not from yesterday, not from the day-before, not (even) since you have spoken to your servant, / for heavy of mouth and heavy of tongue am I!" (*EX,* 4. 10).

The equivocal legacy of this more than human naming of what cannot be named inhabits all concepts of anonymity, of the without name. As Derrida suggested, naming the without name is a *unity* of chance and rule that cannot be reduced to an assured programme, to a system without a swerve. It is at once the chance of meeting and the risk of not meeting. We are always (not) meeting without name.

WAR WITHOUT NAME

War has nothing to say, nothing at least that philosophy could make into a concept, which it could harness to an *epistēmē*. Nor does literature, at least when viewed in the presumption of naming all its animals and all its objects, tell us what war cannot tell us. For Derrida, on the contrary, the *récits* of Blanchot hover in the vicinities (*parages*) of not what war can tell us, but in what war *leaves* us with, with what remains and remains to come of war: the *sans nom*, which Lévinas argued ends all works on the proper name.[12]

The silent resonance of the *sans* in Blanchot's *récits*, of the name *Blanchot*, tears itself from all "filiation with the name" (*PA,* 59). The *sans* is an affirmation, but an affirmation without redemption, a narrative that is always undone by what cannot be named, a narrative without name. "It is nameless [*sans nom*] before *viens*" (*PA,* 74). "Heard from the *come* [le *viens*] that they hear and that they emit, they belong to the nameless since it is only 'starting from' the come that they would be able to shout their name" (*PA,* 75).[13] This is neither making use of a deprivation without name, nor is it a celebration of a chosen anonymity. One cannot avoid "the anonymity in the name", Derrida argues, in friendship, in writing, in bearing witness to "a secret duel", in war, in (not) meeting (*PA,* 104–5; LO).[14]

One can see this unavoidable anonymity not only in works without name where the principal characters have no name or discernable marks of identity, but also in the great works of the nineteenth century that labour without rest to name everything, and most of all when it comes to war, to war and its other. As we have seen, in *War and Peace* the young Nikolai Rostov has his first experiences of war between the disastrous battles of Ulm and Austerlitz in 1805.[15] Tolstoy writes:

> The squadron in which Rostov served had just had time to mount its horses when it was halted facing the enemy. Again, as on the Enns bridge, there was no one between the squadron and the enemy, and there lay between them, separating them, the same terrible line of the unknown and of fear, like the line separating the living from the dead. All men sensed that line, and the question

of whether they would or would not cross that line, and how they would cross it, troubled them. (*WP,* 188).

In this chance encounter on the battlefield, the Russians and the French find themselves "facing" each other with "no one between" them and, at the same time, all are affected by the absolute "line" between life and death. It is in this chance proximity, of proximity *as* chance, that the soldiers encounter an unassailable distance, a "terrible line of the unknown" that can be crossed at any moment.

At the command to charge, Rostov drives his horse Little Rook forward and crosses into "the middle the line [between the two armies] that had seemed so terrible". Exhilarated at surviving this crossing, Rostov inadvertently gallops ahead of the rest of his squadron:

> "'Well, now let anybody at all come along,' thought Rostov, spurring Little Rook and outstripping the others, sending him into a full gallop" (*WP,* 188). Out in front, beyond the line, Rostov's horse is shot from under him, and the next moment he finds himself "alone in the middle of the field. Instead of moving horses and hussar backs, he saw the immobile earth and stubble around him" (*WP,* 189). These displacements – sudden proximity and insurmountable distance, crossing lines and closing gaps that end in solitude, silence and emptiness – register the strange spatial and temporal anonymity of war: "Where ours were, where the French were – he did not know. There was no one around" (*WP,* 189).

Rostov can now no longer find "that line which had so sharply separated the two armies", he no longer knows how to orientate himself in relation to the battle" (*WP,* 189). This disorientation becomes deadly when he fails to recognize that the enemy is running towards him:

> "Well, here are some people," he thought joyfully, seeing several men running towards him. "They'll help me!" In front of these people ran one in a strange shako and a blue greatcoat, dark, tanned, with a hooked nose. Two more and then many came running behind him. [. . .] "What men are these?" Rostov kept thinking, not believing his eyes. "Can they be Frenchmen?" He looked at the approaching Frenchmen and, though a moment before he had been galloping only in order to meet these Frenchmen and cut them to pieces, their closeness now seemed so terrible to him that

he could not believe his eyes. "Who are they? Why are they running? Can it be they're running at me? Can it be? And why? To kill me? *Me*, whom everybody loves so?" [. . .] The first French-man with the hooked nose came so close that the expression on his face could already be seen. And the flushed alien physiognomy of this man who, lowered bayonet, holding his breath, was running lightly towards him, frightened Rostov. He seized his pistol and, instead of firing it, threw it at the Frenchman, and ran for the bushes as fast as he could. (*WP*, 189)

What remains of war, the former soldier Tolstoy suggests, is an inexorable and disorientating *gaining* of anonymity. In war, one not only loses one's own bearings, crossing the line and running ahead of oneself, but one is also unable to recognize or to name the enemy. In war, the enemy is without name. Literature accounts for this (not) meeting without name. Placed in an unbelievable proximity, and pursued by a man without a name, by an anonymous French soldier, Nikolai Rostov can only run away.

Tolstoy counterbalances this early scene of Rostov's fleeing in terror with his experiences of paralysis in the battle of Austerlitz. At one point, by chance, Rostov comes across the Tsar, Alexander I. The Tsar is almost alone in the midst of battle and stuck on his horse before a wide ditch. While Rostov tries to find the courage to approach his "adored sovereign", another solider comes and helps the Tsar (*WP*, 287). Rostov cannot meet his sovereign: the moment is "unsuitable, improper, and impossible". From "a distance" that he can never cross, Rostov watches his monarch sitting under an apple tree and weeping, as the battle is lost (*WP*, 287–8). It is now Rostov who has become a witness without name to the loss of the absolute anonymity of the sovereign.

Seven years later in 1812, Rostov is once again in action and fight-ing the French. Once again, he is rushing forward into battle: "With the feeling with which he raced to intercept a wolf, Rostov, giving his Don horse free rein, galloped to intercept the disordered lines of the French dragoons" (*WP*, 653). Catching a French officer, "Rostov, not knowing why himself, raised his sabre and struck the Frenchman with it." Tolstoy goes on to write:

The moment he did this, all Rostov's animation suddenly vanished. The officer fell, not so much from the stroke of the sword, which only cut his arm slightly above the elbow, as from the jolt to his horse and from fear. Reining in his horse, Rostov sought his enemy with his eyes, to see whom he had vanquished. The French dragoon officer was hopping on the ground with one foot, the other being caught in the stirrup. Narrowing his eyes fearfully, as if expecting a new blow any second, he winced, glancing up at Rostov from below with an expression of terror. His face, pale and mud-spattered, fair-haired, young, with a dimple on the chin and light blue eyes, was not at all for the battlefield, not an enemy's face, but a most simple, homelike face. Before Rostov decided what to do with him, the officer cried out: "*Je me rends!*" (*WP*, 653–4)

While it has become a cliché today to see one's brother or oneself in an enemy on the battlefield, Tolstoy suggests that war is a terrible ever-increasing proximity with anonymity, with the eyes, the face, and body of the other who has no name. This anonymity is the only possibility for the state-run imperative to kill and, at the same time, it is this nameless other, this broken mirror, that announces the (im)possibility of a proximity without name, and the persistence of the "invisible line" that cuts across the frail privilege of every state-given name.

Tolstoy returns to this connection between anonymity and war in his account of Pierre's experiences during the French occupation of Moscow. As much as a reaction to witnessing the battle of Borodino and his wife's announcement that she wants a divorce as concern for his own safety, when he is arrested by the French Count Pierre Bezukhov is unable to give his name. As he is processed by the occupying army Pierre is officially designated "as *celui qui n'avoue pas son nom* [he who does not divulge his name]" (*WP*, 962–3). Named as the one-who-has-no-name by the new power of the state, when he believes that he has been sentenced to death, Pierre experiences the full force of the anonymity of the state-run imperative to kill:

There was one thought in Pierre's head all that time. It was the thought of who, finally, had sentenced him to be executed. It was not the people of the commission that had interrogated him: not one of them would or obviously could have done it. It was not Davout, who had given him such a human look. Another moment and Davout would have understood that they were doing a bad thing, but the adjutant who came in had prevented that moment. And that adjutant obviously had not wanted anything bad, but he

Figure 7 Brussels, 2007 © Jane Brown 2009.

also might not have come in. Who was it, finally, who was executing, killing, depriving of life, him – Pierre – with all his memories, longings, hopes, thoughts? Who was doing it? And Pierre felt that it was no one. (*WP,* 965)

As we shall see, it is perhaps not fortuitous that Tolstoy goes on to link this terrible anonymity of the state to the anonymity of an animal, a dog, that belongs to no one and that has lost all marks of identity: its name, its breed and its colour. Spared execution, Pierre has been imprisoned with other regular soldiers. Tolstoy writes:

> On the sixth of October, early in the morning, Pierre stepped out of the shed and, on his way back, stopped by the door, playing with a long, purplish dog on short, bowed legs that were fidgeting around him. This dog lived in their shed, spending the nights with Karataev, but occasionally went to town somewhere and came back again. It had probably never belonged to anyone, and now, too, it was no one's and had no name at all. The French called it Azor, the storytelling soldier called it Femgalka, Karataev and the others sometimes called it Grey, sometimes Floppy. Its not belonging to anyone, and the absence of a name and even of a breed, even of a definite colour, seemed not to bother the purplish dog in the least. (*WP,* 1008–9)

Later, Tolstoy makes this "purplish dog", this animal without identity, the only possible witness to the murder of Karataev on the forced march of the Russian prisoners from Moscow. Tolstoy writes:

> A dog began to howl behind, in the place where Karataev had been sitting. "What a fool, what's it howling about?" thought Pierre.
> Like him, his soldier comrades, walking beside Pierre, did not turn to look at the place from which the shot had been heard and then the howling of the dog; but there was a stern look on all their faces. (*WP,* 1064)

ANIMALNIMITY

Tolstoy links the anonymity of war to the question of the animal in Nikolai Rostov's struggle with both combat and his relation to the absolute anonymity of the sovereign. In his last conference paper in France, "Le souverain bien – ou l'Europe en mal de souveraineté" (2004), Derrida explored this connection between the animal and sovereignty.[16] Derrida and Tolstoy are both interested in the wolf.[17] "With the feeling with which he raced to intercept a wolf" Rostov pursues the French enemy at Borodino (*WP,* 653). Tolstoy reiterates this link between war and hunting animals in his account of Rostov's involvement in tracking down and killing a wolf in 1810. "Austerlitz [. . .] vividly but fleetingly flashed in his imagination. 'If only once in my life I could chase down a seasoned wolf, I'd ask for nothing more' he thought, straining his hearing and sight, looking to the left and then to the right, and listening to the smallest nuances in the sounds of the chase" (*WP,* 500).

What is striking in Tolstoy's description of the hunt is that every hunting dog has a name while the wolf remains nameless: "each dog knew its master and its name" (*WP,* 495). The loss of anonymity in the hunt is absolute: "Suddenly the wolf's entire physiognomy changed; he shuddered at the sight of human eyes, which he had probably never seen before, directed at him, and turning his head slightly towards the hunter, stopped – go back or go on?" (*WP,* 500). When Rostov's favourite dog, Karay, brings the wolf down, it is "the happiest moment of his life" (*WP,* 501). Before he can stab the wolf, Rostov is persuaded to capture it alive. Tolstoy then tells us that the dogs had killed five of the wolf's cubs. With a "stake thrust between her jaws" and her legs bound, the wolf is carried away:

> everyone came to look at the wolf, who with her broad-browed head hanging down and the bitten stick between her jaws, gazed with great glassy eyes at the crowd of dogs and the men surrounding her. When they touched her she jerked her bound legs and looked wildly yet simply at them all.[18]

While Rostov has no scruples about the wolf's terrible loss of anonymity, he is still unable to overcome the anonymity of his enemy in battle. Derrida begins his 2004 paper by noting the sexual difference between "the beast" and "the sovereign", and one could add Tolstoy's description of the capture of the she-wolf to the many instances of his problematic representation of women (*LSB,* 110). As Anna Akhmatova remarked to Isaiah Berlin, during a conversation about *Anna Karenina*:

Why did Tolstoy make her commit suicide? As soon as she leaves Karenin, everything changes. She suddenly turns into a fallen woman, a *traviata*, a prostitute. Who punishes Anna? God? No, not God – society – that same society whose hypocrisies Tolstoy is constantly denouncing.[19]

Examining the history of the political links between the development of concepts of sovereignty and the many fables and proverbs about wolves, Derrida concentrates on an idiomatic phrase in French, "*à pas de loup*", which can be translated roughly as to act stealthily, furtively, silently (*LSB,* 111). For Derrida, this phrase links a historical use of the concept of the animal, of the wolf, to war, to the commander-in-chief of the army, to the sovereign.

As Derrida points out, the concept "wolf" has long been "allegorising the hunt and war, the prey, predation" (*LSB,* 113). He takes great care to distinguish a "real wolf" from the political concept of the wolf or she-wolf (*la louve*), warning that in speaking of an animal, we are not already speaking for the animal or assuming that the animal cannot speak for itself, in a language that we have yet to understand. One can see an example of this easy idealization or automatic "allegorising" of the animal in *War and Peace* when Pierre dreams that he is "surrounded by dogs" and writes in his journal, "suddenly one small dog seized my left thigh with its teeth and would not let go." Pierre immediately interprets these dogs as symbols of his own spiritual struggles: "Lord, Great Architect of nature! help me to tear off the dogs – my passions" (*WP,* 443).

Derrida marks his own caution around the uses and abuses of the "wolf" by emphasizing that the phrase "*à pas de loup*" implies what has *not yet* been seen or heard. In other words, in this bracketing Derrida insists that the "wolf" has not yet been named, and resists all the names that have been imposed on it:

If I have chosen the locution that names the "pas" [step/not] of the wolf in "*à pas de loup*," it is without doubt because the wolf itself is named *in absentia*, if one can say this. The wolf is named where one neither sees nor hears it coming yet; where it is still absent, save his name. It announces itself, one apprehends it, one names it, one refers to it, one even calls it by its name, one imagines it or one projects on it an image, a trope, a figure, a myth, a fable, a phantasm, but always by referring to someone who, stealthily advancing, is not there, not yet there, to someone who neither presents or represents itself yet. (*LSB,* 113)

At stake in this stealthily slipping away from being named is not only a presentation or making present, a presumption of putting to use, but also a warning against treating this furtive absence as a resource, as "*la ruse de guerre*", as an act of mastery or sovereignty (*LSB,* 115). For Derrida, the "wolf" as a political concept has acted as a critique of the tyranny and violence of an indivisible sovereignty and as a dark mirror that supports the claims of sovereignty to be – like the "wolf" – outside of and above the law (*LSB,* 119–26). "The beast *is* the sovereign", Derrida concludes; it is at once the possibility and the ruin of an absolute sovereignty.[20]

In *War and Peace*, Tolstoy appears both to reinforce and to under- mine this traditional link between the "wolf", war and sovereignty. Wanting to find the logic or force to kill in battle, to fight for the sov- ereign, Rostov relies on his passion in hunting and killing the she-wolf. Rostov relies on the absolute anonymity of the she-wolf (redolent symbol, as Derrida says, of foundation and institution, not least of the monarchy, republic, empire and decline of Rome). The violence of the beast, of what cannot be named or tamed, is the possibility of killing the enemy in war. While Tolstoy does all he can to break away from this powerful trope of animal anonymity as the possibility of state-sanctioned murder, not least by shattering the exceptional ano- nymity of the sovereign as Rostov sees the Tsar weeping under an apple tree at Austerlitz, he neither challenges this tradition of *animal- nimity*, nor, despite his best intentions, diminishes the aura around the greatest sovereign of all, Napoleon. As Isaiah Berlin suggested in his celebrated essay on two differing concepts of animalnimity, one that embraces multiplicity (the fox) and another that yearns for unity (the hedgehog), Tolstoy was a fox who always wanted to be a hedge- hog.[21] In *War and Peace*, "Napoleon" remains the oldest of names for when "the beast becomes the sovereign who becomes the beast" (*LSB,* 126; *WP,* 891).

As Derrida had suggested in "The Animal That Therefore I Am (More to Follow)" (1999), the animal has always been *waiting to see* how it will be addressed or represented, asking of the human "what is he going to call me?" (*ATT,* 387). This tradition of animalnimity, of relying on and exploiting the animal that can never be named *and* that is always being named in philosophy and literature, of the animal as a never ending loss of an inexhaustible anonymity, has always been political, always stood as a witness *sans nom*, for the most equivocal political events of our times, for the wars without end (*ATT,* 379, 381, 384–8, 410). I would like to cite only two remarkable examples from the first half of the twentieth century: Mikhail Bulgakov's *The Heart of a Dog* (1925) and S. Y. Agnon's *Only Yesterday* (1945).

GRIEF CAME TO ME ONLY THROUGH OTHERS

Bulgakov's satirical novel was written in 1925, and only published (in English) in 1968 and did not appear in Russia until 1987: it is truly a work of the twentieth century. Nonetheless, it was written only a year after Lenin died and cannot be seen as a veiled and exuberant commentary on Stalinism – Bulgakov would leave that to *The Master and Margarita*. Why does Bulgakov use a medical experiment on a dog that goes terribly wrong to illustrate the great experiment of the Bolshevik revolution? And why does he link this monstrous experiment, which creates a half dog-half man, an animal-man, to the violent impossibility of naming the animal? The book opens – in its English translation – both with what cannot be translated and with an implicit act of translation: "Ooow-ow-ooow-owow! Oh, look at me, I'm dying."[22] Injured, hungry and freezing on a cold night in Moscow, the dog encounters a woman in the street: "Here, doggy, here, boy! Here, Sharik [. . .] What are you whining for, poor little fellow? Did somebody hurt you, then?" The dog then reflects on this act of naming, on this temporary loss of anonymity:

> "Sharik" she had called him [. . .] What a name to choose! Sharik is the sort of name for a round, fat, stupid dog that's fed on porridge, a dog with a pedigree, and he was a tattered, scraggy, filthy stray mongrel with a scalded side. (*HD*, 8–9)

This misnaming is not only a social error, a sign that there are still social inequalities and hierarchies in Soviet Russia, but also a recognition of an implacable resistance: no matter what it is called no one can ever get the name right, no one can ever get the right name for the dog. The dog has a name that can never be translated, or it may not have a name, it may not even need a name, a proper name. Starving and weak, the dog is then enticed into the company of a man with a sausage in his hand: "'Here, doggy,' the gentleman whistled, and added sternly, 'Come on! Take it, Sharik!' He's christened me Sharik too. Call me what you like. For this you can do anything you like to me" (*HD*, 11).

This man, Philip Preobrazhensky, a professor of medicine, will go on to implant human testes and a human pituitary gland in the dog. At their first meeting, the professor also greets the dog with the same wrong name. Desperate, the dog appears to take on this name, as a momentary strategy or as a thing of indifference: "His flank hurt unbearably, but for the moment Sharik forgot about it." This chance name, this naming in a chance meeting, then takes on the accoutrements of a proper name that will always be improper: "'Come in, Mr Sharik,' said the gentleman ironically and Sharik respectfully obeyed, wagging his tail" (*HD*, 17). Fattened up, pampered and indulged for the forthcoming operation, the dog sees himself in the mirror and begins, almost, to accept this change in social status, though he still retains the secret of his name, of his *sans nom*: "I am handsome. Perhaps I'm really a dog prince, living incognito" (*HD*, 43).

Dragged to the operating theatre the dog loses consciousness. In the journal that records the procedure, the dog is identified by his name: "Name: 'Sharik.'" (*HD*, 58). After the operation, which results in "total humanisation", Sharik begins to laugh and soon to talk, calling the professor a bastard and accusing him of being bourgeois (*HD*, 62, 64). But it is not the dog that is speaking: it is Sharik, or more properly Elim Grigorievich Chugunkin, the deceased petty criminal and Bolshevik sympathizer that has provided the testes and pituitary gland (*HD*, 68). The dog without name has gone. This dog becoming human then chooses his own name, Poligraph Poligraphovich Sharikov, insisting that Sharikov is his "real name" (*HD*, 77–8). After Sharikov is registered with the state and has his papers, he gets a job strangling cats in Moscow, and will eventually denounce the professor (*HD*, 115, 120). Drinking, stealing and assaulting the women in the house, the professor comes to see that Sharikov is not "a man with a dog's heart", but a dog with "a *human heart*", the "rottenest heart in all creation" (*HD*, 110–11). In the end, after the professor has removed the testes and pituitary gland and Sharikov has reverted to Sharik, the heart of the dog – from the title of the book – has returned, and still retains its secrets, the stubborn secret of name or its without name, the chance of its frail anonymity in a totalitarian state.

Twenty years later, and five years after Bulgahov died in 1940, leaving the Devil and his gun-totting cat as the last figures of anarchic redemption and impossible escape in the atheistic absolutism of Stalinism, S. Y. Agnon published *Only Yesterday*. Again, as Derrida warned, one has to take great care with the animal as political analogy. Agnon was writing in Palestine under the British Mandate, and his book was published three years before the foundation of the State of Israel.[23] The conflict between the competing nationalisms of the Jews and Arabs in Palestine had been going on since the end of World War I, and Agnon's book, published at the end of the World War II, is as much about the *Shoah* and what Amos Oz calls "the silence of heaven".[24] *Only Yesterday* is set in the first decade of the twentieth century, and charts the difficult wanderings and perpetual displacement of Isaac Kumer, an idealistic European emigrant who loses his way and cannot find his place in Palestine, moving back and forth between the secular settlements in what will soon become Tel Aviv and the religious orthodoxy of Jerusalem.

Kumer becomes a house and sign painter, and one day on a whim he paints the words "crazy dog" on a dog. After this chance encounter, the narrative moves back and forth between Kumer and the dog. The dog is shunned and beaten because he is thought to be rabid until he goes mad and bites and kills Kumer on his wedding day. Isaac Kumer's first meeting with the dog takes place in a chapter entitled "Stray Dog" and this is the first name that is given to this dog, his first loss of anonymity: this is a dog that wanders without a fixed destination, that inadvertently digresses from the path or diverges from the group.

Kumer is given a job to paint a sign recording the name of the donor of a house for the poor: "the name of the donor he painted in gold."[25] It is just after he has written this name in gold of a charitable man who has undertaken to house the nameless poor, to house those without name or status, that Kumer paints a second name:

As he was about to wipe his brushes, he chanced on a stray dog, with short ears, a sharp nose, a stub of a tail, and hair that looked maybe white or maybe brown or maybe yellow, one of those dogs who roamed around in Jerusalem until the English entered the Land. Isaac picked up one of his brushes and didn't know if he wanted to threaten the dog with it or if he wanted to wipe it off on the dog's skin [. . .] Isaac just stroked the dog's skin, like a clerk stroking the paper before writing. Once again he dipped his brush and leaned toward the dog and wrote a few letters on his back [. . .] And so, by the time Isaac stood up, he had written in calligraphy on the dog the letters d-o-g [*KaLBa*]. He patted his back and told him, From now on, folks won't mistake you, but will know that you're a dog. And you won't forget you're a dog either. (*OY,* 286)

The dog remains standing next to Kumer, and Kumer asks him, "What else do you want? [. . .] Are you crazy? You want me to make spots on your skin, or do you want me to paint your name in gold?" Kumer then paints on the dog "the words Crazy Dog" (*OY,* 286–7). While this third name, "crazy" – after "stray" and "dog" – will lead to the dog's madness and to Kumer's death, it is the second name, "dog", that seems to capture all the vulnerability and violence of the *sans nom*, of (not) meeting without name.

(Not) meeting without name is always the possibility of a violent naming, of a duel or war that ends in a name, in a profound loss of anonymity. But it also ceaselessly announces the edges and borders, the limitations of what can be named (*ATT,* 416).[26] This violent limitation, this imposition that cannot help but impose on itself, is found in writing the name as a noun, in threatening the assurance that a proper name is always more and less than a noun. The proper name cannot avoid the (mis)chance of *la chance de la rencontre* (*OG,* 279–80). In times of war, it is in the politics of anonymity, of finding strategic resistances to the sovereign anonymity and the ceaseless sovereign effort to either leave the enemy nameless or to name what cannot be named, that there is a chance for the other of war. In such times, literature confronts us with the voices of the *sans nom* and the injunction to respond to Derrida's question: what are *sans-papiers* lacking?

In *Only Yesterday*, Agnon follows this scene of naming, of the three names imposed on the dog, "stray", "dog" and "crazy", with a fourth name. A school principal sees the name-noun "dog" (*KaLBa*) written on the skin of the dog, and reading it backwards (*BaLaK*), gives the dog another name: "The people of Jerusalem are experts in Humash and know that there was a wicked man Balak and so they name their dogs after him" (*OY,* 303). Moving backwards and forwards, the noun can be read as a proper name and the proper name as a noun. As this dog with a name-becoming-noun and noun-becoming-name painted on his skin moves away, Agnon writes:

Well then, we can call him Balak. And what was his name, perhaps he had a name and it sank and perhaps he didn't have a name, as in some communities, where a man whose sons don't survive doesn't name his son in order to confound the Angel of Death, so he won't know that there is a creature so-and-so. Balak wagged his tail and said, That's it, exactly what I said, that grief came to me only through others. (*OY*, 303)

NOTES

PREFACE

[1] Jacques Derrida, "Demeure, Athènes", in Jean-François Bonhomme, *Athènes à l'ombre de l'acropole* (Athens: Olkos, 1996), 60. Henceforth cited as *DA*.

For more on Jane Brown's work see: www.janebrownphotography.com

PROLOGUE: A SERIES OF INTERVALS

[1] Plato, *Timaeus*, trans. R. G. Bury (Cambridge, MA: Harvard University Press, 2005), 37d. Henceforth cited as *TM*. See also, John Sallis, *Chorology: On Beginning in Plato's Timaeus* (Bloomington: Indiana University Press, 1999).

[2] Jacques Derrida, *The Archaeology of the Frivolous: Reading Condillac*, (1973), trans. John P. Leavey, Jr. (Pittsburgh: Duquesne University Press, 1980), 33. Henceforth cited as *AF*; *L'archéologie du frivole* (Paris: Éditions Galilée, 1990), 14. Henceforth cited as *AdF*.

[3] On Derrida's reading of a series of photographs see also, Jacques Derrida and Marie-Françoise Plissart, *Right of Inspection*, (1985) (New York: Monacelli, 1997).

[4] Deleuze offers a different reading of the *aiōn*, which he contrasts to *khronos* in *Logic of Sense*, (1969), trans. Mark Lester and Charles Stivale (London: Continuum, 2004), 186–93. See also, D. N. Rodowick, *Gilles Deleuze's Time Machines* (Durham: Duke University Press, 1997).

[5] J. Hillis Miller, *Fiction and Repetition: Seven English Novels* (Cambridge, MA: Harvard University Press, 1982), 6.

[6] Jean-Jacques Rousseau, *Discourse on the Origin of Inequality*, (1755), intro. Patrick Coleman, trans. Franklin Philip (Oxford: Oxford University Press, 1999), 24.

[7] Jean-Jacques Rousseau, *Confessions*, (1770), trans. Angela Scholar, ed. Patrick Coleman (Oxford: Oxford University Press, 2000), 218. Henceforth cited as *CF*.

8 Maurice Blanchot, "The Experience of Proust", (1943), *Faux Pas*, trans. Charlotte Mandell (Stanford: Stanford University Press, 2001), 44, 46.

9 Maurice Blanchot, *L'entretien infini*, (1969), (Paris: Gallimard, 2006), 607–11.

10 Nicholas Royle, *The Romantic Imagination in relation to War and Apocalypse in the Later Poetry of Wallace Stevens* (Oxford, 1984: Bodleian Ms. D. Phil c. 5132).

11 Jacques Derrida, *Of Grammatology*, trans. Gayatri Chakravorty Spivak (Baltimore: Johns Hopkins University Press, 1976), 195. Henceforth cited as *OG*.

12 Jean-Jacques Rousseau, *Essay On the Origin of Languages and Writings Related to Music*, trans. and ed. John T. Scott (Hanover: University Press of New England, 1998), 329.

13 See also, *OG,* 249–50, 262.

14 Jacques Derrida, "Auto-immunités, suicides réels et symboliques", in *Le "concept" du 11 septembre: Dialogues à New York (octobre-décembre 2001)* avec Giovanna Borradori (Paris: Éditions Galilée, 2003), 133.

15 Jacques Derrida and Giovanna Borradori, "Autoimmunity: Real and Symbolic Suicides", in *Philosophy in a Time of Terror: Dialogues with Jürgen Habermas and Jacques Derrida*, trans. Giovanna Borradori (Chicago: University of Chicago Press, 2003), 97. Henceforth cited as *AU*.

16 Alexandre Kojève, *Introduction to the Reading of Hegel*, (1937–1938), ed. Raymond Queneau and Alan Bloom, trans. James H. Nichols (Ithaca: Cornell University Press, 1991), 69–70. Henceforth cited as *IRH*.

17 Jacques Derrida, *Demeure: Fiction and Testimony*, (1998), trans. Elizabeth Rottenberg (Stanford: Stanford University Press, 2000), 112–13, n. 16. Henceforth cited as *DFT*; *Demeure – Maurice Blanchot* (Paris: Éditions Galilée, 1998), 109–10, n. 1. Derrida quotes from G. F. W. Hegel, *Correspondance I. 1785–1812*, trans. J. Carrère (Paris: Gallimard, 1962), 115–19.

18 See Jacques Derrida, "Envois", (1980), in *The Post Card: From Socrates to Freud and Beyond,* trans. Alan Bass (Chicago: University of Chicago Press, 1987), 129, 246–7. Henceforth cited as *E*.

19 Jacques Derrida, "Outwork, Prefacing", (1972), in *Dissemination*, trans. Barbara Johnson (Chicago: University of Chicago Press, 1981), 8. Henceforth cited as *OWP*. See also, Jacques Derrida, "LIVING ON. Border lines", in *Deconstruction and Criticism*, trans. James Hulbert (New York: Continuum, 1979), 127, 147. Henceforth cited as *LO*.

20 Jacques Derrida, "Cartouches", (1978), in *The Truth in Painting*, trans. Geoff Bennington and Ian McLeod (Chicago: University of Chicago Press, 1987), 186. Henceforth cited as *C*.

21 See also, Jacques Derrida, "Et Cetera . . . (and so on, und so weiter, and so forth, *et ainsi de suite*, und so überall, etc.)", in *Deconstructions: A User's Guide*, ed. Nicholas Royle, trans. Geoffrey Bennington (Basingstoke: Palgrave, 2000), 282, 288–91. See J. Hillis Miller, "'Don't count me in': Derrida's Refraining", *Textual Practice* 21 no. 2 (2007): 279–94.

22 Jacques Derrida, *Adieu: To Emmanuel Levinas*, trans. Anne Pascale-Brault and Michael Naas (Stanford: Stanford University Press, 1999), 86. Henceforth cited as *AD*.

[23] Jacques Derrida, "At This Very Moment in This Work Here I Am", (1980), in *Psyche: Inventions of the Other, Volume I*, trans. Ruben Berezdivin and Peggy Kamuf, ed. Peggy Kamuf and Elizabeth Rottenberg (Stanford: Stanford University Press, 2007), 147, 157, 165. 168. Henceforth cited as *ATV*.

[24] Stendhal, *The Charterhouse of Parma*, (1839), trans. Margaret R. B. Shaw (London: Penguin, 1958), 43. Henceforth cited as *CP*.

[25] Leo Tolstoy, *War and Peace*, (1865–1869), trans. Richard Pevear and Larissa Volokhonsky (London: Vintage, 2007), 126, 258. Henceforth cited as *WP*.

[26] Carl von Clausewitz, *On War*, (1832), ed. and trans. Michael Howard and Peter Paret (Princeton: Princeton University Press, 1989), 518. Henceforth cited as *OW*.

1 AN INHERITED DIS-INHERITANCE

[1] A shorter version of this chapter was read at a one day Derrida workshop marking the fortieth anniversary of the publication of *De la grammatologie* at Brunel University in October 2007. I would like to thank the participants: Nicholas Royle, Paul Davies, Joanna Hodge, Sarah Wood and Michael Syrotinski.

[2] The English translations of these works have since been published: Jacques Derrida, *The Animal That Therefore I Am*, ed. Marie-Louis Mallett, trans. David Wills (Stanford: Stanford University Press, 2008). Hélène Cixous, *Insister of Jacques Derrida*, trans. Peggy Kamuf (Edinburgh: Edinburgh University Press, 2007).

[3] Jacques Derrida, "Cogito and the History of Madness", (1964), in *Writing and Difference*, trans. Alan Bass (Chicago: University of Chicago Press, 1978), 31–63. Henceforth cited as *CHM*. Jacques Derrida, "Violence and Metaphysics: An Essay on the Thought of Emmanuel Levinas", in *Writing and Difference*, trans. Alan Bass (Chicago: University of Chicago Press, 1978), 79–153. Henceforth cited as *VM*. Friedrich Nietzsche, *Beyond Good and Evil, in Basic Writings of Nietzsche*, (1886), trans. Walter Kaufman (New York: Modern Library, 1968), 203. Henceforth cited as *BGE*.

[4] Jacques Derrida, "'Dead Man Running': *Salut, Salut* – Notes for a Letter to '*Les Temps Modernes*'", (1996), in *Negotiations: Interventions and Interviews 1971–2001*, trans. Elizabeth Rottenberg (Stanford: Stanford University Press, 2002), 257. Henceforth cited as *DMR*. On the relationship between Derrida and Sartre, see: Christina M. Howells, "Sartre and Derrida: The Promises of the Subject", in *Derrida: Negotiating the Legacy*, ed. Madeleine Fagan, Ludovic Glorieux, Indira Hašimbegović and Marie Suetsugu (Edinburgh: Edinburgh University Press, 2007), 161–71; Steve Martinot, *Forms in the Abyss: A Philosophical Bridge between Sartre and Derrida* (Philadelphia: Temple University Press, 2006).

[5] Jean Paul Sartre, *La nausée*, (1938) (Paris: Gallimard, 2005), 11, 13. My translation.

[6] Jean Paul Sartre, *Les mots*, (1964) (Paris: Gallimard, 2006), 15. Henceforth cited as *M*. My translation.

[7] Sartre writes, *"je ne cesse de me créer; je suis le donateur et la donation"*.

[8] See also, Jacques Derrida, "Plato's Pharmacy", (1968), in *Dissemination*, trans. Barbara Johnson (Chicago: University of Chicago Press, 1981), 61–171.

[9] See *OG*, 137, 231–2, 237, 254, 277–8, 302. See also, Jacques Derrida, "Heidegger's Ear: Philopolemology (*Geschlecht* IV)", (1989), in *Reading Heidegger: Commemorations*, ed. John Sallis, trans. John Leavey Jr. (Bloomington: Indiana University Press, 1992), 187, 209. Henceforth abbreviated as *HE*. Martin Heidegger, *What is Called Thinking?*, (1951), trans. Fred D. Wieck and J. Glenn Gray (New York: Harper and Row, 1968), 3, 11. Henceforth cited as *WCT*. Martin Heidegger, *Was heisst Denken?* (Frankfurt am Main: Vittoria Klostermann, 2002), 5, 13. See also, David Wood, *Thinking After Heidegger* (Cambridge: Polity, 2002).

[10] Jacques Derrida, *De la grammatologie* (Paris: Les Éditions du Minuit, 1967), 331. Translation modified. Henceforth cited as *Dlg*.

[11] See Ginette Michaud, "Literature in Secret: Crossing Derrida and Blanchot", *Angelaki* 7 no. 2 (2002), 69–90; Timothy Clark, *Derrida, Heidegger, Blanchot: Sources of Derrida's Notion and Practice of Literature* (Cambridge: Cambridge University Press, 1992).

[12] Jacques Derrida, "Pas", (1976), in *Parages*, nouvelle édition revue et augmentée (Paris: Éditions Galilée, 2003), 13. Henceforth cited as *PA*. My translation. On the link between this essay and Derrida's reading of Heidegger, Herman Rapaport, *Heidegger and Derrida: Reflections on Time and Language* (Lincoln: University of Nebraska Press, 1991).

[13] See, Jacques Derrida, *The Other Heading: Reflections on Today's Europe*, (1991), trans. Pascale-Anne Brault and Michael Naas (Bloomington: Indiana University Press, 1992). On the family, see also Jacques Derrida, *Glas*, (1974), trans. John P. Leavey Jr. and Richard Rand (Lincoln: University of Nebraska Press, 1986). Henceforth cited as *G*.

[14] Jacques Derrida, " 'Il courait mort' Salut, Salut: Notes pour un courrier aux *Les Temps Modernes*", in *Papier Machine: Le ruban de machine à écrire et autres réponses* (Paris: Éditions Galilée, 2001), 194.

[15] The echo of the Beatles's song 'Sgt. Peppers's Lonely Hearts Club Band' can also be read in Derrida's "Back from Moscow, in the USSR", (1990), in *Politics, Theory, and Contemporary Culture*, ed. Mark Poster, trans. Mary Quaintaire (New York: Columbia University Press 1993), 197–235.

[16] Jacques Derrida, "The 'World' of the Enlightenment to Come (Exception, Calculation and Sovereignty)", in *Rogues: Two Essays on Reason*, (2003), trans. Pascale-Anne Brault and Michael Naas (Stanford: Stanford University Press, 2005), 150. See also, 141–2, 148–51. Henceforth cited as *WEC*. See also, Jacques Derrida, "The Reason of the Strongest (Are there Rogue States?)", (2002), in *Rogues: Two Essays on Reason*, (2003), trans. Rachel Bowlby (Stanford: Stanford University Press, 2005), 48–55. Henceforth cited as *RS*.

[17] The title of Derrida's 1967 Doctorat en Philosophie, *Essai sur la permanence des concepts platonicien, aristotélicien et scolastique du signe écrit*, is

cited by Eddie Yeghiayan at http://sun3.lib.uci.edu/~scctr/Wellek/jacques.
html (Accessed 22 May 2007). Derrida refers to his unwritten book in a
1999 interview, Jacques Derrida and Dominique Janicaud, "Interview
with Jacques Derrida", (1999) *Heidegger en France*, 2 vols (Paris: Hachette,
2005), I: 96. Henceforth cited as *IJD*.

[18] Jacques Derrida, "Implications: Interview with Henri Ronse", (1967), in
Positions, trans. Alan Bass (Chicago: University of Chicago Press, 1982),
3–4. Henceforth cited as *IMP*. Jacques Derrida, "Implications: entretien
avec Henri Ronse", in *Positions* (Paris: Les Éditions du Minuit, 1972),
11–12.

[19] Gayatri Chakravorty Spivak, "Ghostwriting", *Diacritics* 25 no. 2 (1995):
65–84. See also, Michael Syrotinski, *Deconstruction and the Postcolonial:
At the Limits of Theory* (Liverpool: Liverpool University Press, 2007).

[20] Jacques Derrida, *The Problem of Genesis in Husserl's Philosophy*, (1953–
1954), trans. Marian Hobson (Chicago: University of Chicago Press,
2003), xvii–xix, 168–9, n. 11 189. Henceforth cited as *PG*. See also, Jacques
Derrida, *Edmund Husserl's Origin of Geometry: An Introduction*, (1962),
trans. John P. Leavey, Jr. (Lincoln: University of Nebraska Press, 1989),
59–62, 135–42. Henceforth cited as *EHO*. Jacques Derrida, "'Genesis and
Structure' and Phenomenology", (1959), in *Writing and Difference*, trans.
Alan Bass (Chicago: University of Chicago Press, 1978), 154–68. Henceforth cited as *GS*.

[21] Jacques Derrida, "Some Statements and Truisms about Neologisms,
Newisms, Postisms, Parasitisms, and Other Small Seismisms", in
The States of "Theory": History, Art and Critical Discourse, ed. David
Carroll, trans. Anne Tomiche (New York: Columbia University Press,
1990), 91–2.

[22] See also, *OG* 59–60. See also, Jacques Derrida and Derek Attridge, "This
Strange Institution Called Literature: An interview with Jacques Derrida",
in *Acts of Literature*, ed. Derek Attridge (New York and London:
Routledge, 1992), 33–75.

[23] Jacques Derrida, "Structure, Sign and Play in the Discourse of the Human
Sciences", (1966), *Writing and Difference*, trans. Alan Bass (Chicago:
University of Chicago Press, 1978), 278–94.

[24] Jacques Derrida, "The Ends of Man", (1968), in *Margins of Philosophy*,
trans. Alan Bass (Chicago: University of Chicago Press, 1982), 111.
Henceforth cited as *EM*. See also, Jacques Derrida, *Who's Afraid of
Philosophy: Right to Philosophy 1*, trans. Jan Plug (Stanford: Stanford
University Press, 2002); Jacques Derrida, *Eyes of the University: Right to
Philosophy 2*, trans. Jan Plug (Stanford: Stanford University Press, 2005).

[25] Jacques Derrida, "Force et signification", *Critique* 19 nos. 193 and 194
(1963): 483–99, 619–36. Derrida's later articles in *Critique* were: "Edmond
Jabès et la question du livre", *Critique* 20 no. 201 (1964): 99–115; "De la
grammatologie I" and "De la grammatologie II", *Critique* 21 nos. 223 and
224 (1965–1966): 16–42, 23–53; "Le théatre de la cruauté et la clôture de la
representation", *Critique* 22 no. 230 (1966): 595–618; "La dissémination I"
and "La dissémination II", *Critique* 25 nos. 261 and 262 (1969): 99–139,
215–49. With the exception of "De la grammatologie" I and II, which

appeared in a revised form in *De la grammatologie*, the rest of these articles are found in the collections, *L'écriture et la différence* (1967) and *La dissémination* (1972). The editorial board of *Critique* in the early 1960s included Raymond Aron, Maurice Blanchot, Fernand Braudel, René Char, Jean Wahl and Eric Weil. The editorial team for the 1965–1966 issue included Roland Barthes, Michel Deguy and Michel Foucault. As far as I am aware, after the 1960s Derrida did not publish another article in *Critique*, though he had joined the editorial board by January 1974 and today, along with Maurice Blanchot, remains part of the honorary and posthumous board of *Critique*.

26 Paul de Man, "La circularité de l'interprétation dans l'oeuvre de Maurice Blanchot", *Critique* 19, no. 229 (1966): 547–60; "Vérité et méthode dans l'oeuvre de Georges Poulet", *Critique* 25 no. 266 (1969): 608–23. See, Paul de Man, "Impersonality in the Criticism of Maurice Blanchot" and "The Literary Self as Origin: The Work of Georges Poulet", in *Blindness and Insight: Essays in the Rhetoric of Contemporary Criticism*, 2ⁿᵈ edn (Minneapolis: University of Minnesota Press, 1983), 60–78, 79–101. Samuel Weber, "Lecture de Benjamin", *Critique* 26, no. 267–68 (1969), 699–712.

27 Jacques Derrida, "From Restricted to General Economy: A Hegelianism without Reserve", (1967), in *Writing and Difference*, trans. Alan Bass (Chicago: University of Chicago Press, 1978), 256; "De l'économie restreinte à l'économie générale: un hegelianisme sans réserve", in *L'écriture et la différence* (Paris: Éditions du Seuil, 1967), 376.

28 See also, *OG,* 119, 135, 184, 218, 242.

29 See also, Jacques Derrida, "The Animal That Therefore I am (More to Follow)", trans. David Wills, *Critical Inquiry* 28 (2002), 405. Henceforth cited as *ATT*.

30 Spivak translates *s'étend* as "spreads out more and more", and one could also translate this as "extends" and an oblique reference to the relation of *différance* to the Cartesian notion of *extensio* and the Heideggerian critique of it in *Being and Time*. René Descartes, *Meditations on First Philosophy*, (1641), trans. John Cottingham, intro. Bernard Williams (Cambridge: Cambridge University Press, 1986), 21, 44, 54–5. Henceforth cited as *MF*. Martin Heidegger, *Being and Time*, (1927), trans. John Macquarrie and Edward Robinson (Oxford: Blackwell, 1990), 89–101. The pages numbers refer to the marginal page numbers. Henceforth cited as *BT*. See also Jacques Derrida, *On Touching – Jean-Luc Nancy*, (2000), trans. Christine Irizarry (Stanford: Stanford University Press, 2005), 11–20. Henceforth cited as *OT*.

31 My translation.

32 See also, Geoffrey Bennington, "Derridabase", in *Jacques Derrida* (Chicago: University of Chicago Press, 1992), 252; Nicholas Royle, *Jacques Derrida* (London: Routledge, 2003), 37–8; Michael Payne and John Schad, eds., *Life. After. Theory: Jacques Derrida, Frank Kermode, Toril Moi, Christopher Norris* (London: Continuum, 2004), 32–6.

33 See Jacques Derrida, "Restitutions of the Truth in Pointing", (1978), in *The Truth in Painting*, trans. Geoff Bennington and Ian McLeod (Chicago:

University of Chicago Press, 1989), 255–382; Jacques Derrida, *Parages*, nouvelle édition revue et augmentée (Paris: Éditions Galilée, 2003).

[34] Derrida later quotes Rousseau remarking, "the superstition of etymology gives rise to as many inconsistencies in its small domain, as superstition properly speaking does in graver matters. Our orthography is an assemblage of *bizarrerie* and contradictions" (*OG* 228).

[35] See also, *OG* 244.

[36] See, Jacques Derrida, "Différance", in *Margins of Philosophy*, (1968), trans. Alan Bass (Chicago: University of Chicago Press, 1982), 24. Henceforth cited as *DF*. Martin Heidegger, "Language", (1950), in *Poetry, Language, Thought*, trans. Albert Hofstadler (New York: Harper and Row, 1971), 199; "Die Sprache", in *Unterwegs zur Sprache* (Frankfurt am Main: Kletti-Cotta, 1985), 19.

[37] See also, Jacques Derrida, "Otobiographies: The Teaching of Nietzsche and the Politics of the Proper Name", (1979–1982), in *The Ear of the Other*, ed. Christie McDonald, trans. Avital Ronell (Lincoln: University of Nebraska Press, 1988), 1–38. Henceforth cited as *O*. Jacques Derrida, *Memories – for Paul de Man*, trans. Cecile Lindsay, Jonathan Culler and Eduardo Cadava (New York: Columbia University Press, 1986), 89–150; "Circumfession", in *Jacques Derrida*, (1991), trans. Geoffrey Bennington (Chicago: University of Chicago Press, 1993); Jacques Derrida, "Typewriter Ribbon: Limited Ink (2)", (1998–2001), in *Without Alibi*, trans. Peggy Kamuf (Stanford: Stanford University Press, 2002), 71–160. See also, Peggy Kamuf, "To Do Justice to 'Rousseau': Irreducibly", *Eighteenth-Century Studies* 40.3 (2007), 395–404; Robert Bernasconi, "No More Stories, Good or Bad: de Man's Criticisms of Derrida on Rousseau", in *Derrida: A Critical Reader*, ed. David Wood (Oxford: Blackwell, 1992), 137–66; Christie V. McDonald, "Jacques Derrida's Reading of Rousseau", *Eighteenth Century: Theory and Interpretation* 20 (1979): 164–81.

[38] Jean-Jacques Rousseau, *Les confessions*, ed. Alain Grosrichard, 2 vols (Paris: Flammarion, 2002), I: 81. Henceforth cited as *LC*.

[39] Jacques Derrida, "To Speculate – on 'Freud'", (1975–1980), in *The Post Card: From Socrates to Freud and Beyond*, (1980), trans. Alan Bass (Chicago: University of Chicago Press, 1987), 257–409. Henceforth cited as *TS*.

[40] Maurice Blanchot, "Rousseau" (1958), in *The Book to Come*, (1958), trans. Charlotte Mandell (Stanford: Stanford University Press, 2003), 42–3.

[41] See also the passage where Rousseau writes, "for some bizarre reason that escapes me, I decided to pass myself off as English: I presented myself as a Jacobite, which seemed to satisfy them, called myself Dudding, and was known to the company as *M*. Dudding" (*CF* 244). See Geoffrey Bennington, *Dudding: des noms de Rousseau* (Paris: Éditions Galilée, 1991); Peggy Kamuf, *Signature Pieces: On the Institution of Authorship* (Ithaca: Cornell University Press, 1988).

[42] See also, *OG*, 258; *Dlg*, p. 364. I have attempted to explore the relation between *écart* and *écarter* in Derrida's work in *The Impossible Mourning of Jacques Derrida* (London: Continuum, 2006).

⁴³ William Shakespeare, *The Tragedy of King Lear*, (1608), in *The Norton Shakespeare, Based on the Oxford Edition*, ed. Stephen Greenblatt and others (New York: Norton, 1997), V. III. 298–301.

2 ABSENCE AS PURE POSSIBILITY

[1] The first version of this chapter was written in July 2006, at the kind suggestion of Simon Morgan Wortham. I would like thank him and to dedicate this chapter to William Watkin, a far better reader of Agamben than myself.

[2] The following pages develop earlier work of mine in *Derrida and Disinterest* (London: Continuum, 2006), and *Starting With Derrida: Plato, Aristotle and Hegel* (London: Continuum, 2007).

[3] Edmund Husserl, *Ideas: General Introduction to Pure Phenomenology*, (1913), trans. W. R. Boyce Gibson (New York: Collier, 1962), 190–91. Henceforth cited as *I*. See also, Joanna Hodge, *Derrida on Time* (London: Routledge, 2007).

[4] Jacques Derrida, "'Genèse et structure' et la phenomenologie", in *L'écriture et la différence* (Paris: Éditions du Éditions du Seuil, 1967), 242.

[5] For other references to the diaphanous in this period, see: *CHM*, 55; *EM*, 112; *G*, 169a; *O*, 4; Jacques Derrida, "Edmond Jabès and the Question of the Book", in *Writing and Difference*, (1964), trans. Alan Bass (Chicago: University of Chicago Press, 1978), 74. Henceforth cited as *EJ*. See also, Jacques Derrida, *Memoirs of the Blind: The Self-Portrait and Other Ruins*, (1990), trans. Pascale-Anne Brault and Michael Naas (Chicago: University of Chicago Press, 1993).

[6] Jacques Derrida, "Force and Signification", (1963), in *Writing and Difference*, trans. Alan Bass (Chicago: University of Chicago Press, 1978), 27. Henceforth cited as *FS*. Jacques Derrida, 'Force et signification', in *L'écriture et la différence* (Paris: Éditions du Seuil, 1967), 45. Henceforth cited as *FeS*.

[7] Giorgio Agamben, "On Potentiality", (1986), in *Potentialities*, ed. and trans. Daniel Heller-Roazen (Stanford: Stanford University Press, 1999), 180. Henceforth cited as *OP*.

[8] *Glas* (French edition), 122a. Translation modified.

[9] This is Daniel Heller-Roazen's translation. For a broader account of Agamben's reading of *De Anima*, see Melinda Cooper, , "The Living and the Dead: Variations on De Anima", *Angelaki* 7 no. 3 (2002): 80–104. For the Greek text, see *On the Soul*, trans. W. S. Hett (Cambridge, MA: Harvard University Press, 1986).

[10] Aristotle, *On the Soul*, in *The Complete Works of Aristotle,* ed. Jonathan Barnes, trans. J. A Smith, 2 vols (Princeton: Princeton University Press, 1984), II: 417a. I have used J. A. Smith's translation for all subsequent quotations from *On the Soul* and consulted W. S. Hett's translation in the standard Loeb edition for the passages in Greek. Henceforth cited as *S*.

[11] This phrase from the *Metaphysics* 1050b has been translated by Daniel Heller-Roazen. See Agamben's discussion of this passage in *Homo Sacer: Sovereign Power and Bare Life*, (1995), trans. Daniel Heller-Roazen (Stanford: Stanford University Press, 1998), 44–8. See also, Andrew Gibson, *Beckett and Badiou: The Pathos of Intermittancy* (Oxford: Oxford University Press, 2007), 273–84.

[12] On the relation between potentiality and literature in Agamben, see Alexander Cooke, "Resistance and Potentiality and the Law: Deleuze and Agamben on 'Bartleby'", *Angelaki* 10 no. 3 (2005): 79–89; Claire Colebrook, "Agamben: Aesthetics, Potentiality, and Life", *South Atlantic Quarterly* 107, no. 1 (2008): 107–20.

[13] Jacques Derrida, "Tympan", (1972), in *Margins of Philosophy*, trans. Alan Bass (Chicago: University of Chicago Press, 1982), xv–xvi. See also, *S,* 419b.

[14] See, Jacques Derrida, "Psyche: Invention of the Other", (1984), in *Psyche: Inventions of the Other, Volume I*, trans. Catherine Porter, ed. Peggy Kamuf and Elizabeth Rottenberg (Stanford: Stanford University Press, 2007), 1–47. Henceforth cited as *PIO*.

[15] See Thomas Carl Wall, *Radical Passivity: Levinas, Blanchot, and Agamben* (Albany: State University of New York Press, 1999).

[16] On time as a dividing continuity, see Aristotle, *Physics*, in *The Complete Works of Aristotle*, ed. Jonathan Barnes, 2 vols (Princeton: Princeton University Press, 1984), I: 220b.

[17] Jacques Derrida, "Deconstruction and the Other", in Richard Kearney, *Dialogues with Contemporary Continental Thinkers: The Phenomenological Heritage* (Manchester: Manchester University Press, 1984), 117.

[18] See also, Jacques Derrida, "*Ousia* and *Grammē*: Note on a note from *Being and Time*", (1968), in *Margins of Philosophy*, trans. Alan Bass (Chicago: University of Chicago Press, 1982), 60. Henceforth cited as *OU*.

[19] Aristotle, *Metaphysics*, trans. Hugh Tredennick, 3 vols (London: Heinemann, 1993), I: 1050b.

[20] For the fragments of Parmenides, see *Early Greek Philosophers*, ed. Jonathan Barnes (London: Penguin, 1987), 129–49.

[21] In *Idea of Prose*, (1985), trans. Michael Sullivan and Sam Whitsitt (New York: State University Press of New York, 1995), Agamben writes "light is only the coming to itself of the dark", 119.

[22] Giorgio Agamben, "*Pardes*: The Writing of Potentiality", (1990), in *Potentialities*, ed. and trans. Daniel Heller-Roazen (Stanford: Stanford University Press, 1999), 218. See also, 216. On the differences between Derrida and Agamben, see David E. Johnson, "As If the Time Were Now: Deconstructing Agamben", *South Atlantic Quarterly* 106 no. 2 (2007): 268–90.

[23] Giorgio Agamben, "The Passion of Facticity", (1988), in *Potentialities*, ed. and trans. Daniel Heller-Roazen (Stanford: Stanford University Press, 1999), 298 n. 47. Henceforth cited as *PF*.

[24] Martin Heidegger, *Aristotle's Metaphysics Θ 1-3: On the Essence and Actuality of Force*, (1931), trans. Walter Brogan and Peter Warnek (Bloomington: Indiana University Press, 1995), 2–3. Henceforth cited as *AM*. See, Walter A. Brogan, *Heidegger and Aristotle: The Twofoldedness of*

Being (New York: State University of New York Press, 2005), xi, 19, 107, 110–37. See also, William McNeill, *The Glance of the Eye: Heidegger, Aristotle, and the Ends of Being* (New York: State University of New York Press, 1999).

25 Martin Heidegger, *Aristoteles, Metaphysik Theta 1-3: Vom Wesen und Wirklichkeit der Kraft* (Frankfurt am Main: Vittorio Klostermann, 1981), 27. Henceforth cited as *MT*.

3 (NOT) MEETING HEIDEGGER

1 Jacques Derrida, "Le 'monde' des Lumières à venir (Exception, calcul et souveraineté)", in *Voyous: Deux essais sur la raison* (Paris: Éditions Galilée, 2003), 165.

2 Dominique Janicaud, *Heidegger en France*, (2001), 2 vols (Paris: Hachette, 2005). Henceforth cited as *HF*. All subsequent translations of this text are my own.

3 Philippe Lacoue-Labarthe, "In the Name of . . . ", in Philippe Lacoue-Labarthe and Jean-Luc Nancy, *Retreating the Political*, ed. Simon Sparks (London: Routledge, 1997), 58.

4 See also, Jacques Derrida, Jean-Luc Nancy and Philippe Lacoue-Labarthe, *Penser à Strasbourg* (Paris: Éditions Galilée, 2004).

5 I am writing this a few days after the death of Philippe Lacoue-Labarthe at the end of January 2007.

6 Jacques Derrida, "Shibboleth: For Paul Celan", 1986, in *Sovereignties in Question: The Poetics of Paul Celan*, ed. Thomas Dutoit and Outi Pasanen (New York: Fordham University Press, 2005), 1. See also , OWP8; David Couzens Hoy, *Critical Resistance: From Post-Structuralism to Post-Critique* (Cambridge, MA: MIT Press, 2005).

7 See also, Diane P. Michelfelder and Richard E. Palmer, *Dialogue and Deconstruction: The Gadamer-Derrida Encounter* (Albany: State University of New York Press, 1989).

8 Jacques Derrida, *Speech and Phenomena and Other Essays on Husserl's Theory of Signs*, trans. David B. Allison (Evantson: Northwestern University Press, 1973).

9 Herman Rapaport makes much of this *faux-bond* in his *The Theory Mess: Deconstruction in Eclipse* (New York: Columbia University Press, 2001).

10 This 1975 interview was published in two parts: "Between Brackets I", (1975–1976), and "Ja, or the *faux-bond* II". (1975–1977). Jacques Derrida, "Between Brackets I" in *Points: Interviews 1974–1994*, ed. Elisabeth Weber, trans. Peggy Kamuf (Stanford: Stanford University Press, 1995), 9. Jacques Derrida, "Entre crochets I", in *Points de suspension: Entretiens*, choisis et présentés par Elisabeth Weber (Paris: Éditions Galilée, 1992), 18.

11 Jacques Derrida, "Ja, or the *faux-bond* II", in *Points . . . . .: Interviews 1974–1994*, ed. Elisabeth Weber, trans. Peggy Kamuf (Stanford: Stanford University Press, 1995), 30. Henceforth cited as *JA*. Jacques Derrida, "Ja, ou le faux-bond", in *Points de suspension: Entretiens*, choisis et présentés par Elisabeth Weber (Paris: Éditions Galilée, 1992), 37. Henceforth cited

Notes

as *JO*. On Heidegger's use of exclamation marks, see also, Jacques Derrida, "*Geschlecht* I: Sexual Difference, Ontological Difference", (1963), in *Psyche: Inventions of the Other, Volume II*, trans. Ruben Bevezdivin and Elizabeth Rottenberg, ed. Peggy Kamuf and Elizabeth Rottenberg (Stanford: Stanford University Press, 2008), 10. Henceforth cited as *GSD*. See also, Jacques Derrida, "A Number of Yes", (1987), in *Psyche: Inventions of the Other, Volume II*, trans. Brian Holmes, eds Peggy Kamuf and Elizabeth Rottenberg (Stanford: Stanford University Press, 2008), 234.

[12] See, Jacques Derrida, "The *Retrait* of Metaphor", (1978), in *Psyche: Inventions of the Other, Volume I*, trans. Peggy Kamuf, ed. Peggy Kamuf and Elizabeth Rottenberg (Stanford: Stanford University Press, 2007), 48–80.

[13] See also, Roger Laporte, "Heidegger, Beaufret et le politique: Témoignage et réflexions sur une longue occultation", *Lendemains* 17 (1992): 72–4.

[14] Recalling his later meetings with Blanchot, Derrida writes, "the silences, the necessary respiration of ellipsis and discretion, during these interviews, were also, as far as I remember, the blessed time, without the least interruption, the unbroken time of a smile, a trusting and benevolent waiting", Jacques Derrida, "À Maurice Blanchot", in *Chaque fois unique, la fin du monde*, présenté par Pascale-Anne Brault et Michael Naas (Paris: Éditions Galilée, 2003), 324–5. My translation.

[15] Jacques Derrida, *The Post Card: From Socrates to Freud and Beyond*, trans. Alan Bass (Chicago: University of Chicago Press, 1987). See also, Jacques Derrida, "Envoi", (1980), in *Psyche: Inventions of the Other, Volume I*, trans. Peter and Mary Ann Caws, ed. Peggy Kamuf and Elizabeth Rottenberg (Stanford: Stanford University Press, 2007), 104, 108–10, 120–22.

[16] Martin Heidegger, "Time and Being", (1962), in *On Time and Being*, trans. Joan Stambaugh (Chicago: University of Chicago Press, 2002), 1–24.

[17] Jacques Derrida, "*Ousia* et *Grammè*: note sur une note de *Sein und Zeit*", in *Marges – de la philosophie* (Paris: Les Éditions du Minuit, 1972), 72 n. 25.

[18] Friedrich Nietzsche, *Thus Spoke Zarathustra*, (1885), ed. Adrian Del Caro and Robert B. Pippin, trans. Adrian del Caro (Cambridge: Cambridge University Press, 2006), 28. Henceforth cited as *TSZ*.

[19] Jacques Derrida, "Désistance", (1987), in *Psyche: Inventions of the Other, Volume II*, trans. Christopher Fynsk. ed. Peggy Kamuf and Elizabeth Rottenberg (Stanford: Stanford University Press, 2008), 197–98. Henceforth cited as *DE*. See also, Philippe Lacoue-Labarthe, *Typography: Mimesis, Philosophy, Politics*, intro. Jacques Derrida, trans. Christopher Fynsk (Stanford: Stanford University Press, 1998).

[20] Jacques Derrida, "Je suis en guerre contre moi-même", in *Le Monde* Jeudi 19 Août, 2004: 13. My translation.

[21] Plato, *Parmenides,* in *The Dialogues of Plato*, trans. Benjamin Jowett, 5 vols (Oxford: Clarendon Press, 1892), IV, 137a.

[22] J. Hillis Miller, *The Ethics of Reading* (New York: Columbia University Press, 1989).

23 See also, Nicholas Royle, "On Not Reading: Derrida and Beckett", in *Reading Reading: Essays on the Theory and Practice of Reading* (Finland: Tampere, 1993), 201–19; Geoffrey Bennington, "Le temps de la lecture", *Etudes Françaises* 38 (2002): 77–85; Patrick Poirier, "À Demeure: Le lire comme un hôte", *Etudes Françaises* 38 (2002): 145–64.

24 Jacques Derrida, *Specters of Marx: The State of the Debt, the Work of Mourning, and the New International*, trans. Peggy Kamuf (London: Routledge, 1994), 13. Henceforth cited as *SM*. Jacques Derrida, *Spectres de Marx: L'État de la dette, le travail du deuil et la nouvelle Internationale* (Paris: Éditions Galilée, 1993), xvii. Derrida will later contrast this to Heidegger's emphasis on "learning to think" (*apprendre à penser*), in "Heidegger's Hand (*Geschlecht* II)", in *Psyche: Inventions of the Other*, Volume II, trans. John P. Leavey Jr. and Elizabeth Rottenberg (Stanford: Stanford University Press, 2008), 36. Henceforth cited as *HH*. Jacques Derrida, "La main de Heidegger (*Geschlecht* II)", (1985), in *Psyche: Inventions de l'autre*, 2 vols (Paris: Éditions Galilée, 1998–2003), II: 44. Henceforth cited as *MH*. See also, Ginette Michaud, " 'Comme après la vie': Derrida et Cixous, ou Apprendre à lire enfin", *Mosaic* 39 no. 3 (2006): 133–50.

25 Maurice Blanchot, "Literature and the Right to Death", (1949), in *The Work of Fire*, trans. Charlotte Mandell (Stanford: Stanford University Press, 1995), 335–6. Henceforth cited as *LRD*. Maurice Blanchot, "La littérature et le droit à la mort", in *La part du feu* (Paris: Gallimard, 1949), 337.

26 See Jacques Derrida, "If there is cause for translation I: Philosophy in its national language (towards a "literature en français")", and "If there is cause for translation II: Decartes' romances, or the economy of words", (1984), in *Eyes of the University: The Right to Philosophy 2*, trans. Sylvia Söderlind and Rebecca Coma (Stanford: Stanford University Press, 2005), 1–19, 20–42.

27 René Descartes, *Méditations sur la philosophie première*, in *Oeuvres philosophiques*, ed. Ferdinand Alquie, 2 vols (Paris: Garnier Frères, 1967), II: 387. Henceforth cited as *MPP*.

28 Descartes writes: "il faudrait plus de temps pour le lire, que nous n'en avons pour demeurer en cette vie" (MPP 1107).

29 Martin Heidegger, *Sein und Zeit* (Frankfurt am Main: Klostermann, 1977), 168–9.

30 Martin Heidegger, *Introduction to Metaphysics*, (1935), trans. Gregory Fried and Richard Polt (New Haven: Yale University Press, 2000), 99–100. Henceforth cited as *IM*. Martin Heidegger, *Einführung in die Metaphysik* (Frankfurt am Main: Vittorio Klostermann, 1983), 103. Henceforth cited as *EidM*.

31 Emmanuel Lévinas, *Nine Talmudic Readings*, (1963–1975), trans. Annette Aronowicz (Bloomington: Indiana University Press, 1994), 8.

32 See also, Martin Heidegger, *Parmenides*, (1942–1943), trans. André Schuwer and Richard Rojcewicz, (Bloomington: Indiana University Press, 1982), 80–4; Martin Heidegger, "Was heißt Lesen?", (1954), in *Aus der Erfahrung des Denkens* (Frankfurt am Main: Vittorio Klostermann, 1983), 111. See also, Kenneth May, "Reading and Thinking: Heidegger and the

Hinting Greeks", in *Martin Heidegger: Critical Assessments*, ed. Christopher Macann, 4 vols (London: Routledge, 1992), 55–6.

33 See also, Timothy Clark, *Poetics of Singularity: The Counter-Culturalist Turn in Heidegger, Derrida and Blanchot and the later Gadamer* (Edinburgh: Edinburgh University Press, 2005).

34 Timothy Clark, *Martin Heidegger* (London: Routledge, 2001), 111.

35 Jacques Derrida, "L'oreille de Heidegger: Philopolémologie (*Geschlecht IV*)", in *Politiques de l'amitié* (Paris: Éditions Galilée, 1994), 378.

36 Jacques Derrida, "Désistance", in *Psyche: Inventions de l'autre*, 2 vols (Paris: Éditions Galilée, 1998–2003), II: 203. Henceforth cited as *Des*.

37 Jacques Derrida, "Telepathy", (1981), in *Psyche: Inventions of the Other, Volume I*, trans. Nicholas Royle, ed. Peggy Kamuf and Elizabeth Rottenberg (Stanford: Stanford University Press, 2007), 235. Henceforth cited as *TEL*. Jacques Derrida, "Télépathie", in *Psyché: Inventions de l'autre*, 2 vol (Paris: Éditions Galilée, 1998–2003), 245.

38 Jacques Derrida, "Me – Psychoanalysis", (1979–1982), in *Psyche: Inventions of the Other, Volume I*, trans. Richard Klein, ed. Peggy Kamuf and Elizabeth Rottenberg (Stanford: Stanford University Press, 2007), 129, 131.

39 Jacques Derrida, "Fifty-two Aphorisms for a Foreword", (1987), in *Psyche: Inventions of the Other, Volume II*, trans. Andrew Benjamin, ed. Peggy Kamuf and Elizabeth Rottenberg (Stanford: Stanford University Press, 2008), 120. Henceforth cited as *FT*. Jacques Derrida, "Cinquante-deux aphorismes pour un avant propos", in *Psyché: Inventions de l'autre*, 2 vols (Paris: Éditions Galilée, 1998–2003), II: 124. Henceforth cited as *CD*.

40 Jacques Derrida, *Signéponge / Signsponge*, trans. Richard Rand (New York: Columbia University Press, 1988), 52–3.

41 Jacques Derrida, "The Deaths of Roland Barthes", in *Psyche: Inventions of the Other, Volume I*, (1981), trans. Ruben Berezdivin and Peggy Kamuf, ed. Peggy Kamuf and Elizabeth Rottenberg (Stanford: Stanford University Press, 2007), 280.

4 (MIS)CHANCES

1 Plato, *Lysis*, in *The Dialogues of Plato*, trans. Benjamin Jowett, 5 vols (Oxford: Clarendon Press, 1892), I: 203a; *Republic*, in *The Dialogues of Plato*, trans. Benjamin Jowett, 5 vols (Oxford: Clarendon Press, 1892), III: 327a.

2 Jacques Derrida, "My Chances/*Mes Chances*: A Rendezvous with Some Epicurean Stereophonies", (1982), in *Psyche: Inventions of the Other, Volume I*, trans. Irene Harvey and Avital Ronell, ed. Peggy Kamuf and Elizabeth Rottenberg (Stanford: Stanford University Press, 2007), 344–76. Henceforth cited as *MC*.

3 Jacques Derrida, "Mes chances. Au rendez-vous de quelques stérophonies épicuriennes", (1991), in *Psyché: inventions de l'autre*, 2 vols (Paris: Éditions Galilée, 1998–2003), I: 354. On Derrida's writings on the *rencontre* before "Mes chances" see: *VM*, 95; *EJ*, 74; *ATV*, 146, *GSD*, 26. See also,

Jacques Derrida, *Given Time: 1. Counterfeit Money*, trans. Peggy Kamuf (Chicago: University of Chicago Press, 1992), 125, 133. See also *E*.
4   Jacques Derrida, "Rams: Uninterrupted dialogue – between two infinities, the poem", (2003), in *Sovereignties in Question: The Poetics of Paul Celan*, ed. Thomas Dutoit and Outi Pasanen (New York: Fordham University Press, 2005), 159–60.
5   Immanuel Kant, *Critique of Pure Reason*, (1781, 1787), trans. Paul Guyer (Cambridge: Cambridge University Press, 1998), A 855/B 883. It is possible that Kant was thinking of a fragment of Democritus in Diogenes Laertius, "in reality we know nothing – for truth is in the depths", *Lives of Eminent Philosophers*, trans. R. D. Hicks, 2 vols (Cambridge, MA: Harvard University Press, 1980), II: IX 72. See also, Democritus, "Fragments", in *Early Greek Philosophers*, ed. Jonathan Barnes (London: Penguin, 1987), 244–88. Henceforth cited as *F*. Immanuel Kant, *The Critique of Judgement*, (1790), trans. James Creed Meredith (Oxford: Oxford University Press, 1952), 43; *Critique of Practical Reason*, (1788), in *Practical Philosophy*, trans. Mary J. Gregor, intro. Paul Guyer (Cambridge: Cambridge University Press, 1999), 241–42.
6   Walter G. Englert, *Epicurus on the Swerve and Voluntary Action* (Atlanta: Scholars Press, 1987), 14–19. See also, Epicurus, *The Extant Remains*, ed. and trans. Cyril Bailey (Oxford: Oxford University Press, 1926).
7   Lucretius, *De Reum Natura Libri Sex*, 3 vols, ed. and trans. Cyril Bailey (Oxford: Clarendon Press, 1947), I: 250–51 [II: 292]. See also, Michel Serres, *La naissance de la physique dans le texte de Lucrece: Fleuves et turbulences* (Paris: Les Éditions du Minuit, 1977).
8   Cicero, *De Fato*, in *De Oratore*, trans. H. Rackham, 3 vols (Cambridge, MA: Harvard University Press, 1942), III, X.22; XX.46.
9   In *Marx dans le jardin d'épicure* (Paris: Les Éditions du Minuit, 1974), her study of Marx's early work on the difference between Democritus and Epicurus, Francine Markovits writes:

"Déplacement de l'identité des éléments du corps dans une rencontre, déplacement de l'identité du corps du fait de son existence qui est pour d'autres corps (et la connaissance est elle même un tel phénomène de rencontre et de hasard – *tuchē*), le clinamen est la loi générale de l'épicurisme. Le terme de rencontre est explicité à la fois par les termes de *tuchē* et de *sumptôma*: variation d'identité autant que changement de rôle, déclinaison des cas du substantif, l'identité est ce qui choit, le retour périodique, le temps: *sumptôma sumptomatôn*". (60)

10 Catherine Malabou, "Another Possibility", *Research in Phenomenology* 36 no. 1 (2006): 115–29.
11 Michel de Montaigne, "On Democritus and Heraclitus", (1580–1592), in *The Complete Essays*, trans. M. A. Screech (London: Penguin, 1993), 337–40.
12 G. W. F. Hegel, *Lectures on the History of Philosophy I: Greek Philosophy to Plato*, (1805–1831), trans. E. S. Haldane, intro. Frederick C. Beister (Lincoln: University of Nebraska Press, 1995), 166.

13 Jacques Derrida, "Why Peter Eisenman Writes Such Good Books", (1987), in *Psyche: Inventions of the Other, Volume II*, trans. Sarah Whiting, ed. Peggy Kamuf and Elizabeth Rottenberg (Stanford: Stanford University Press, 2008), 106. Henceforth cited as *WH*.

14 See also, *RS,* 52–3.

15 See also, Geoffrey Bennington, "Deconstruction and the Philosophers" (The Very Idea)", in *Legislations: The Politics of Deconstruction* (London: Verso, 1994), 60 n. 73. Earlier in "The Double Session", Derrida had linked the necessary difference of the moving gaps and spacings of the text to Mallarmé's *Un coup de dés*. "For difference", he writes, "is the necessary interval, the suspense between two outcomes, the 'lapse of time' between two shots, two rolls, two chances", "The Double Session", (1970), in *Dissemination*, trans. Barbara Johnson (Chicago: University of Chicago Press, 1981), 277. On the differences between Nietzsche and Mallarmé, see also Gilles Deleuze, *Nietzsche and Philosophy*, (1962), trans. Hugh Tomlinson (London: Continuum, 2006), 24, 30–31. On Mallarmé and chance, see also Maurice Blanchot, "The Book to Come", in *The Book to Come*, trans. Charlotte Mandell (Stanford: Stanford University Press, 2003), 224–44.

16 Jacques Derrida and Catherine Malabou, *Counterpath; Travelling with Jacques Derrida*, trans. David Wills (Stanford: Stanford University Press, 2004), 55–6. See also, *BT,* 105–10.

17 See also Jacques Derrida, *Politics of Friendship*, (1994), trans. George Collins (London: Verso, 2005), 1; Jacques Derrida, "Punctuations: The Time of the Thesis", (1980), in *Eyes of the University: Right to Philosophy 2*, trans. Kathleen McLauglin (Stanford: Stanford University Press, 2005), 113.

18 Jacques Derrida, *Schibboleth – pour Paul Celan* (Paris: Éditions Galilée, 1986), 23.

19 Jacques Derrida, "No Apocalypse, Not Now: Full Speed Ahead, Seven Missiles, Seven Missives", (1984), in *Psyche: Inventions of the Other, Volume I*, trans. Catherine Porter and Philip Lewis, ed. Peggy Kamuf and Elizabeth Rottenberg (Stanford: Stanford University Press, 2007), 393.

20 Once asked what a realistic war movie would be like, the World War Two veteran and film director Samuel Fuller is reported to have said: "nothing more than deafening noises and blurred images".

21 Jacques Derrida, "Majesties", (2002), in *Sovereignties in Question: The Poetics of Paul Celan*, ed. and trans. Thomas Dutoit and Outi Pasanen (New York: Fordham University Press, 2005), 119. Henceforth cited as *MAJ*.

22 Jacques Derrida, "Pourquoi Peter Eisenman écrit de si bons livres", in *Psyché: inventions de l'autre*, 2 vols (Paris: Éditions Galilée, 1987–2003), II: 110.

23 Jacques Derrida, *Genèses, généalogies, genres et le génie: Les secrets de l'archive* (Paris: Éditions Galilée, 2003), 75. My translation. See also, 16–17, 74. See also, *PIO* 23, 30–33; Jacques Derrida, *Monolingualism of the Other, or, The Prothestic Origin*, (1992), trans. Patrick Menash (Stanford: Stanford University Press, 1998), 55–6. Derrida first addresses the *se trouver* in *AF* 63–5.

[24] Paul Celan, "The Bright Stones", in *Selected Poems and Prose,* trans. John Felstiner (New York: Norton, 2001), 176–77.

> DIE HELLEN
> STEINE gehn durch die Luft, die hell-
> weissen, die Licht-
> bringer.
>
> Sie wollen
> nicht niedergehen, nicht stürzen,
> nicht treffen.

[25] Paul Celan, "Radix, Matrix", in *Selected Poems and Prose,* trans. John Felstiner (New York: Norton, 2001), 166–9.

[26]

> Wie man zum Stein spricht, wie
> du,
> mir vom Abgrund her, von
> einer Heimat her Ver-
> schwisterte, Zu-
> geschleuderte, du,
> du mir im Nichts einer Nacht,
> du in der Aber-Nacht Be-
> gegnete, du
> Aber-Du —:

[27] Jacques Derrida, *Of Spirit: Heidegger and the Question*, (1987), trans. Geoffrey Bennington and Rachel Bowlby (Chicago: University of Chicago Press, 1989), 47–57. Henceforth cited as *OS*.

5 WAR AND ITS OTHER

[1] Plato, *The Republic*, trans. G. M. A. Grube and C. D. C. Reeve (Indianapolis: Hackett, 1992), 599e–600a.

[2] Samuel Richardson, *Clarissa, or The History of a Young Lady*, (1747–1748), ed. Angus Ross (London: Penguin, 2004), 39.

[3] William Godwin, *Things as They Are; or, The Adventures of Caleb Williams*, (1794), ed. Maurice Hindle (London: Penguin, 2005), 4, 79, 155.

[4] Thomas Hardy, *Tess of the D'Urbervilles*, (1891), ed. Tim Dolin, intro. Margaret R. Higonnet (London: Penguin, 2003), 305, 303. See, Thomas Hardy, *Far From the Madding Crowd*, (1874), ed. Rosemarie Morgan and Shannon Russell (London: Penguin, 2003), 44. Henceforth cited as *FMC*. Thomas Hardy, *The Mayor of Casterbridge*, (1886), ed. Keith Wilson (London: Penguin, 2003), 170. Henceforth cited as *CA*. See also, Bert G. Hornbach, *The Metaphor of Chance: Vision and Technique in the Works of Thomas Hardy* (Athens: Ohio University Press, 1971), 6.

[5] See also, Thomas Hardy, *Jude the Obscure*, (1895), ed. Dennis Taylor (London: Penguin, 1998), 258; *FMC* 260; Thomas Hardy, *The Woodland-*

ers, (1887), ed. Patricia Ingham (London: Penguin, 1998), 135. Henceforth cited as *WD*. Thomas Hardy, *The Return of the Native*, (1878), ed. Tony Slade, intro. Penny Boumelha (London: Penguin, 1999), 235–41. See also, J Hillis Miller, *Thomas Hardy: Distance and Desire* (Cambridge, MA: Belknap, 1970).

6 David Hume, *An Enquiry Concerning the Principles of Morals*, (1751), ed. L. A. Selby-Bigge and P. H. Nidditch, 3rd edn (Oxford: Clarendon Press, 1994), 187.

7 David Hume, *The History of England*, (1754–1762), intro. William B. Todd, 6 vols (Indianapolis: Liberty Classics, 1983), II: 415. Henceforth cited as *HOE*.

8 David Hume, *A Treatise of Human Nature: Being An Attempt to introduce the experimental Method of Reasoning into Moral Subjects*, (1739–1740), ed. L. A. Selby-Bigge and P. H. Nidditch (Oxford: Oxford University Press, 1978), p. 441. Henceforth cited as *T*.

9 V. G. Kiernan, *The Duel in European History: Honour and the Reign of the Aristocracy* (Oxford: Oxford University Press, 1989); Lewis Melville and Reginald Hergreaves, *Famous Duels and Assassinations* (London: Jarrolds, 1929).

10 Ivan Turgenev, *Fathers and Sons*, (1862), trans. Rosemary Edmonds, intro. Isaiah Berlin (London: Penguin, 1972), 237. Henceforth cited as *TUR*.

11 Heinrich von Kleist, "The Duel", (1811), in *The Marquise of O – and Other Stories*, trans. and intro. David Luke and Nigel Reeves (London: Penguin, 2004), 302. Henceforth cited as *K*. I would like to thank Thomas Dutoit for bringing this work to my attention.

12 This witness, the chambermaid Rosalie, will also turn out to be the "third party": the true perpetrator (*K*, 315).

13 See Denys Dye, *The Stories of Kleist: A Critical Study* (London: Duckworth, 1977), 174, 182; John M. Ellis, *Heinrich von Kleist: Studies in the Character and Meaning of his Writings* (Chapel Hill: University of North Carolina Press, 1979), pp. 58, 66; Séan Allan, *The Stories of Heinrich von Kleist: Fictions of Security* (Rochester: Camden House, 2001), 94–5, 101–2; Eystan Griffiths, *Political Change and Human Emancipation in the works of Heinrich von Kleist* (Rochester: Camden House, 2005), 146.

14 Jacques Derrida, "Aphorism Countertime", (1981), in *Psyche: Inventions of the Other, Volume II*, trans. Nicholas Royle, ed. Peggy Kamuf and Elizabeth Rottenberg (Stanford: Stanford University Press, 2008), 132.

15 William Shakespeare, *The Most Excellent and Lamentable Tragedy of Romeo and Juliet*, in *The Norton Shakespeare, Based on the Oxford Edition*, ed. Stephen Greenblatt and others (New York: Norton, 1997), 3. 1. Henceforth cited as *RJ*.

16 Francis Bacon, *The Charge Touching Duels*, in *Francis Bacon: The Major Works*, (1613), ed. Brian Vickers (Oxford: Oxford University Press, 2002), 304. Henceforth cited as *CTD*.

17 See also, Jennifer Low, *Manhood and the Duel: Masculinity in Early Modern Drama and Culture* (New York: Palgrave, 2003).

[18] Jacques Derrida, "Provocation: Forewords", (1999), in *Without Alibi,* trans. Peggy Kamuf (Stanford: Stanford University Press, 2002), xix–xx. See also, Jacques Derrida, "The University Without Condition", in *Without Alibi*, trans. Peggy Kamuf (Stanford: Stanford University Press, 2002), 235.

[19] Immanuel Kant, *The Metaphysics of Morals,* (1797), in *Practical Philosophy,* trans. Mary J. Gregor, Intro. Paul Guyer (Cambridge: Cambridge University Press, 1999), 476–77. Henceforth cited as *MOM.*

[20] Jacques Derrida and Elisabeth Roudinesco, *For What Tomorrow . . . .: Dialogue,* (1989–1990), trans. Jeff Fort (Stanford: Stanford University Press, 2004), 149–50. Henceforth cited as *FWT.*

[21] See also, Jacques Derrida, "Before the Law", (1982–1985), in *Acts of Literature*, ed. Derek Attridge (London: Routledge, 1992), 181–220.

[22] Immanuel Kant, "Toward Perpetual Peace", (1795), in *Practical Philosophy,* trans. Mary J. Gregor, intro. Paul Guyer (Cambridge: Cambridge University Press, 1999), 317. Henceforth cited as *TPP.* See also, *MOM* 482–88.

[23] See, Jacques Derrida, "Globalization, Peace, and Cosmopolitanism", (1999), in *Negotiations: Interventions and Interviews, 1971–2001*, trans. Elizabeth Rottenberg (Stanford: Stanford University Press, 2002), 384–85. See also, Nick Mansfield, "Under the Black Light: Derrida, War, and Human Rights", *Mosaic* 40 no. 2 (2007), 151–64.

[24] See, Jacques Derrida, "The Deconstruction of Actuality", (1993), in *Negotiations: Interventions and Interviews, 1971–2001*, trans. Elizabeth Rottenberg (Stanford: Stanford University Press, 2002), 85–116. See also *SM, DFT.*

[25] Jacques Derrida, "Le facteur de la vérité", (1971–1975), in *The Post Card: From Socrates to Freud and Beyond*, trans. Alan Bass (Chicago: University of Chicago Press, 1987), 411–96.

[26] See also, Jacques Derrida, *The Gift of Death and Literature in Secret,* (1999), trans. David Wills (Chicago: University of Chicago Press, 2008), 130–31.

[27] William Makepeace Thackeray, *Vanity Fair: A Novel Without A Hero,* (1847–1848) (London: Penguin, 1985), 364. Henceforth cited as *VF.* See also, Mary Hammond, "Thackeray's Waterloo: History and War in *Vanity Fair*", *Literature and History* 11 (2002), 19–38.

[28] William Makepeace Thackeray, *Barry Lyndon,* (1844) (Oxford: Oxford University Press, 1999).

[29] Friedrich Schiller, *Wallenstein,* (1799), in *The Robbers and Wallenstein*, trans. F. J. Lamport (London: Penguin, 1979), 212. Henceforth cited as *W.* Friedrich Schiller, *Wallenstein*, in *Werke und Briefe* 4, ed. Fritjof Stock (Frankfurt am Main: Deutscher Klassiker Verlag, 2000), 52. Henceforth cited as *Wa.*

> Der dem Tod ins Angesicht schauen kann,
> Der Soldat allein, ist der freie Mann.

[30]
> Und setzet ihr nicht das Leben ein,
> Nie wird euch das Leben gewonnen sein (*Wa* 53)

[31]
> Denn hört der Krieg im Kriege nicht schon auf,
> Woher soll Friede kommen? (*Wa* 74)

[32] On Schiller's ambivalent relation to the war of his times, see Elisabeth Krimmer, "Transcendental Soldiers: Warfare in Schiller"s *Wallenstein* and *Die Jungfrau von Orleans*", *Eighteenth Century Fiction* 19 (2006), 99–121. See also, David L. Clark , "Schelling's Wartime: Philosophy and Violence in the Age of Napoleon", *European Romantic Review* 19 no. 2 (2008): 139–48.

[33] Michel Foucault, *"Society Must be Defended": Lectures at the College de France, 1975–1976*, ed. Mauro Bertani and Alessandro Fontana, trans. David Macey (London: Allen Lane, 2003), 5. Henceforth cited as *SMD*. See, Lucy Hartley, "War and Peace, or Governmentality as the Ruin of Democracy", in *Foucault in an Age of Terror: Essays on Biopolitics and the Defense of Society*, ed. Stephen Morton and Stephen Byrgave (New York: Palgrave, 2008), 133–51. See also Derrida's careful comments on the concept of war in *AU*.

[34] Gilles Deleuze and Felix Guattari, *A Thousand Plateaus: Capitalism and Schizophrenia*, (1980), trans. Brian Massumi (London: Continuum, 2004), 388–467, 514–16. See, Friedrich Nietzsche, *On the Genealogy of Morals*, (1887), in *Basic Writings of Nietzsche*, trans. Walter Kaufman (New York: Modern Library, 1968), 522–23. See also, Paul Virilio, *Speed and Politics: An Essay on Dromology* (1977) (New York: Semiotext(e), 1986).

[35] Carl von Clausewitz, *Vom Kriege: Hinterlassenes Werke*, ed. Werner Hahlweg (Bonn: Ferd. Dümmlers Verlag, 1952), 77. Henceforth cited as *VK*.

[36] See also *OWP*.

[37] See also, W. B. Gallie, *Philosophers of Peace and War: Kant, Clausewitz, Marx, Engels, and Tolstoy* (Cambridge: Cambridge University Press, 1978).

[38] See also *EM*.

[39] See also Maurice Blanchot, "The Essential Solitude", (1953), in *The Space of Literature*, trans. Ann Smock (Lincoln: University of Nebraska Press, 1982), 26.

[40] On the more than one as an uncertain doubling, see Nicholas Royle, *The Uncanny* (Manchester: Manchester University Press, 2003).

[41] See also, Katherine L. Herbig, "Chance and Uncertainty in *On War*", in *Clausewitz and Modern Strategy*, ed. Michael Handel (Oxford: Frank Cass, 2005), 95–116.

[42] See also, *WP* 709, 773.

[43]
　　　Recht stets behält das Schicksal, denn das Herz
　　　In uns ist sein gebietrischer Vollzieher (*Wa* 176)

[44]
　　　Mit Pflichten streiten Pflichten.
　　　Du mußt Partei ergreifen in dem Krieg,
　　　Der zwischen deinem Freund und deinem Kaiser
　　　Sich jetzt entzündet (*Wa* 176)

[45]
　　　Krieg! Ist das der Name?
　　　Der Krieg ist schrecklich, wie des Himmels Plagen,
　　　Doch er ist gut, ist ein Geschick, wie sie.
　　　Ist das ein guter Krieg, den du dem Kaiser
　　　Bereitest mit des Kaisers eignem Heer? (*Wa* 179)

46   Des Menschen Taten und Gedanken, wißt!
Sind nicht wie Meeres blind bewegte Wellen.
Die innre Welt, sein Mikrokosmus, ist
Der tiefe Schacht, aus dem sie ewig quellen (*Wa* 186)

47   Es denkt der Mensch die freie Tat zu tun,
Umsonst! Er ist das Spielwerk nur der blinden
Gewalt, die aus der eignen Wahl ihm schnell
Die furchtbare Notwendigkeit erschafft (*Wa* 255)

48 G. W. F. Hegel, "On Wallenstein", (1800–1801), trans. Ido Geiger, *Idealist Studies* 35 nos. 2–3 (2005): 196–7. Henceforth cited as *Wall.* G. W. F., "Über Wallenstein", in *Werke I* (Surkamp: Frankfurt am Main, 1986), 618–20.

49 Jacques Derrida, "Psychoanalysis Searches the States of Its Soul: The Impossible Beyond of a Sovereign Cruelty (Address to the States General of Psychoanalysis)", (2000), in *Without Alibi*, ed. and trans. Peggy Kamuf (Stanford: Stanford University Press, 2002), 280. Henceforth cited as *PSS*. Jacques Derrida, *États d'âme de la psychanalyse: L'impossible au-delà d'une souveraine cruauté* (Paris: Éditions Galilée, 2000), 90. Henceforth cited as *EAD*.

50 See also, Dieter Borchmeyer, *Macht und Melancholie: Schillers Wallenstein* (Frankfurt am Main: Athenäum, 1988).

51 Sigmund Freud, *Introductory Lectures on Psychoanalysis*, (1915–1917), trans. James Strachey, ed. James Strachey and Angela Richards (London: Penguin, 1991), 62. Freud had been interested in this passage from *Wallenstein* since at least the *Psychopathology of Everyday Life* (1901), trans. Andrea L. Bell, ed. Paul Keegan (London: Penguin, 2002).

52 See also, Jacques Derrida, "Geopsychoanalysis: 'and the rest of the world'", (1981), in *Psyche: Inventions of the Other, Volume I*, trans. Peggy Kamuf, ed. Peggy Kamuf and Elizabeth Rottenberg (Stanford: Stanford University Press, 2007), 339. See also Derrida's remarks on war in *WEC* 154–9.

53 Friedrich Nietzsche, "On Truth and Lie in an Extra-Moral Sense", (1874), in *The Portable Nietzsche,* ed. trans. Walter Kaufmann (London: Penguin, 1982), 44. Henceforth cited as *OTL*. Nor – despite the claims of Deleuze and Guattari – can the concept of war be described as a concept that is *always* particular and contingent, Gilles Deleuze and Félix Guattari, *What is Philosophy?*, (1991), trans. Graham Burchell and Hugh Tomlinson (London: Verso, 1994), 7.

54 Sigmund Freud, "Thoughts for the Times on War and Death", (1915), in *The Standard Edition of the Complete Works of Sigmund Freud*, trans. James Strachey (London: The Hogarth Press, 1962), XIV: 275. Henceforth cited as *TT*. Sigmund Freud, "*Zeitgemässes über Krieg und Tod*", in *Das Unbewußte: Schriften zur Psychoanalyse* (Frankfurt am Main: S. Fischer Verlag, 1960), 187. Henceforth cited as *ZUK*. See also, See Anthony Sampson, "Freud on the State, Violence, and War", *Diacritics* 35 no. 3 (2005), 78–91; Samuel Weber, *Targets of Opportunity: On the Militarization of Thinking* (New York: Fordham University Press, 2005); "Wartime", in

Violence, Identity, and Self-Determination, ed. Hent de Vries and Samuel Weber (Stanford: Stanford University Press, 1997), 80–105.

55 See also, Maurice Blanchot, "Death as Possibility", (1952), in *The Space of Literature*, trans. Ann Smock (Lincoln: University of Nebraska Press, 1989), 87–107.

56 In his later reading of Heidegger, Derrida also challenged the movement of a return to a position or thesis in Heidegger's use of *Auseinandersetzung* as a dialogue (*Zwiesprache*) or debate with the other. See, *OS* 89–90, 93, 113 and *HE* 209. See also, Joanna Hodge, *Heidegger and Ethics* (London: Routledge, 1995), 112–33.

57 See also, Jacques Derrida, "The Pit and the Pyramid: Introduction to Hegel's Semiology", (1968), in *Margins of Philosophy*, trans. Alan Bass (Chicago: University of Chicago Press, 1982), 88.

58 Maurice Blanchot, "Encountering the Imaginary", (1954), in *The Book to Come*, trans. Charlotte Mandell (Stanford: Stanford University Press, 2003), 7–9; "La rencontre de l'imaginaire", in *Le Livre à venir* (Paris: Gallimard, 1959), 14–16.

59 Maurice Blanchot, "War and Literature", in *Friendship*, (1971), trans. Elizabeth Rottenberg (Stanford: Stanford University Press, 1997), 109. Henceforth cited as *WL*.

60 Jacques Derrida, "Ethics and Politics Today", (1987), in *Negotiations: Interventions and Interviews, 1971-2001*, trans. Elizabeth Rottenberg (Stanford: Stanford University Press, 2002), 296.

6 CONRAD AND THE ASYMMETRICAL DUEL

1 Joseph Conrad, "The Duel", (1908), in *A Set of Six* (London: Dent, 1954), 165. Henceforth cited as *TD*. On Napoleon and the duel see, John Dunlop, *Anti-Duel; or a Plan for the Abrogation of Duelling* (London: Houlston and Stoneman, 1843), 43. A shorter version of this chapter was read in the English Department at the University of Edinburgh in October 2007. I would like to thank Robert Irvine, Kenneth Millard, Alex Thompson and Laura Marcus for their exceptional and kind hospitality.

2 Joseph Conrad, "Autocracy and War", (1905), in *Notes on Life and Letters*, ed. J. H. Stape with Andrew Busza (Cambridge: Cambridge University Press, 2004), 73.

3 Joseph Conrad, "Author's Note", (1920), in *A Set of Six* (London: Dent, 1954), viii. Henceforth cited as *AN*.

4 Irina Reyfman, *Ritualized Violence Russian Style: The Duel in Russian Culture and Literature* (Stanford: Stanford University Press, 1999), 3. Henceforth cited as *RVR*. See also, David Richards, "'Pistols for Two': Duelling in Nineteenth Century Russian Literature", *Journal of Russian Studies* 49 (1985), 37–41; Jeffrey Meyers, "The Duel in Fiction", *North Dakota Quarterly* 51 no. 4 (1983): 129–50.

5 Anton Chekhov, "The Duel", (1890), in *The Steppe and Other Stories, 1887-1891*, trans. Ronald Wilkes, intro. Donald Rayfield (London: Penguin, 2001), 348. See also, Andrew Durkin, "Allusion and Dialogue in

Notes

'The Duel'", in *Reading Chekhov's Text*, ed. Robert L. Jackson (Evanston: Northwestern University Press, 1993), 169–78.

[6] Nietzsche writes of the "Napoleonic tempo" in Stendhal's works, *BGE* 384. See also, Dennis Porter, "Stendhal and the Lesson of Napoleon", *PMLA* 85.3 (1970): 456–62.

[7] See David F. Bell, *Chance in the Literary Text* (Lincoln: University of Nebraska Press, 1993), 82–7.

[8] W. G. Sebald, *Vertigo*, trans. Michael Hulse (London: Harvill, 1999), 5–7. See Stendhal, *Vie de Henry Brulard*, (1835–1836), ed. Béatrice Didier (Paris: Gallimard, 2006), 427.

[9] See also Paul Stock, "Imposing on Napoleon: Romantic Appropriation of Bonaparte", *Journal of European Studies* 36 no. 4 (2006): 363–88.

[10] See, Stendhal, *The Red and the Black*, (1830), trans. Roger Gard (London: Penguin, 2002), 32, 67, 72; *Napoleon: Vie de Napoleon, Mémoires sur Napoleon*, (1816–1818, 1836), ed. Catherine Mariette (Paris: Stock, 1998). See also, Marcel Heisler, *Stendhal et Napoleon* (Paris: A. G. Nizet, 1969); Pierre Laubriet, "La légende et le mythe Napoléoniens chez Balzac", in *L'année Balzacienne 1968* (Paris: Éditions Garnier Frères, 1968), 285–301.

[11] On the recent use of the language of "asymmetric war", see David Rodin, "The Ethics of Aysmmetric War", in *The Ethics of War: Shared Problems in Different Traditions*, ed. Richard Sorabji and David Rodin (London: Ashgate, 2006), 153–68.

[12] Joseph Roth, *The Radetzky March*, (1932), trans. Joachim Neugroshchel, intro. Nadine Gordimer (London: Penguin, 1995), 72. Henceforth cited as *RM*. See also, Andrew C. Wisely, *Arthur Schitzler and the Discourse of Honour and Duelling* (New York: Peter Lang, 1996).

[13] Zdzislaw Najder, *Joseph Conrad: A Chronicle* (New Brunswick: Rutgers University Press, 1983), 326–7. See also, "Sources for Conrad's *The Duel*", in Joseph Conrad, *The Nigger of The "Narcissus" and Other Stories*, eds. J. A. Stape and Allan H. Simmons, intro. Gail Fraser (London: Penguin, 2007), 415–18.

[14] Frederick R. Krall, *Joseph Conrad: The Three Lives* (London: Faber and Faber, 1979), 32, 58–60.

[15] Delancy J. Ferguson, "The Plot of Conrad's 'The Duel'", *MLN* 1 (1935): 385–90; Roger Tenant, *Joseph Conrad* (New York: Atheneum, 1981), 174.

[16] Jeffrey Meyers, *Joseph Conrad: A Biography* (London: John Murray, 1991), 243–45. See, Alexander Pushkin, "The Shot", *The Queen of Spades*, trans. Alan Myers, ed. Andrew Kahn (Oxford: Oxford University Press, 1999), 7–18.

[17] Fyodor Dostoyevsky, *The Devils*, (1871), trans. David Margashack (London: Penguin, 1971), 288. Henceforth cited as *DEV*.

[18] Norman Sherry, ed. *Conrad: the Critical Heritage* (London: Routledge & Kegan Paul, 1973), 220. 242. Mikhail Lermontov, *A Hero of Our Time*, (1841), trans. Paul Foote (London: Penguin, 2001), 132. Henceforth cited as *HOT*.

[19] See, Robert L. Jackson, "Pierre and Dolochov at the Barrier: The Lesson of the Duel", *Scando-Slavica* 39 (1993): 52–61.

[20] On Stavrogin's response to duelling, see *RVR,* 192–261.

Notes

²¹ Walter Scott, *The Tale of Old Mortality*, (1816), ed. Douglas S. Mack (London: Penguin, 1999).
At one point Scott's hero Henry Morton says, "I join a cause supported by men engaged in open war, which it is proposed to carry on according to the rules of civilized nations; and do not in any respect subscribe to the act of violence which gave immediate rise to it", 175.

²² G. W. F. Hegel, *Phenomenology of Spirit*, 1807, trans. A.V. Miller (Oxford: Oxford University Press, 1977), 10.

²³ Joseph Conrad, *The Secret Agent*, 1907, ed. John Lyon (Oxford: Oxford University Press, 2004), 37. Henceforth cited as *SA*.

²⁴ William Wordsworth, *Lyrical Ballads, and Other Poems, 1797-1800*, ed. James Butler and Karen Green (Ithaca: Cornell University Press, 1992), 747; *S* 422b. See also, *OT*.

²⁶ Having had his eardrums ruptured, Razumov's last words are "*Je suis sourd*", Joseph Conrad, *Under Western Eyes*, (1911), ed. Allan H. Simmons (London: Penguin, 2007), 305.

²⁷ Reported Thursday, 3 October, 2002. See *news.bbc.co.uk* In February 2007, Taha Yassin Ramadan was sentenced to death by hanging. He was executed on 20 March 2007, the day after the fourth anniversary of the start of the American led invasion of Iraq.

7 (NOT) MEETTING WITHOUT NAME

¹ An earlier version of this chapter appears in *Symploke* 16, no. 2 (2008). I would like to thank Jeffrey Di Leo and Northwestern University Press, and to dedicate this chapter to Simon Morgan Wortham.

² Emmanuel Lévinas, *Noms propres* (Paris: Fata Morgana, 1976).

³ In contrast to those who, for some strategic, political, institutional or creative reason (and perhaps some form of good conscience) have embraced anonymity, if such a thing is possible.

⁴ Emmanuel Lévinas, "Nameless", in *Proper Names*, trans. Michael B. Smith (London: Athlone, 1996), 119; "Sans nom", in *Noms propres* (Paris: Fata Morgana, 1976), 141.

⁵ See also, Jacques Derrida, "Force of Law: 'The Mystical Foundation of Authority'", in *Acts of Religion*, ed. and intro. Gil Anjdar, trans. Mary Quaintance, (London; Routledge, 2002), 296.

⁶ Jacques Derrida, "Dereliction of the Right to Justice (But what are the 'sans-papiers' lacking?)", (1996), in *Negotiations: Interventions and Interviews 1971-2001*, trans. Elizabeth Rottenberg (Stanford: Stanford University Press, 2002), 133. Henceforth cited as *DRJ*.

⁷ Pliny, The *Historie of the World: Commonly called, The Naturall Historie of C. Plinus Secondus*, trans. Philemon Holland, 2 vols. (London: G. B., 1601), II: 274.

⁸ See Herbert F. Tucker, ed. *Anonymity*, New Literary History, 33 no. 2 (2002); Robert J. Griffin, ed. *The Faces of Anonymity: Anonymous and Pseudonymous Publication from the Sixteenth to the Twentieth Century*

(New York: Palgrave, 2003); John Mullan, *Anonymity: A Secret History of English Literature* (London: Faber and Faber, 2007); Nancy Yousef, *Isolated Cases: The Anxieties of Autonomy in Enlightenment Philosophy and Romantic Literature* (Ithaca: Cornell University Press, 1999).

9   *Exodus*, in *The Five Books of Moses*, trans. Everett Fox (London: Harvill, 1995), 2: 1–2. Henceforth cited as *EX*.

10   See also, *ATT* 384–87.

11   Maurice Blanchot, "Gog and Magog", (1959), in *Friendship*, trans. Elizabeth Rottenberg (Stanford: Stanford University Press, 1997), 230–31.

12   Martin Heidegger, "The Thing", (1950), in *Poetry, Language, Thought*, trans. Albert Hofstadter (New York: Harper and Row, 1975), 165–6.

13   See also, *PA* 81, 92–3, 99–105.

14   See also *DFT* 17–18, 32, 65–6.

15   See also, John Bayley, *Tolstoy and the Novel* (London: Chatto & Windus, 1968), 163–76; Leo Tolstoy, "Sevastopol Stories", in *The Cossacks and Other Stories*, trans. David McDuff and Paul Foote, intro. Paul Foote (London: Penguin, 2006), 185–333.

16   Jacques Derrida, "Le souverain bien – ou l'Europe en mal de souveraineté", (2004), *Cités* 30 (2007): 103–40. My translation. Henceforth cited as *LSB*.

17   For Derrida's argument against using "the general singular that is *the animal*", see *ATT* 402, 408–9, 415–16.

18   I have chosen to follow Edmonds's translation in this case, Leo Tolstoy, *War and Peace*, trans. Rosemary Edmonds (London: Penguin, 1982), 592. In Edmonds's translation the wolf is identified as a female. This is the only significant discrepancy I have found in the quoted passages with the new translation by Pevear and Volokhonsky, see *WP* 502. Subsequent to this note, my good friend Stephen Farrow has kindly looked at the Russian text. The wolf is male (*volk*), not a she-wolf (*volchika, volchitsa*). As Derrida suggests, translation is always encountering and registering the snags of sexual difference.

19   Isaiah Berlin, "Conversations with Akhmatova and Pasternak", (1980), in *The Proper Study of Mankind: An Anthology of Essays*, ed. Henry Hardy and Roger Hausheer, foreword Noel Annan (London: Pimlico, 1998), 545. See also, Ruth Crego Benson, *Women in Tolstoy: The Ideal and the Erotic* (Urbana: University of Illinois Press, 1973).

20   On Derrida's work on sovereignty, see Peggy Kamuf, "Introduction: Event of Resistance", in Jacques Derrida, *Without Alibi*, ed. trans. Peggy Kamuf (Stanford: Stanford University Press, 2002), 14–16; Michael Naas, "'One Nation . . . Indivisible': Jacques Derrida on the Autoimmunity of Democracy and the Sovereignty of God", *Research in Phenomenology* 36.1 (2006), 15–44; Geoffrey Bennington, "The Fall of Sovereignty", *Epoché* 10 no. 2 (2006): 395–406.

21   Isaiah Berlin, "The Hedgehog and the Fox", (1951–1953), in *The Proper Study of Mankind: An Anthology of Essays*, ed. Henry Hardy and Roger Hausheer, foreword Noel Annan (London: Pimlico, 1998), 450–66.

Notes

[22] Mikhail Bulgakov, *The Heart of a Dog*, (1925), trans. Michael Glenny (London: Vintage, 1968), 5. Henceforth cited as *HD*.

[23] On this period see, Tom Segev, *One Palestine, Complete: Jews and Arabs under the British Mandate*, trans. Haim Watzman (London: Abacus, 2000); Amos Oz, *Panther in the Basement*, trans. Nicholas de Lange (London: Vintage, 1997), and *A Tale of Love and Darkness*, trans. Nicholas de Lange (London: Chatto & Windus, 2004). See also, Jacques Derrida, "Interpretations at War: Kant, the Jew, the German", (1988–1990), in *Psyche: Inventions of the Other, Volume II*, trans. Moshe Ron and Dana Hollander, ed. Peggy Kamuf and Elizabeth Rottenberg (Stanford: Stanford University Press, 2008), 241–98; Gil Anidjar, *The Jew, The Arab: A History of the Enemy* (Stanford: Stanford University Press, 2003), 241–98.

[24] Amos Oz, *The Silence of Heaven: Agnon's Fear of God*, trans. Barbara Harshav (Princeton: Princeton University Press, 2000).

[25] S. Y. Agnon, *Only Yesterday: A Novel*, (1945), trans. Barbara Harshav (Princeton: Princeton University Press, 2000), 285. Henceforth cited as *OY*.

[26] See also: Emmanuel Lévinas, "The Name of a Dog, or Natural Rights", (1975), in *Difficult Freedom: Essays on Judaism*, trans. Séan Hand (Baltimore: Johns Hopkins University Press, 1990), 151–53; Matthew Calarco, *Zoographies: The Question of the Animal from Heidegger to Derrida* (New York: Columbia University Press, 2008).

This book is dedicated to Etai and Maya Koren, Alice, Joel and Louis-Gabriel Penrose, and Darcey and Erin Snape – and to Carmella Elan-Gaston.

BIBLIOGRAPHY

Agamben, Giorgio. *Homo Sacer: Sovereign Power and Bare Life* (1995). Trans. Daniel Heller-Roazen. Stanford: Stanford University Press, 1998.

―――― *Idea of Prose* (1985). Trans. Michael Sullivan and Sam Whitsitt. New York: State University Press of New York, 1995.

―――― "On Potentiality" (1986). *Potentialities*. Ed. and Trans. Daniel Heller-Roazen, 177–84. Stanford: Stanford University Press, 1999.

―――― "*Pardes*: The Writing of Potentiality" (1990). *Potentialities*. Ed. and Trans, 205–19. Daniel Heller-Roazen. Stanford: Stanford University Press, 1999.

―――― "The Passion of Facticity" (1988). *Potentialities*. Ed. and Trans, 185–204. Daniel Heller-Roazen. Stanford: Stanford University Press, 1999.

Agnon, S. Y. *Only Yesterday: A Novel* (1945). Trans. Barbara Harshav. Princeton: Princeton University Press, 2000.

Allan, Séan. *The Stories of Heinrich von Kleist: Fictions of Security*. Rochester: Camden House, 2001.

Anidjar, Gil. *The Jew, The Arab: A History of the Enemy*. Stanford: Stanford University Press, 2003.

Aristotle. *The Metaphysics*. Trans. Hugh Lawson-Tancred. London: Penguin, 2004; *Metaphysics*. Trans. Hugh Tredennick. 3 Vols. London: Heinemann, 1993.

―――― *On the Soul. The Complete Works of Aristotle*. Ed. Jonathan Barnes. Trans. J. A. Smith, 2 Vols. Princeton: Princeton University Press, 1984. I; *On the Soul*. Trans. W. S. Hett Cambridge, MA: Harvard University Press, 1986.

―――― *Physics. The Complete Works of Aristotle*. Ed. Jonathan Barnes. 2 Vols, I. Princeton: Princeton University Press, 1984. I.

Bacon, Francis. *The Charge Touching Duels*. *Francis Bacon: The Major Works* (1613). Ed. Brian Vickers, 304–13. Oxford: Oxford University Press, 2002.

Balzac, Honoré de. *Colonel Chabert* (1832). Trans. Andrew Brown. Intro A. N. Wilson. London: Hesperus, 2003.

Bayley, John. *Tolstoy and the Novel*. London: Chatto & Windus, 1968.

Bell, David F. *Chance in the Literary Text*. Lincoln: University of Nebraska Press, 1993.

Bennington, Geoffrey. "Deconstruction and the Philosophers (The Very Idea)". *Legislations: The Politics of Deconstruction*, 11–60. London: Verso, 1994.

——— "Derridabase". *Jacques Derrida*. Chicago: University of Chicago Press, 1992.

——— *Dudding: des noms de Rousseau*. Paris: Éditions Galilée, 1991.

——— "The Fall of Sovereignty". *Epoché* 10 no. 2 (2006): 395–406.

——— "Le temps de la lecture". *Etudes Françaises* 38 (2002): 77–85.

Benson, Ruth Crego. *Women in Tolstoy: The Ideal and the Erotic*. Urbana: University of Illinois Press, 1973.

Berlin, Isaiah. "Conversations with Akhmatova and Pasternak" (1980). *The Proper Study of Mankind: An Anthology of Essays*. Ed. Henry Hardy and Roger Hausheer. Foreword by Noel Annan, 525–52. London: Pimlico, 1998.

——— "The Hedgehog and the Fox" (1951–1953). *The Proper Study of Mankind: An Anthology of Essays*. Ed. Henry Hardy and Roger Hausheer. Foreword. Noel Annan, 436–98. London: Pimlico, 1998.

Bernasconi, Robert. "No More Stories, Good or Bad: de Man's Criticisms of Derrida on Rousseau". *Derrida: A Critical Reader*. Ed. David Wood, 137–66. Oxford: Blackwell, 1992.

Blanchot, Maurice. "The Book to Come" (1957). *The Book to Come*. Trans. Charlotte Mandell, 224–44. Stanford: Stanford University Press, 2001.

——— "Death as Possibility" (1952). *The Space of Literature*. Trans. Ann Smock, 87–107. Lincoln: University of Nebraska Press, 1989.

——— "Encountering the Imaginary" (1954). *The Book to Come*. Trans. Charlotte Mandell, 3–10. Stanford: Stanford University Press, 2001. "La rencontre de l'imaginaire". *Le Livre à venir*, 9–18. Paris: Gallimard, 1959.

——— "The Essential Solitude" (1953). *The Space of Literature*. Trans, Ann Smock, 19–34. Lincoln: University of Nebraska Press, 1982.

———— The Experience of Proust" (1943). *Faux Pas*. Trans. Charlotte Mandell, 42–6. Stanford: Stanford University Press, 2001.

———— "Gog and Magog" (1959). *Friendship*. Trans. Elizabeth Rottenberg, 228–39. Stanford: Stanford University Press, 1997.

———— *The Infinite Conversation* (1969). Trans. Susan Hanson. Minneapolis: University of Minnesota Press, 1992; *L'entretien infini*. Paris: Gallimard, 2006.

———— "Literature and the Right to Death" (1949). *The Work of Fire*. Trans. Charlotte Mandell, 300–44. Stanford: Stanford University Press, 1995. "La littérature et le droit à la mort". *La part du feu*, 303–45. Paris: Gallimard, 1949.

———— "Rousseau" (1958). *The Book to Come*. Trans. Charlotte Mandell, 41–8. Stanford: Stanford University Press, 2003.

———— "War and Literature" (1971). *Friendship*. Trans. Elizabeth Rottenberg, 109–11. Stanford: Stanford University Press, 1997.

Borchmeyer, Dieter. *Macht und Melancholie: Schillers Wallenstein*. Frankfurt am Main: Athenäum, 1988.

Brogan, Walter A. *Heidegger and Aristotle: The Twofoldness of Being*. New York: State University of New York Press, 2005.

Bulgakov, Mikhail. *The Heart of a Dog* (1925). Trans. Michael Glenny. London: Vintage, 1968.

———— *The Master and Margarita* (1938). Trans. Michael Glenny. London: Collins Harvill, 1988.

Calarco, Matthew. *Zoographies: The Question of the Animal from Heidegger to Derrida*. New York: Columbia University Press, 2008.

Celan, Paul. *Selected Poems and Prose*. Trans. John Felstiner. New York: Norton, 2001.

Chekhov, Anton. "The Duel" (1890). *The Steppe and Other Stories, 1887-1891*. Trans. Ronald Wilkes. Intro. Donald Rayfield, 251–357. London: Penguin, 2001.

Cicero. *De Fato*. Trans. H. Rackham. 3 Vols, 187–249. Cambridge, MA: Harvard University Press, 1942. III.

Cixous, Hélène. *Insister of Jacques Derrida*. Trans. Peggy Kamuf. Edinburgh: Edinburgh University Press, 2007; *À insister – à Jacques Derrida*. Paris: Éditions Galilée, 2006.

Clark, David L. "Schelling's Wartime: Philosophy and Violence in the Age of Napoleon". *European Romantic Review*. 19 no. 2 (2008): 139–48.

Clark, Timothy. *Derrida, Heidegger, Blanchot: Sources of Derrida's Notion and Practice of Literature.* Cambridge: Cambridge University Press, 1992.

—— *Martin Heidegger.* London: Routledge, 2001.

—— *Poetics of Singularity: The Counter-Culturalist Turn in Heidegger, Derrida and Blanchot and the later Gadamer.* Edinburgh: Edinburgh University Press, 2005.

Clausewitz, Carl von. *On War* (1832). Ed. and Trans. Michael Howard and Peter Paret. Princeton: Princeton University Press, 1989; *Vom Kriege: Hinterlassenes Werke.* Ed. Werner Hahlweg. Bonn: Ferd. Dümmlers Verlag, 1952.

Colebrook, Claire. "Agamben: Aesthetics, Potentiality, and Life". *South Atlantic Quarterly* 107 no. 1 (2008): 107–20.

Conrad, Joseph. "Author's Note" (1920). *A Set of Six,* v–ix. London: Dent, 1954.

—— "Autocracy and War" (1905). *Notes on Life and Letters.* Ed. J. H. Stape with Andrew Busza, 1–93. Cambridge: Cambridge University Press, 2004.

—— "The Duel" (1908). *A Set of Six,* 165–266. London: Dent, 1954.

—— *The Secret Agent* (1907). Ed. John Lyon. Oxford: Oxford University Press, 2004.

—— *Under Western Eyes* (1911). Ed. Allan H. Simmons. London: Penguin, 2007.

Cooke, Alexander. "Resistance and Potentiality and the Law: Deleuze and Agamben on 'Bartleby'". *Angelaki* 10 no. 3 (2005): 79–89.

Cooper, Melinda. "The Living and the Dead: Variations on *De Anima*". *Angelaki* 7 no. 3 (2002): 80–104.

Deleuze, Gilles. *Logic of Sense* (1969). Trans. Mark Lester and Charles Stivale. London: Continuum, 2004.

—— *Nietzsche and Philosophy* (1962). Trans. Hugh Tomlinson. London: Continuum, 2006.

Deleuze, Gilles and Felix Guattari. *A Thousand Plateaus: Capitalism and Schizophrenia* (1980). Trans. Brian Mascumi. London: Continuum, 2004.

—— *What is Philosophy?* (1991). Trans. Graham Burchell and Hugh Tomlinson. London: Verso, 1994.

De Man, Paul. "Impersonality in the Criticism of Maurice Blanchot". *Blindness and Insight: Essays in the Rhetoric of Contemporary*

Criticism. 2ⁿᵈ edn, 60–78. Minneapolis: University of Minnesota Press, 1983. "La circularité de l'interprétation dans l'oeuvre deMaurice Blanchot", *Critique* 19, no. 229 (1966): 547–60.

———— "The Literary Self as Origin: The Work of Georges Poulet". *Blindness and Insight: Essays in the Rhetoric of Contemporary Criticism.* 2ⁿᵈ edn, 79–101. Minneapolis: University of Minnesota Press, 1983. "Vérité et méthode dans l'oeuvre de Georges Poulet", *Critique* 25 no. 266 (1969): 608–23.

Democritus. "Fragments". *Early Greek Philosophers.* Ed. Jonathan Barnes, 244–88. London: Penguin, 1987.

Derrida, Jacques. *Adieu: To Emmanuel Levinas.* Trans. Anne Pascale-Brault and Michael Naas. Stanford: Stanford University Press, 1999; *Adieu – à Emmanuel Lévinas.* Paris: Galilée, 1997.

———— "The Animal That Therefore I am (More to Follow)" (1997). Trans. David Wills. *Critical Inquiry* 28 (2002): 369–418; *L'animal Que Donc Je Suis.* Ed. Marie-LouisMallett. Paris: Éditions Galilée, 2006; *The Animal That Therefore I Am.* Ed. Marie Louis Mallett, Trans. David Wills. Stanford: Stanford University Press, 2008.

———— "Aphorism Countertime" (1981). *Psyche: Inventions of the Other, Volume II.* Trans. Nicholas Royle. Ed. Peggy Kamuf and Elizabeth Rottenberg, 127–42. Stanford: Stanford University Press, 2008. "L'aphorisme à contretemps". *Psyché: Inventions de l'autre.* 2 Vols, 131–44. Paris: Éditions Galilée, 1998–2003.

———— *The Archaeology of the Frivolous: Reading Condillac* (1973). Trans. John P. Leavey, Jr. Pittsburgh: Duquesne University Press, 1980; *L'archéologie du frivole.* Paris: Éditions Galilée, 1990.

———— "At This Very Moment in This Work Here I Am" (1980). *Psyche: Inventions of the Other, Volume I.* Trans. Ruben Berezdivin and Peggy Kamuf. Ed. Peggy Kamuf and Elizabeth Rottenberg, 143–90. Stanford: Stanford University Press, 2007. "En cemoment même dans cet ouvrage me voici". *Psyché: Inventions de l'autre.* 2 Vols, I: 159–202. Paris: Éditions Galilée, 1998–2003.

———— "Back from Moscow, in the USSR" (1990). *Politics, Theory, and Contemporary Culture.* Ed. Mark Poster. Trans. Mary Quaintaire, 197–235. New York: Columbia University Press 1993. *Moscou aller-retour.* Paris, Éditions de l'Aube, 1995.

———— "Before the Law" (1982–1985). *Acts of Literature.* Ed. Derek Attridge, 181–220. London: Routledge, 1992. "Préjugés: devant la loi". *La faculté de juger*, 87–139. Paris: Les Éditions de Minuit, 1985.

———— "Between Brackets I" (1975–1976). *Points: Interviews 1974-1994*. Ed. Elisabeth Weber. Trans. Peggy Kamuf, 5–29. Stanford: Stanford University Press, 1995. "Entre crochets I". *Points de suspension: Entretiens*, choisis et présentés par Elisabeth Weber, 13–36. Paris: Éditions Galilée, 1992.

———— "Cartouches" (1978). *The Truth in Painting*. Trans. Geoff Bennington and Ian McLeod, 183–247. Chicago: University of Chicago Press, 1987. "Cartouches". *La vérité en peinture*, 211–90. Paris: Flammarion, 1978.

———— "Circumfession". *Jacques Derrida*. Trans. Geoffrey Bennington. Chicago: University of Chicago Press, 1993; "Circonfession". *Jacques Derrida*. Paris: Éditions du Seuil, 1991.

———— "Cogito and the History of Madness" (1964). *Writing and Difference*. Trans. Alan Bass, 31–63. Chicago: University of Chicago Press, 1978. "Cogito et histoire de la folie." *L'écriture et la différence*, 51–98. Paris: Éditions du Seuil, 1967.

———— "Countersignature". *Genet*. Ed. Mairéad Hanrahan. *Paragraph* 27 no. 2, 7–42. Edinburgh: Edinburgh University Press, 2004.

———— "'Dead Man Running': *Salut, Salut* – Notes for a Letter to '*Les Temps Modernes*'" (1996). *Negotiations: Interventions and Interviews 1971-2001*. Trans. Elizabeth Rottenberg, 257–92. Stanford: Stanford University Press, 2002. "'Il courait mort' *Salut, Salut*: Notes pour un courrier aux *Les Temps Modernes*". *Papier Machine: Le ruban de machine à écrire et autres réponses*, 167–214. Paris: Éditions Galilée, 2001.

————"The Deaths of Roland Barthes" (1981). *Psyche: Inventions of the Other, Volume I*. Trans. Ruben Berezdivin and Peggy Kamuf. Ed. Peggy Kamuf and Elizabeth Rottenberg, 264–98. Stanford: Stanford University Press, 2007. "Les morts de Roland Barthes". *Psyche: Inventions de l'autre*. 2 Vols, 273–304. Paris: Éditions Galilée, 1998–2003.

Derrida, Jacques, and Richard Kearney. "Deconstruction and the Other". *Dialogues with Contemporary Continental Thinkers: The Phenomenological Heritage*, 105–26. Manchester: Manchester University Press, 1984.

———— "The Deconstruction of Actuality" (1993). *Negotiations: Interventions and Interviews, 1971–2001*. Trans. Elizabeth Rottenberg, 85–116. Stanford: Stanford University Press, 2002.

———— "De la grammatologie I" and "De la grammatologie II". *Critique* 21 nos. 223 and 224 (1965–1966): 16–42, 23–53.

—— "Demeure, Athènes". Jean-François Bonhomme. *Athènes à l'ombre de l'acropole, 39–64.* Athens: Olkos, 1996.

—— *Demeure: Fiction and Testimony* (1998). Trans. Elizabeth Rottenberg. Stanford: Stanford University Press, 2000; *Demeure – Maurice Blanchot.* Paris: Éditions Galilée, 1998.

—— "Dereliction of the Right to Justice (But what are the 'sans-papiers' lacking?)" (1996). *Negotiations: Interventions and Interviews 1971–2001.* Trans. Elizabeth Rottenberg, 133–44. Stanford: Stanford University Press, 2002. "Manquements du droit à la justice (mais que manque-t-il donc aux 'sans papiers'?)". *Marx en jeu*, 73–91. Paris: Descartes and Cie, 1997.

—— "Désistance" (1987). *Psyche: Inventions of the Other, Volume II.* Trans. Christopher Fynsk. Ed. Peggy Kamuf and Elizabeth Rottenberg, 196–230. Stanford: Stanford University Press, 2008. "Désistance". *Psyche: Inventions de l'autre*, 2 Vols, 201–38. Paris: Éditions Galilée, 1998–2003.

—— "Différance" (1968). *Margins of Philosophy.* Trans. Alan Bass, 1–27. Chicago: University of Chicago Press, 1982. "La Différance". *Marges – de la philosophie*, 1–29. Paris: Les Éditions de Minuit, 1972.

—— "Dissemination". *Dissemination.* Trans. Barbara Johnson, 287–366. Chicago: University of Chicago Press, 1981. "La dissémination". *La dissémination*, 349–445. Paris: Éditions du Seuil, 1972. Originally published as: "La dissémination I" and "La dissémination II". *Critique* 25, nos. 261 and 262 (1969): 99–139, 215–49.

—— *La dissémination.* Paris: Éditions du Seuil, 1972; *Dissemination.* Trans. Barbara Johnson. Chicago: University of Chicago Press, 1981.

—— "The Double Session" (1970). *Dissemination.* Trans. Barbara Johnson, 173–286. Chicago: University of Chicago Press, 1981. "La double séance". *La disséminationm*, 215–346. Paris: Éditions du Seuil, 1972.

—— *L'écriture et la différence.* Paris: Éditions du Seuil, 1967; *Writing and Difference.* Trans. Alan Bass. Chicago: University of Chicago Press, 1978.

—— *Edmund Husserl's Origin of Geometry: An Introduction* (1962). Trans. John P. Leavey, Jr. Lincoln: University of Nebraska Press, 1989; *L'origine de la géométrie, de Husserl, Introduction et traduction.* Paris: P.U.F, 1974.

———— "Edmond Jabès and the Question of the Book". *Writing and Difference*. Trans. Alan Bass, 64–78. Chicago: University of Chicago Press, 1978. "Edmond Jabès et la question du livre". *L'écriture et la différence,* 99–118. Paris: Éditions du Seuil, 1967. Originally published as: "Edmond Jabès et la question du livre". *Critique* 20 no. 201 (1964): 99–115.

———— "The Ends of Man" (1968). *Margins of Philosophy*. Trans. Alan Bass, 109–36. Chicago: University of Chicago Press, 1982. "Les fins de l'homme". *Marges – de la philosophie,* 129–66. Paris: Les Éditions de Minuit, 1972.

———— "Envoi" (1980). *Psyche: Inventions of the Other, Volume I*. Trans. Peter and Mary Ann Caws. Ed. Peggy Kamuf and Elizabeth Rottenberg, 94–128. Stanford: Stanford University Press, 2007. "Envoi". *Psyche: Inventions de l'autre*. 2 Vols, 109–44. Paris: Éditions Galilée, 1998–2003.

———— "Envois" (1980). *The Post Card: From Socrates to Freud and Beyond*. Trans. Alan Bass, 1–256. Chicago: University of Chicago Press, 1987. "Envois". *La carte postale: de Socrate à Freud et au-delà,* 5–273. Paris: Aubier Flammarion, 1980.

———— "Et Cetera . . . (and so on, *und so weiter*, and so forth, *et ainsi de suite, und so überall*, etc.)". *Deconstructions: A User's Guide*. Ed. Nicholas Royle. Trans. Geoffrey Bennington, 282–305. Basingstoke: Palgrave, 2000. "Et cetera . . . (and so on, und so weiter, and so forth, *et ainsi de suite*, und so überall, etc.)". *Derrida, Cahiers de l'Herne 83*. Ed. Marie-Louise and Ginette Michaud, 21–34. Paris: L'Herne, 2004.

———— "Ethics and Politics Today" (1987). *Negotiations: Interventions and Interviews, 1971–2001*. Trans. Elizabeth Rottenberg, 295–314. Stanford: Stanford University Press, 2002.

———— *Eyes of the University: Right to Philosophy 2*. Trans. Jan Plug. Stanford: Stanford University Press, 2005; Second part of *Du droit à la philosophie*. Paris: Éditions Galilée, 1990.

———— "Le facteur de la vérité" (1971–1975). *The Post Card: From Socrates to Freud and Beyond*. Trans. Alan Bass, 411–96. Chicago: University of Chicago Press, 1987. "Le facteur de la vérité". *La carte postale: de Socrate à Freud et au-delà,* 439–524. Paris: Aubier Flammarion, 1980.

———— "Fifty-two Aphorisms for a Foreword" (1987). *Psyche: Inventions of the Other, Volume II*. Trans. Andrew Benjamin. Ed. Peggy Kamuf and Elizabeth Rottenberg, 117–26. Stanford: Stanford

University Press, 2008. "Cinquante-deux aphorismes pour un avant propos". *Psyché: Inventions de l'autre.* 2 Vols, II: 121–30. Paris: Éditions Galilée, 1998 2003.

——— "Force and Signification". *Writing and Difference.* Trans. Alan Bass, 3–30. Chicago: University of Chicago Press, 1978. "Force et signification". *L'écriture et la différence,* 9–49. Paris: Éditions du Seuil, 1967. Originally published as "Force et signification". *Critique* 19 nos. 193 and 194 (1963): 483–99, 619–36.

——— "Force of Law: 'The Mystical Foundation of Authority'" (1989–1990). *Acts of Religion.* Ed. and Intro. Gil Anjdar. Trans. Mary Quaintance, 230–98. London: Routledge, 2002. *Force de loi: Le "Fondement mystique de l'autorité".* Paris: Éditions Galilée, 1994.

——— "From Restricted to General Economy: A Hegelianism without Reserve" (1967). *Writing and Difference.* Trans. Alan Bass, 251–77. Chicago: University of Chicago Press, 1978. "De l'économie restreinte à l'économie générale: un hegelianisme sans réserve". *L'écriture et la différence,* 369–407. Paris: Éditions du Seuil, 1967.

——— *Geneses, Genealogies, Genres, and Genius: The Secrets of the Archive.* Trans. Beverley Bie Brahic. Edinburgh: Edinburgh University Press, 2006; *Genèses, généalogies, genres et le génie: Les secrets de l'archive.* Paris: Éditions Galilée, 2003.

——— "'Genesis and Structure' and Phenomenology" (1959). *Writing and Difference.* Trans. Alan Bass, 154–68. Chicago: University of Chicago Press, 1978. "'Genèse et structure' et la phénoménologie". *L'écriture et la différence,* 409–28. Paris: Éditions du Seuil, 1967.

——— "Geopsychoanalysis: 'and the rest of the world'" (1981). *Psyche: Inventions of the Other, Volume I.* Trans. Peggy Kamuf. Ed. Peggy Kamuf and Elizabeth Rottenberg, 318–43. Stanford: Stanford University Press, 2007. "Géopsychanalyse 'and the rest of the world'". *Psyche: Inventions de l'autre.* 2 Vols, 305–26. Paris: Éditions Galilée, 1998–2003.

——— "*Geschlecht* I: Sexual Difference, Ontological Difference" (1963). *Psyche: Inventions of the Other, Volume II.* Trans. Ruben Bevezdivin and Elizabeth Rottenberg. Ed. Peggy Kamuf and Elizabeth Rottenberg, 7–26. Stanford: Stanford University Press, 2008. "*Geschlecht* I: différence sexuelle, différence ontologique". *Psyche: Inventions de l'autre.* 2 Vols, II: 15–34. Paris: Éditions Galilée, 1998–2003.

—— *The Gift of Death and Literature in Secret* (1999). Trans. David Wills. Chicago: University of Chicago Press, 2008.

—— *Given Time: 1. Counterfeit Money*. Trans. Peggy Kamuf. Chicago: University of Chicago Press, 1992; *Donner le temps: I. La fausse monnaie*. Paris: Éditions Galilée, 1991.

—— *Glas*. Trans. John P. Leavey Jr. and Richard Rand. Lincoln: University of Nebraska Press, 1986; *Glas*. Paris: Éditions Galilée, 1974.

—— "Globalization, Peace, and Cosmopolitanism" (1999). *Negotiations: Interventions and Interviews, 1971-2001*. Trans. Elizabeth Rottenberg, 371–86. Stanford: Stanford University Press, 2002.

—— *H. C. for Life, That is to Say*. Trans. Laurent Milesi and Stefan Herbrechter. Stanford: Stanford University Press, 2006; *H. C. pour la vie, c'est à dire . . .* Paris: Éditions Galilée, 2002.

—— "Heidegger's Ear: Philopolemology (*Geschlecht* IV)" (1989). *Reading Heidegger: Commemorations*. Ed. John Sallis. Trans. John Leavey Jr. 163–218. Bloomington: Indiana University Press, 1992. "L'oreille de Heidegger: Philopolémologie (*Geschlecht* IV)". *Politiques de l'amitié*, 341–419. Paris: Éditions Galilée, 1994.

—— "Heidegger's Hand (*Geschlecht* II)" (1985). *Psyche: Inventions of the Other, Volume II*. Trans. John P. Leavey Jr. and Elizabeth Rottenberg, 27–62. Stanford: Stanford University Press, 2008. "La main de Heidegger (*Geschlecht* II)". *Psyche: Inventions de l'autre*. 2 Vols, II: 35–68. Paris: Éditions Galilée, 1998–2003.

—— "If there is cause for translation I: Philosophy in its national language (towards a 'licerature en François')" (1984). *Eyes of the University: The Right to Philosophy 2*. Trans. Sylvia Söderlind, 1–19. Stanford: Stanford University Press, 2005. "S'il y a lieu de traduire I: La philosophie dans sa langue nationale (vers une 'licterature en françois') *Du droit à la philosophie*", 283–09. Paris: Éditions Galilée, 1990.

—— "If there is cause for translation II: Descartes' romances, or the economy of words" (1984). *Eyes of the University: The Right to Philosophy 2*. Trans. Rebecca Coma, 20–42. Stanford: Stanford University Press, 2005. "S'il y a lieu de traduire II: Les romans de Descartes ou l'économie des mots". *Du droit à la philosophie*, 311–41. Paris: Éditions Galilée, 1990.

—— "Implications: Interview with Henri Ronse" (1967). *Positions*. Trans. Alan Bass, 1–14. Chicago: University of Chicago Press, 1982. "Implications: entretien avec Henri Ronse". *Positions*, 9–24. Paris: Les Éditions de Minuit, 1972.

—— "Interpretations at War: Kant, the Jew, the German" (1988–1990). *Psyche: Inventions of the Other, Volume II.* Trans. Moshe Ron and Dana Hollander. Ed. Peggy Kamuf and Elizabeth Rottenberg, 241–98. Stanford: Stanford University Press, 2008. "Interpretations at War: Kant, le Juif, l'Allemand". *Psyché: Inventions de l'autre.* 2 Vols, II: 249–305. Paris: Éditions Galilée, 1998–2003.

—— "Ja, or the *faux-bond* II" (1975–1977). *Points: Interviews 1974-1994.* Ed. Elisabeth Weber. Trans. Peggy Kamuf, 30–77. Stanford: Stanford University Press, 1995. "Ja, ou le faux-bond". *Points de suspension: Entretiens,* choisis et présentés par Elisabeth Weber, 37–81. Paris: Éditions Galilée, 1992.

—— *The Last Interview: Learning to Live Finally.* Trans. Pascale-Anne Brault and Michael Naas. London: Melville House, 2007; *Apprendre à vivre: Entretien avec Jean Birnbaum.* Paris: Éditions Galilée, 2005. Originally published as, "Je suis en guerre contre moi-même". *Le Monde.* Jeudi 19 Août, 2004: 12–13.

—— "LIVING ON. Border lines". *Deconstruction and Criticism.* Trans. James Hulbert. New York: Continuum, 1979, 75–176. "Survivre". *Parages,* nouvelle edition revue et augmentée, 109–203. Paris: Éditions Galilée, 2003.

—— "Majesties" (2002). *Sovereignties in Question: The Poetics of Paul Celan.* Ed. and Trans. Thomas Dutoit and Outi Pasanen, 108–34. New York: Fordham University Press, 2005.

—— "À Maurice Blanchot". *Chaque fois unique, la fin du monde,* présenté par Pascale-Anne Brault et Michael Naas, 323–32. Paris: Éditions Galilée, 2003.

——"'Maurice Blanchot est mort'". *Parages,* nouvelle édition revue et augmentée, 271–82. Paris: Éditions Galilée, 2003.

—— *Memoirs of the Blind: The Self-Portrait and Other Ruins.* Trans. Pascale Anne Brault and Michael Naas. Chicago: University of Chicago Press, 1993; *Mémoires d'aveugle: L'autoportrait et autres ruines.* Paris: Réunion des musées nationaux, 1990.

—— *Memories – for Paul de Man.* Trans. Cecile Lindsay, Jonathan Culler and Eduardo Cadava. New York: Columbia University Press, 1986; *Mémoires – pour Paul de Man.* Paris: Éditions Galilée, 1988.

——"Me – Psychoanalysis" (1979–1982). *Psyche: Inventions of the Other, Volume I.* Trans. Richard Klein. Ed. Peggy Kamuf and Elizabeth Rottenberg, 129–42. Stanford: Stanford University

Press, 2007. "Moi – la psychanalyse". *Psyche: Inventions de l'autre.* 2 Vols, 145–58. Paris: Galilée, 1998–2003.

———— *Monolingualism of the Other; or, The Prothestic Origin* (1992). Trans. Patrick Menash. Stanford: Stanford University Press, 1998; *Le monolinguisme de l'autre, ou la prothèse d'origine.* Paris: Éditions Galilée, 1996.

———— "My Chances/*Mes Chances*: A Rendezvous with Some Epicurean Stereophonies" (1982). *Psyche: Inventions of the Other, Volume I.* Trans. Irene Harvey and Avital Ronell. Ed. Peggy Kamuf and Elizabeth Rottenberg, 344–76. Stanford: Stanford University Press, 2007. "Mes chances. Au rendez-vous de quelques stérophonies épicuriennes". *Psyché: inventions de l'autre.* 2 Vols, 353–84.. Paris: Éditions Galilée, 1998–2003.

———— "No Apocalypse, Not Now: Full Speed Ahead, Seven Missiles, Seven Missives" (1984). *Psyche: Inventions of the Other, Volume I.* Trans. Catherine Porter and Philip Lewis. Ed. Peggy Kamuf and Elizabeth Rottenberg, 387–410. Stanford: Stanford University Press, 2007. "*No apocalypse, not now* à toute vitesse, sept missiles, sept missives". *Psyche: Inventions of the Other.* 2 Vols, 395–418. Paris: Éditions Galilée, 1998–2003.

———— "A Number of Yes" (1987). *Psyche: Inventions of the Other, Volume II.* Trans. Brian Holmes. Ed. Peggy Kamuf and Elizabeth Rottenberg, 231–40. Stanford: Stanford University Press, 2008. "Nombre de oui". *Psyché: Inventions de l'autre.* 2 Vols, II: 239–48. Paris: Éditions Galilée, 1998–2003.

———— *Of Grammatology.* Trans. Gayatri Chakravorty Spivak. Baltimore: Johns Hopkins University Press, 1976); *De la grammatologie.* Paris: Les Éditions de Minuit, 1967.

———— *Of Spirit: Heidegger and the Question* (1987). Trans. Geoffrey Bennington and Rachel Bowlby. Chicago: University of Chicago Press, 1989; "De l'esprit". *Heidegger et la question,* 9–143. Paris: Champs/Flammarion, 1990.

———— *On Touching – Jean-Luc Nancy.* Trans. Christine Irizarry. Stanford: Stanford University Press, 2005; *Le toucher, Jean-Luc Nancy.* Paris: Éditions Galilée, 2000.

———— *The Other Heading: Reflections on Today's Europe.* Trans. Pascale-Anne Brault and Michael Naas. Bloomington: Indiana University Press, 1992; *L'autre cap.* Paris: Les Éditions de Minuit, 1991.

————— "Otobiographies: The Teaching of Nietzsche and the Politics of the Proper Name" (1979–1982). *The Ear of the Other*. Ed. Christie McDonald. Trans. Avital Ronell, 1–38. Lincoln: University of Nebraska Press, 1988. *Otobiographies: l'enseignement de Nietzsche et la politique du nom propre*. Paris: Éditions Galilée, 1984.

————— "*Ousia* and *Grammé*: Note on a note from *Being and Time*" (1968). *Margins of Philosophy*. Trans. Alan Bass, 29–63. Chicago: University of Chicago Press, 1982. "*Ousia* et *Grammé*: note sur une note de *Sein und Zeit*". *Marges – de la philosophie*, 33–78. Paris: Les Éditions de Minuit, 1972. 03.

————— "Outwork, Prefacing" (1972). *Dissemination*. Trans. Barbara Johnson, 1–59. Chicago: University of Chicago Press, 1981. "Hors livre: préfaces". *La dissémination*, 7–68. Paris: Éditions du Seuil, 1973.

————— *Parages*, nouvelle édition revue et augmentée. Paris: Éditions Galilée, 2003.

————— "Pas" (1976). *Parages*, nouvelle édition revue et augmentée, 17–108. Paris: Éditions Galilée, 2003.

————— "The Pit and the Pyramid: Introduction to Hegel's Semiology".(1968) *Margins of Philosophy*. Trans. Alan Bass, 69–108. Chicago: University of Chicago Press, 1982. "Le puits et la pyramide: introduction à la sémiologie de Hegel". *Marges – de la philosohie*, 79–128. Paris: Les Éditions de Minuit, 1972.

————— "Plato's Pharmacy" (1968). *Dissemination*. Trans. Barbara Johnson, 61–171. Chicago: University of Chicago Press, 1981. "La pharmacie de Platon". *La dissémination*, 69–167. Paris: Éditions du Seuil, 1972 .

————— *Politics of Friendship*. Trans. George Collins. London: Verso, 2005; *Politiques de l'amitié*. Paris: Éditions Galilée, 1994.

————— *The Post Card: From Socrates to Freud and Beyond* (1980). Trans. Alan Bass. Chicago: University of Chicago Press, 1987.

————— *The Problem of Genesis in Husserl's Philosophy*. (1953–1954) Trans. Marian Hobson. Chicago: University of Chicago Press, 2003; *Le problème de la genèse dans la philosophie de Husserl*. Paris: Presses Universitaires de France, 1990.

————— "Provocation: Forewords". *Without Alibi*. Trans. Peggy Kamuf, xv–xxxv. Stanford: Stanford University Press, 2002.

————— "Psyche: Invention of the Other" (1984). *Psyche: Inventions of the Other, Volume I*. Trans. Catherine Porter. Ed. Peggy Kamuf and Elizabeth Rottenberg, 1–47. Stanford: Stanford University

Press, 2007. "Psyché: Invention de l'autre". *Psyché: Inventions de l'autre.* 2 Vol. Paris: Éditions Galilée, I: 11–62. 1998–2003.

———— "Psychoanalysis Searches the States of Its Soul: The Impossible Beyond of a Sovereign Cruelty (Address to the States General of Psychoanalysis)" (2000). *Without Alibi.* Ed. and Trans. Peggy Kamuf, 38–80. Stanford: Stanford University Press, 2002. *États d'âme de la psychanalyse: L'impossible au-delà d'une souveraine cruauté.* Paris: Éditions Galilée, 2000.

———— "Punctuations: The Time of the Thesis" (1980). *Eyes of the University: Right to Philosophy 2.* Trans. Kathleen McLauglin, 113–28. Stanford: Stanford University Press, 2005. "Ponctuations: le temps de la thèse". *Du droit à la philosophie,* 439–59. Paris: Éditions Galilée, 1990.

———— "Rams: Uninterrupted dialogue – between two infinities, the poem". *Sovereignties in Question: The Poetics of Paul Celan.* Ed. Thomas Dutoit and Outi Pasanen, 135–63. New York: Fordham University Press, 2005. *Béliers – Les dialogue ininterrompu: entre deux infinis, le poème.* Paris: Éditions Galilée, 2003.

———— "The Reason of the Strongest (Are there Rogue States?)" (2002). *Rogues: Two Essays on Reason.* Trans. Rachel Bowlby, 1–114. Stanford: Stanford University Press, 2005. "La raison du plus fort (Y a-t-il des états voyous?)". *Voyous: Deux essais sur la raison,* 19–161. Paris: Éditions Galilée, 2003.

———— "Restitutions of the Truth in Pointing" (1978). *The Truth in Painting.* Trans. Geoff Bennington and Ian McLeod, 255–382. Chicago: University of Chicago Press, 1989. "Restitutions de la vérité en pointure". *La Vérité en peinture,* 291–436. Paris: Flammarion, 1978.

———— "The *Retrait* of Metaphor" (1978). *Psyche: Inventions of the Other, Volume I.* Trans. Peggy Kamuf, 48–80. Ed. Peggy Kamuf and Elizabeth Rottenberg, 48–8. Stanford: Stanford University Press, 2007. "Le retrait de la métaphore". *Psyche: Inventions de l'autre.* 2 Vols, I: 63–94. Paris: Éditions Galilée, 1998–2003.

———— *Rogues: Two Essays on Reason* (2003). Trans. Pascale-Anne Brault and Michael Naas. Stanford: Stanford University Press, 2005.

———— "Shibboleth: For Paul Celan" (1986). *Sovereignties in Question: The Poetics of Paul Celan.* Ed. Thomas Dutoit and Outi Pasanen, 1–64. New York: Fordham University Press, 2005. *Schibboleth – pour Paul Celan.* Paris: Éditions Galilée, 1986.

——— *Signéponge/Signsponge*. Trans. Richard Rand. New York: Columbia University Press, 1988.

——— "Some Statements and Truisms about Neologisms, Newisms, Postisms, Parasitisms, and Other Small Seismisms". *The States of "Theory": History, Art and Critical Discourse*. Ed. David Carroll. Trans. Anne Tomiche, 63–94. New York: Columbia University Press, 1990.

——— "Le souverain bien – ou l'Europe en mal de souveraineté." (2004) *Cités* 30 (2007): 103–40.

——— *Specters of Marx: The State of the Debt, the Work of Mourning, and the New International*. Trans. Peggy Kamuf. London: Routledge, 1994; *Spectres de Marx: L'État de la dette, le travail du deuil et la nouvelle Internationale*. Paris: Éditions Galilée, 1993.

——— *Speech and Phenomena and Other Essays on Husserl's Theory of Signs* (1967). Trans. David B. Allison. Evantson: Northwestern University Press, 1973; *La voix et le phénomène: Introduction au probleme du signe dans la phénoménologie de Husserl*. Paris: Presses Universitaires de France, 1993.

——— "Structure, Sign and Play in the Discourse of the Human Sciences" (1966). *Writing and Difference*. Trans. Alan Bass, 278–94. Chicago: University of Chicago Press, 1978. "La structure, le signe et le jeu dans le discours des sciences humaines". *L'écriture et la différence,* 409–28. Paris: Éditions du Seuil, 1978.

——— "Telepathy" (1981). *Psyche: Inventions of the Other, Volume I*. Trans. Nicholas Royle, 226–61. Ed. Peggy Kamuf and Elizabeth Rottenberg, 226–61. Stanford: Stanford University Press, 2007. "Télépathie". *Psyché: Inventions de l'autre*. 2 Vol, 237–70. Paris: Éditions Galilée, 1998–2003.

——— "The Theatre of Cruelty and the Closure of Representation" (1966). *Writing and Difference*. Trans. Alan Bass, 232–50. Chicago: University of Chicago Press, 1978. "Le théâtre de la cruauté et la clôture de la representation". *L'écriture et la différence,* 341–68. Paris: Éditions du Seuil, 1967. Originally published as, "Le théatre de la cruauté et la clôture de la représentation". *Critique* 22 no. 230 (1966): 595–618.

——— "To Speculate – on 'Freud'" (1975–1980). *The Post Card: From Socrates to Freud and Beyond*. Trans. Alan Bass, 257–409. Chicago: University of Chicago Press, 1987. "Spéculer – sur 'Freud'". *La carte postale: de Socrate à Freud et au-delà,* 275–437. Paris: Flammarion, 1980.

——— "Tympan" (1972). *Margins of Philosophy*. Trans. Alan Bass, ix–xxix. (Chicago: University of Chicago Press, 1982), "Tympan". *Marges – de la philosophie, i–xxv*. Paris: Les Éditions de Minuit, 1972.

——— "Typewriter Ribbon: Limited Ink (2)" (1998–2001). *Without Alibi*. Trans. Peggy Kamuf, 71–160. Stanford: Stanford University Press, 2002. "Le ruban de machine à écrire. Limited Ink II". *Papier Machine, 33–147*. Paris: Éditions Galilée, 2001.

——— "The University without Condition". *Without Alibi*. Trans. Peggy Kamuf, 202–37. Stanford: Stanford University Press, 2002. *L'université sans condition*. Paris: Éditions Galilée, 2001.

——— "Violence and Metaphysics: An Essay on the Thought of Emmanuel Levinas". *Writing and Difference*. Trans. Alan Bass, 79–153. Chicago: University of Chicago Press, 1978. "Violence et métaphysique: Essai sur la pensée d'Emmanuel Levinas". *L'écriture et la différence, 117–228*. Paris: Éditions du Seuil, 1967.

——— *Who's Afraid of Philosophy: Right to Philosophy 1*. Trans. Jan Plug. Stanford: Stanford University Press, 2002; first part of *Du droit à la philosophie*. Paris: Éditions Galilée, 1990.

——— "Why Peter Eisenman Writes Such Good Books" (1987). *Psyche: Inventions of the Other, Volume II*. Trans. Sarah Whiting. Ed. Peggy Kamuf and Elizabeth Rottenberg, 104–16. Stanford: Stanford University Press, 2008. "Pourquoi Peter Eisenman écrit de si bons livres". *Psyché: inventions de l'autre. 2 Vols, II: 107–20*. Paris: Éditions Galilée, 1987–2003.

——— "The 'World' of the Enlightenment to Come (Exception, Calculation and Sovereignty)". *Rogues: Two Essays on Reason*. Trans. Pascale-Anne Brault and Michael Naas, 118–60. Stanford: Stanford University Press, 2005. "Le 'monde' des Lumières à venir (Exception, calcul et souveraineté)". *Voyous: Deux essai sur la raison, 163–217*. Paris: Éditions Galilée, 2003.

Derrida, Jacques and Giovanna Borradori. "Autoimmunity: Real and Symbolic Suicides". *Philosophy in a Time of Terror: Dialogues with Jürgen Habermas and Jacques Derrida*. Trans. Giovanna Borradori, 85–136. Chicago: University of Chicago Press, 2003. "Auto-immunités, suicides réels et symboliques" *Le "concept" du 11 septembre: Dialogues à New York (octobre-décembre 2001)* avec Giovanna Borradori, 133–96. Paris: Éditions Galilée, 2003.

Derrida, Jacques and Catherine Malabou. *Counterpath: Travelling with Jacques Derrida*. Trans. David Wills. Stanford: Stanford

University Press, 2004; *Le Contre-allée*. Paris: La Quinzaine littéraire-Louis Vuitton, 1997.

Derrida, Jacques and Elisabeth Roudinesco. *For What Tomorrow . . . Dialogue*. Trans. Jeff Fort. Stanford: Stanford University Press, 2004; *De quoi demain . . .: Dialogue*. Paris: Fayard/Éditions Galilée, 2001.

Derrida, Jacques and Dominique Janicaud, "Interview with Jacques Derrida" (1999) *Heidegger en France*. 2 Vols, II: 89–126. Paris: Hachette, 2005.

Derrida, Jacques, Jean-Luc Nancy and Philippe Lacoue-Labarthe. *Penser à Strasbourg*. Paris: Éditions Galilée, 2004.

Derrida, Jacques and Marie-Françoise Plissart. *Right of Inspection* (1985). New York: Monacelli, 1997.

Derrida, Jacques and Derek Attridge. "This Strange Institution Called Literature: An Interview with Jacques Derrida". *Acts of Literature*. Ed. Derek Attridge, 33–75. New York: Routledge, 1992.

Descartes, René. *Meditations on First Philosophy* (1641). Trans. John Cottingham. Intro. Bernard Williams. Cambridge: Cambridge University Press, 1986; *Méditations sur la philosophie première. Oeuvres philosophiques*. Ed. Ferdinand Alquie. 2 Vols, II. Paris: Garnier Frères, 1967.

Dostoyevsky, Fyodor. *The Devils* (1871). Trans. David Margashack. London: Penguin, 1971.

Dunlop, John. *Anti-Duel; or a Plan for the Abrogation of Duelling*. London: Houlston and Stoneman, 1843.

Durkin, Andrew. "Allusion and Dialogue in 'The Duel'". *Reading Chekhov's Text*, 169–78. Ed. Robert L. Jackson, 169–78. Evanston: Northwestern University Press, 1993.

—— "Pushkin and Conrad: From the Povesti Belkina to the Limits of Parody". *American Contributions to the XII International Congress of Slavists*. Ed. Robert H. Maguire and Alan Timberlake, 77–84. Bloomington: Slavika, 2003.

Dye, Denys. *The Stories of Kleist: A Critical Study*. London: Duckworth, 1977.

Ellis, John M. *Heinrich von Kleist: Studies in the Character and Meaning of his Writings*. Chapel Hill: University of North Carolina Press, 1979.

Englert, Walter G. *Epicurus on the Swerve and Voluntary Action*. Atlanta: Scholars Press, 1987.

Epicurus. *The Extant Remains*. Ed. and Trans. Cyril Bailey. Oxford: Oxford University Press, 1926.

Ferguson, Delancy J. "The Plot of Conrad's 'The Duel'". *MLN* 1 (1935): 385–90.

Foucault, Michel. *"Society Must be Defended": Lectures at the College de France, 1975-1976*. Ed. Mauro Bertani and Alessandro Fontana. Trans. David Macey. London: Allen Lane, 2003.

Fox, Everett. Trans. *Exodus. The Five Books of Moses*. London: Harvill, 1995.

Freud, Sigmund. *Introductory Lectures on Psychoanalysis*. (1915–1917) Trans. James Strachey. Ed. James Strachey and Angela Richards. London: Penguin, 1991.

———— *Psychopathology of Everyday Life* (1901). Trans. Andrea L. Bell. Ed. Paul Keegan. London: Penguin, 2002.

———— "Thoughts for the Times on War and Death" (1915). *The Standard Edition of the Complete Works of Sigmund Freud*. Trans. James Strachey, XIV: 273–300. London: The Hogarth Press, 1962. *"Zeitgemässes über Krieg und Tod." Das Unbewußte: Schriften zur Psychoanalyse,* 185–214. Frankfurt am Main: S. Fischer Verlag, 1960.

Gallie, W. B. *Philosophers of Peace and War: Kant, Clausewitz, Marx, Engels, and Tolstoy*. Cambridge: Cambridge University Press, 1978.

Gaston, Sean. *Derrida and Disinterest*. London and New York: Continuum, 2006.

———— *The Impossible Mourning of Jacques Derrida*. London and New York: Continuum, 2006.

———— *Starting With Derrida: Plato, Aristotle and Hegel*. London and New York: Continuum, 2007.

Gibson, Andrew. *Beckett and Badiou: The Pathos of Intermittancy*. Oxford: Oxford University Press, 2007.

Godwin, William. *Things as They Are; or, the Adventures of Caleb Williams* (1794). Ed. Maurice Hindle. London: Penguin, 2005.

Griffin, Robert J., Ed. *The Faces of Anonymity: Anonymous and Pseudonymous Publication from the Sixteenth to the Twentieth Century*. New York: Palgrave, 2003.

Griffiths, Eystan. *Political Change and Human Emancipation in the Works of Heinrich von Kleist*. Rochester: Camden House, 2005.

Hammond, Mary. "Thackeray's Waterloo: History and War in *Vanity Fair*". *Literature and History* 11 (2002): 19–38.

Hardy, Thomas. *Far from the Madding Crowd* (1874). Ed. Rosemarie Morgan and Shannon Russell. London: Penguin, 2003.
—— *Jude the Obscure* (1895). Ed. Dennis Taylor. London: Penguin, 1998.
—— *The Mayor of Casterbridge* (1886). Ed. Keith Wilson. London: Penguin, 2003.
—— *The Return of the Native* (1878). Ed. Tony Slade. Intro. Penny Boumelha. London: Penguin, 1999.
—— *Tess of the D'Urbervilles* (1891). Ed. Tim Dolin. Intro. Margaret R. Higonnet. London: Penguin, 2003.
—— *The Woodlanders* (1887). Ed. Patricia Ingham. London: Penguin, 1998.
Hartley, Lucy. "War and Peace, or Governmentality as the Ruin of Democracy". *Foucault in an Age of Terror: Essays on Biopolitics and the Defense of Society.* Ed. Stephen Morton and Stephen Byrgave, 133–51. New York: Palgrave, 2008.
Hegel, G. F. W. *Correspondance I. 1785-1812.* Trans. J. Carrère. Paris: Gallimard, 1962.
—— *Lectures on the History of Philosophy I: Greek Philosophy to Plato.* (1805–1831) Trans. E. S. Haldane. Intro. Frederick C. Beister. Lincoln: University of Nebraska Press, 1995.
—— *Phenomenology of Spirit* (1807). Trans. A.V. Miller. Oxford: Oxford University Press, 1977.
—— "On Wallenstein" (1800–1801). Trans. Ido Geiger. *Idealist Studies* 35 nos. 2–3 (2005): 196–97; "Über Wallenstein". *Werke I,* 618–20. Surkamp: Frankfurt am Main, 1986.
Heidegger, Martin. *Aristotle's Metaphysics Θ 1–3: On the Essence and Actuality of Force* (1931). Trans. Walter Brogan and Peter Warnek. Bloomington: Indiana University Press, 1995; *Aristoteles, Metaphysik Theta 1-3: Vom Wesen und Wirklichkeit der Kraft.* Frankfurt am Main: Vittorio Klostermann, 1981.
—— *Being and Time* (1927). Trans. John Macquarrie and Edward Robinson. Oxford: Blackwell, 1990); *Sein und Zeit.* Frankfurt am Main: Vittorio Klostermann, 1977.
—— *Introduction to Metaphysics* (1935). Trans. Gregory Fried and Richard Polt. New Haven: Yale University Press, 2000; *Einführung in die Metaphysik.* Frankfurt am Main: Vittorio Klostermann, 1983.
—— "Language" (1950). *Poetry, Language, Thought.* Trans. Albert Hofstadter, 187–210. New York: Harper and Row, 1975.

"Die Sprache". *Unterwegs zur Sprache,* 7–30. Frankfurt am Main: Klett-Cotta, 1985.

———— *Parmenides* (1942–1943). Trans. André Schuwer and Richard Rojcewicz. Bloomington: Indiana University Press, 1982.

———— "The Thing" (1950). *Poetry, Language, Thought.* Trans. Albert Hofstadter, 165–82. New York: Harper and Row, 1975.

———— "Time and Being" (1962). *On Time and Being.* Trans. Joan Stambaugh, 1–24. Chicago: University of Chicago Press, 2002.

———— "Was heißt Lesen?" (1954). *Aus der Erfahrung des Denkens,* 111. Frankfurt am Main: Vittorio Klostermann, 1983.

———— *What is Called Thinking?* (1951). Trans. Fred D. Wieck and J. Glenn Gray. New York: Harper and Row, 1968; *Was heisst Denken?* Frankfurt am Main: Vittoria Klostermann, 2002.

Heisler, Marcel. *Stendhal et Napoleon.* Paris: A. G. Nizet, 1969.

Herbig, Katherine L. "Chance and Uncertainty in *On War*". *Clausewitz and Modern Strategy,* Ed. Michael Handel, 95–116. Oxford: Frank Cass, 2005.

Hodge, Joanna. *Derrida on Time.* London: Routledge, 2007.

———— *Heidegger and Ethics.* London: Routledge, 1995.

Hornbach, Bert G. *The Metaphor of Chance: Vision and Technique in the Works of Thomas Hardy.* Athens: Ohio University Press, 1971.

Howells, Christina M. "Sartre and Derrida: The Promises of the Subject". *Derrida: Negotiating the Legacy.* Ed. Madeleine Fagan, Ludovic Glorieux, Indira Hašimbegovic´ and Marie Suetsugu, 161–71. Edinburgh: Edinburgh University Press, 2007.

Hoy, David Couzens. *Critical Resistance: From Post-Structuralism to Post-Critique.* Cambridge, MA: MIT Press, 2005.

Hume, David. *An Enquiry Concerning the Principles of Morals* (1751). Ed. L. A. Selby-Bigge and P. H. Nidditch. 3rd edn. Oxford: Clarendon Press, 1994.

———— *The History of England* (1754–1762). Intro. William B. Todd. 6 Vols. Indianapolis: Liberty Classics, 1983.

———— *A Treatise of Human Nature: Being an Attempt to Introduce the Experimental Method of Reasoning into Moral Subjects.* (1739–1740) Ed. L. A. Selby-Bigge and P. H. Nidditch. Oxford: Oxford University Press, 1978.

Husserl, Edmund. *Ideas: General Introduction to Pure Phenomenology* (1913). Trans. W. R. Boyce Gibson. New York: Collier, 1962.

Jackson, Robert L. "Pierre and Dolochov at the Barrier: The Lesson of the Duel". *Scando Slavica* 39 (1993): 52–61.

Janicaud, Dominique. *Heidegger en France*. (1999)2 Vols. Paris: Hachette, 2005.

Johnson, David E. "As If the Time Were Now: Deconstructing Agamben". *South Atlantic Quarterly* 106 no. 2 (2007): 268–90.

Kamuf, Peggy. "Introduction: Event of Resistance". Jacques Derrida. *Without Alibi*. Ed. and Trans. Peggy Kamuf, 1–27. Stanford: Stanford University Press, 2002.

―――― *Signature Pieces: On the Institution of Authorship*. Ithaca: Cornell University Press, 1988.

―――― "To Do Justice to 'Rousseau': Irreducibly". *Eighteenth-Century Studies* 40 no. 3 (2007): 395–404.

Kant, Immanuel. *The Critique of Judgement* (1790). Trans. James Creed Meredith. Oxford: Oxford University Press, 1952.

―――― *Critique of Practical Reason* (1788). *Practical Philosophy*. Trans. Mary J. Gregor. Intro. Paul Guyer, 133–272. Cambridge: Cambridge University Press, 1999.

―――― *Critique of Pure Reason* (1781, 1787). Trans. Paul Guyer. Cambridge: Cambridge University Press, 1998.

―――― *The Metaphysics of Morals*. *Practical Philosophy* (1797). Trans. Mary J. Gregor. Intro. Paul Guyer, 353–603. Cambridge: Cambridge University Press, 1999.

―――― "Toward Perpetual Peace" (1795). *Practical Philosophy*. Trans. Mary J. Gregor. Intro. Paul Guyer, 311–51. Cambridge: Cambridge University Press, 1999.

Kiernan, V. G. *The Duel in European History: Honour and the Reign of the Aristocracy*. Oxford: Oxford University Press, 1989.

Kleist, Heinrich von. "The Duel" (1811). *The Marquise of O – and Other Stories*. Trans. and Intro. David Luke and Nigel Reeves, 287–320. London: Penguin, 2004.

Kojève, Alexandre. *Introduction to the Reading of Hegel* (1937–1938). Ed. Raymond Queneau and Alan Bloom. Trans. James H. Nichols. Ithaca: Cornell University Press, 1991.

Krall, Frederick R. *Joseph Conrad: The Three Lives*. London: Faber and Faber, 1979.

Krimmer, Elisabeth. "Transcendental Soldiers: Warfare in Schiller's *Wallenstein* and *Die Jungfrau von Orleans*". *Eighteenth Century Fiction* 19 (206): 99–121.

Lacoue-Labarthe, Philippe. "In the Name of … ." Philippe Lacoue-Labarthe and Jean-Luc Nancy. *Retreating the Political*. Ed. Simon Sparks, 55–78. London: Routledge, 1997.

———. *Typography: Mimesis, Philosophy, Politics*. Intro. Jacques Derrida. Trans. Christopher Fynsk. Stanford: Stanford University Press, 1998.

Laertius, Diogenes. *Lives of Eminent Philosophers*. Trans. R. D. Hicks. 2 Vols. Cambridge, MA: Harvard University Press, 1980.

Lamport, F. J. "Introduction". Friedrich Schiller. *The Robbers and Wallenstein*. Trans. F. J. Lamport, 7–19. London: Penguin, 1979.

Laporte, Roger. "Heidegger, Beaufret et le politique: Témoignage et réflexions sur une longue occultation". *Lendemains* 17 (1992): 72–4.

Laubriet, Pierre. "La légende et le mythe Napoléoniens chez Balzac". *L'année Balzacienne 1968*, 285–301. Paris: Éditions Garnier Frères, 1968.

Lermontov, Mikhail. *A Hero of Our Time* (1841). Trans. Paul Foote. London: Penguin, 2001.

Lévinas, Emmanuel. *Is It Righteous to Be?: Interviews with Emmanuel Levinas*. Ed. Jill Robbins. Stanford: Stanford University Press, 2001.

———. "Nameless". *Proper Names*. Trans. Michael B. Smith, 119–124. London: Athlone, 1996. "Sans nom". *Noms propres*, 141–46. Paris: Fata Morgana, 1976.

———. "The Name of a Dog, or Natural Rights" (1975). *Difficult Freedom: Essays on Judaism*. Trans. Séan Hand, 151–53. Baltimore: Johns Hopkins University Press, 1990.

———. *Nine Talmudic Readings* (1963–1975). Trans. Annette Aronowicz. Bloomington: Indiana University Press, 1994.

———. *Proper Names*. Trans. Michael B. Smith. London: Athlone, 1996; *Noms propres*. Paris: Fata Morgana, 1976.

———. *Totality and Infinity: An Essay on Exteriority* (1961). Trans. Alphonso Lingis. Pittsburgh: Duquesne University Press, 1996.

Low, Jennifer. *Manhood and the Duel: Masculinity in Early Modern Drama and Culture*. New York: Palgrave, 2003.

Lucretius. *De Reum Natura Libri Sex*. 3 Vols. Ed. and Trans. Cyril Bailey. Oxford: Clarendon Press, 1947.

McDonald, Christie V. "Jacques Derrida's Reading of Rousseau". *The Eighteenth Century: Theory and Interpretation* 20 (1979): 164–81.

McNeill, William. *The Glance of the Eye: Heidegger, Aristotle, and the Ends of Being*. New York: State University of New York Press, 1999.

Malabou, Catherine. "Another Possibility". *Research in Phenomenology* 36 no. 1 (2006): 115–29.

Mandeville, Bernard. *The Fable of the Bees; or, Private Vices, Publick Benefits*. London: J. Roberts, 1714.

Mansfield, Nick. "Under the Black Light: Derrida, War, and Human Rights". *Mosaic* 40 no. 2 (2007): 151–64.

Markovits, Francine. *Marx dans le jardin d'épicure*. Paris: Éditions du Minuit, 1974.

Martinot, Steve. *Forms in the Abyss: A Philosophical Bridge between Sartre and Derrida*. Philadelphia: Temple University Press, 2006.

May, Kenneth. "Reading and Thinking: Heidegger and the Hinting Greeks". *Martin Heidegger: Critical Assessments*. Ed. Christopher Macann. 4 Vols, 37–60. London: Routledge, 1992.

Melville, Lewis and Reginald Hergreaves. *Famous Duels and Assassinations*. London: Jarrolds, 1929.

Meyers, Jeffrey. "The Duel in Fiction". *North Dakota Quarterly* 51 no. 4 (1983): 129–50.

———— *Joseph Conrad: A Biography*. London: John Murray, 1991.

Michaud, Ginette. "'Comme après la vie': Derrida et Cixous, ou Apprendre à lire enfin". *Mosaic* 39 no. 3 (2006): 133–50.

———— "Literature in Secret: Crossing Derrida and Blanchot". *Angelaki* 7 no. 2 (2002): 69–90.

Michelfelder, Diane P. and Richard E. Palmer. *Dialogue and Deconstruction: The Gadamer-Derrida Encounter*. Albany: State University of New York Press, 1989.

Miller, J. Hillis, "'Don't count me in': Derrida's Refraining". *Textual Practice* 21 no. 2 (2007): 279–94.

———— *The Ethics of Reading*. New York: Columbia University Press, 1989.

———— *Fiction and Repetition: Seven English Novels*. Cambridge, MA: Harvard University Press, 1982.

———— *Thomas Hardy: Distance and Desire*. Cambridge, MA: Belknap, 1970.

Montaigne, Michel de. "On Democritus and Heraclitus". (1580–1592) *The Complete Essays*. Trans. M. A. Screech, 337–40. London: Penguin, 1993.

Mullan, John. *Anonymity: A Secret History of English Literature*. London: Faber and Faber, 2007.

Naas, Michael. "'One Nation . . . Indivisible': Jacques Derrida on the Autoimmunity of Democracy and the Sovereignty of God". *Research in Phenomenology* 36 no. 1 (2006): 15–44.

Najder, Zdzislaw. *Joseph Conrad: A Chronicle*. New Brunswick: Rutgers University Press, 1983.

Nietzsche, Friedrich. *Beyond Good and Evil. Basic Writings of Nietzsche* (1886). Trans. Walter Kaufman. New York: Modern Library, 1968.

———— *On the Genealogy of Morals. Basic Writings of Nietzsche* (1887). Trans. Walter Kaufman. New York: Modern Library, 1968.

———— "On Truth and Lie in an Extra-Moral Sense" (1874). *The Portable Nietzsche*. Ed. Trans. Walter Kaufmann, 42–7. London: Penguin, 1982.

———— *Thus Spoke Zarathustra* (1885). Ed. Adrian Del Caro and Robert B. Pippin. Trans. Adrian del Caro. Cambridge: Cambridge University Press, 2006.

Oz, Amos. *Panther in the Basement*. Trans. Nicholas de Lange. London: Vintage, 1997.

———— *The Silence of Heaven: Agnon's Fear of God*. Trans. Barbara Harshav. Princeton: Princeton University Press, 2000.

———— *A Tale of Love and Darkness*. Trans. Nicholas de Lange. London: Chatto & Windus, 2004.

Payne, Michael, and John Schad. Eds. *Life. After.Theory: Jacques Derrida, Frank Kermode, Toril Moi, Christopher Norris*. London: Continuum, 2004.

Plato. *Lysis. The Dialogues of Plato*. Trans. Benjamin Jowett. 5 Vols, I. Oxford: Clarendon Press, 1892.

———— *Parmenides. The Dialogues of Plato*. Trans. Benjamin Jowett. 5 Vols, IV. Oxford: Clarendon Press, 1892.

———— *Phaedrus. The Dialogues of Plato*. Trans. Benjamin Jowett. 5 Vols, I. Oxford: Clarendon Press, 1892.

———— *The Republic*. Trans. G. M. A. Grube and C. D. C. Reeve. Indianapolis: Hackett, 1992; *Republic. The Dialogues of Plato*. Trans. Benjamin Jowett. 5 Vols, III. Oxford: Clarendon Press, 1892.

———— *Sophist. The Dialogues of Plato.* Trans. Benjamin Jowett. 5 Vols, IV. Oxford: Clarendon Press, 1892.

———— *Theaetetus. The Dialogues of Plato.* Trans. Benjamin Jowett. 5 Vols, IV. Oxford: Clarendon Press, 1892.

———— *Timaeus.* Trans. R. G. Bury. Cambridge, MA: Harvard University Press, 2005.

Pliny. *The Historie of the World: Commonly Called, the Naturall Historie of C. Plinus Secondus.* Trans. Philemon Holland. 2 Vols. London: G. B., 1601.

Poirier, Patrick. "À Demeure: Le lire comme un hôte." *Etudes Françaises.* 38 (2002): 145–64.

Porter, Dennis. "Stendhal and the Lesson of Napoleon". *PMLA* 85 no. 3 (1970): 456–62.

Pushkin, Alexander. "The Shot" (1831). *The Queen of Spades.* Trans. Alan Myers. Ed. Andrew Kahn, 7–18. Oxford: Oxford University Press, 1999.

Rapaport, Herman. *Heidegger and Derrida: Reflections on Time and Language.* Lincoln: University of Nebraska Press, 1991.

———— *The Theory Mess: Deconstruction in Eclipse.* New York: Columbia University Press, 2001.

Reyfman, Irina. *Ritualized Violence Russian Style: The Duel in Russian Culture and Literature.* Stanford: Stanford University Press, 1999.

Richards, David. "'Pistols for Two': Duelling in Nineteenth Century Russian Literature". *Journal of Russian Studies* 49 (1985): 37–41.

Richardson, Samuel. *Clarissa, or The History of a Young Lady* (1747–1748). Ed. Angus Ross. London: Penguin, 2004.

Rodin, David. "The Ethics of Asymmetric War". *The Ethics of War: Shared Problems in Different Traditions.* Ed. Richard Sorabji and David Rodin, 153–68. London: Ashgate, 2006.

Rodowick, D. N. *Gilles Deleuze's Time Machines.* Durham: Duke University Press, 1997.

Roth, Joseph. *The Radetzky March* (1932). Trans. Joachim Neugroshchel. Intro. Nadine Gordimer. London: Penguin, 1995.

Rousseau, Jean-Jacques. *Confessions* (1770). Trans. Angela Scholar. Ed. Patrick Coleman. Oxford: Oxford University Press, 2000; *Les confessions.* Ed. Alain Grosrichard. 2 Vols. Paris: Flammarion, 2002.

—— *Discourse on the Origin of Inequality* (1755). Intro. Patrick Coleman. Trans. Franklin Philip. Oxford: Oxford University Press, 1999.

—— *Essay on the Origin of Languages and Writings Related to Music*. Trans. and Ed. John T. Scott, 289–332. Hanover: University Press of New England, 1998.

Royle, Nicholas. *After Derrida*. Manchester: Manchester University Press, 1995.

—— *Jacques Derrida*. London: Routledge, 2003.

—— "Jacques Derrida's Language (Bin Laden on the Telephone)". *Mosaic* 39 no. 3 (2006): 173–95.

—— "On Not Reading: Derrida and Beckett". *Reading Reading: Essays on the Theory and Practice of Reading*, 201–19. Finland: Tampere, 1993.

—— *The Romantic Imagination in Relation to War and Apocalypse in the Later Poetry of Wallace Stevens*. Oxford, 1984. Bodleian Ms. D. Phil c. 5132.

—— *The Uncanny*. Manchester: Manchester University Press, 2003.

Sallis, John. *Chorology: On Beginning in Plato's Timaeus*. Bloomington: Indiana University Press, 1999.

Sampson, Anthony. "Freud on the State, Violence, and War". *Diacritics* 35 no. 3 (2005): 78–91.

Sartre, Jean Paul. *Les mots* (1964). Paris: Gallimard, 2006; *Words*. Trans. I. Clephane. London: Penguin, 2000.

—— *La nausée* (1938). Paris: Gallimard, 2005; *Nausea*. Trans. Robert Baldick. Intro. James Wood. London: Penguin, 2000.

Schiller, Friedrich, "Wallenstein" (1799). in *The Robbers and Wallenstein*. Trans. F. J. Lamport. London: Penguin, 1979; *Wallenstein: Werke und Briefe* 4. Ed. Fritjof Stock. Frankfurt am Main: Deutscher Klassiker Verlag, 2000.

Scott, Walter. *The Tale of Old Mortality* (1816). Ed. Douglas S. Mack. London: Penguin, 1999.

Sebald, W. G. *Vertigo*. Trans. Michael Hulse. London: Harvill, 1999.

Segev, Tom. *One Palestine, Complete: Jews and Arabs under the British Mandate*. Trans. Haim Watzman. London: Abacus, 2000.

Serres, Michel. *La naissance de la physique dans le texte de Lucrece: Fleuves et turbulences*. Paris: Les Éditions de Minuit, 1977.

Shakespeare, William. *The Most Excellent and Lamentable Tragedy of Romeo and Juliet* (1595). *The Norton Shakespeare, Based on the Oxford Edition*. Ed. Stephen Greenblatt and others. New York: Norton, 1997.

—— *The Tragedy of King Lear* (1608). *The Norton Shakespeare, Based on the Oxford Edition*. Ed. Stephen Greenblatt and others. New York: Norton, 1997.

Sherry, Norman. Ed. *Conrad: the Critical Heritage*. London: Routledge & Kegan Paul, 1973.

Spivak, Gayatri Chakravorty. "Ghostwriting". *Diacritics* 25 no. 2 (1995): 65–84.

Stape, J. A. and Allan H. Simmons. Eds. "Sources for Conrad's The Duel". Joseph Conrad, *The Nigger of The "Narcissus" and Other Stories*. Intro. Gail Fraser, 415–18. London: Penguin, 2007.

Stendhal. *The Charterhouse of Parma* (1839). Trans. Margaret R. B. Shaw. London: Penguin, 1958.

—— *Napoleon: Vie de Napoleon, Mémoires sur Napoleon*. (1816–1818, 1836) Ed. Catherine Mariette. Paris: Stock, 1998.

—— *The Red and the Black* (1830). Trans. Roger Gard. London: Penguin, 2002.

—— *Vie de Henry Brulard* (1835–1836). Ed. Béatrice Didier. Paris: Gallimard, 2006.

Stock, Paul. "Imposing on Napoleon: Romantic Appropriation of Bonaparte". *Journal of European Studies* 36 no. 4 (2006): 363–88.

Syrotinski, Michael. *Deconstruction and the Postcolonial: At the Limits of Theory*. Liverpool: Liverpool University Press, 2007.

Tenant, Roger. *Joseph Conrad*. New York: Atheneum, 1981.

Thackeray, William Makepeace. *Barry Lyndon*. Oxford: Oxford University Press, 1999.

—— *Vanity Fair: A Novel without a Hero* (1847–1848) London: Penguin, 1985.

Tolstoy, Leo. "Sevastopol Stories". *The Cossacks and Other Stories*. Trans. David McDuff and Paul Foote. Intro. Paul Foote, 185–333. London: Penguin, 2006.

—— *War and Peace* (1865–1869). Trans. Richard Pevear and Larissa Volokhonsky. London: Vintage, 2007; *War and Peace*. Trans. Rosemary Edmonds. London: Penguin, 1982.

Tucker, Herbert F. Ed. *Anonymity*, *New Literary History*, 33 no. 2 (2002)

Turgenev, Ivan. *Fathers and Sons* (1862). Trans. Rosemary Edmonds. Intro. Isaiah Berlin. London: Penguin, 1972.

Virilio, Paul. *Speed and Politics: An Essay on Dromology* (1977). New York: Semiotext(e), 1986.

Wall, Thomas Carl. *Radical Passivity: Levinas, Blanchot, and Agamben*. Albany: State University of New York Press, 1999.

Weber, Samuel. "Lecture de Benjamin". *Critique* 26 nos. 267–68 (1969): 699–712.

———— *Targets of Opportunity: On the Militarization of Thinking*. New York: Fordham University Press, 2005.

———— "Wartime". *Violence, Identity, and Self-Determination*. Ed. Hent de Vries and Samuel Weber, 80–105. Stanford: Stanford University Press, 1997.

Wisely, Andrew C. *Arthur Schitzler and the Discourse of Honour and Duelling*. New York: Peter Lang, 1996.

Wood, David. *Thinking After Heidegger*. Cambridge: Polity, 2002.

Wordsworth, William. *Lyrical Ballads, and Other Poems, 1797-1800*. Ed. James Butler and Karen Green. Ithaca: Cornell University Press, 1992.

Wortham, Simon Morgan. *Counter-Institutions: Jacques Derrida and the Question of the University*. New York: Fordham University Press, 2006.

Yousef, Nancy. *Isolated Cases: The Anxieties of Autonomy in Enlightenment Philosophy and Romantic Literature*. Ithaca: Cornell University Press, 1999.

INDEX

Blanchot, Maurice vii, 4–5, 18, 24,
    32, 64–5, 67–70, 115–16, 140,
    145, 164
  "Encountering the
    Imaginary" 115
  L'entretien infini 5
  "The Experience of Proust" 4–5
  "Literature and the Right to
    Death" 70, 115, 140
  "Rousseau" 32
  "War and Literature" 116
Bonhomme, Jean-François x
Borodino 9, 148, 151
Braudel, Fernand 164
Braun, Lucien 60
Brecht, Bertolt 109
Breton, André 5
Brown, Jane vi, ix–x, 31, 39, 59, 82,
    101, 137, 149, 159n. 1
Buber, Martin 140
Bulgakov, Mikhail viii, 154–6
  The Heart of a Dog 154–6
  The Master and Margarita 154
Bush, George W. 139

Celan, Paul viii, 60, 85–9, 140
chance vii, viii, x, 2, 5, 9–11, 35, 44,
    45, 56, 57, 62, 65, 67, 76,
    79–89, 90–8, 110, 113, 115,
    119–20, 128, 141, 142–4, 157
  chance and death 113–14
  chance and rule 83, 98, 144
  chance as name meeting 142–4
  chance of the duel 94–8
  la chance de la rencontre vii, 2, 5,
    54–5, 60, 62–3, 76, 79, 84, 90,
    115, 142–4, 157
Char, René 64, 164
Chekhov, Anton viii, 118
  "The Duel" 118
Cicero 80
Cixous, Hélène 15, 87
  Insister of Jacques Derrida 15

Clark, Timothy 74
Clausewitz, Carl von viii, 9, 97,
    102–8, 111
  On War viii, 9, 102–8
  clinamen 80
  Cogito 70–2
Condillac, Étienne Bonnot de 2–4, 5
Conrad, Joseph viii, ix, 103, 117–39
  "Autocracy and War" 117
  "The Duel" viii, ix, 95, 103, 117–39
  "Gaspar Ruiz" 134
  Nostromo 134
  The Secret Agent 117, 134–5
  Suspense 127
  "The Warrior's Soul" 127
  countering institution 76
  Critique 20–2, 28

darkness 36–40, 47–50
Dastur, Françoise 57
date 16, 22, 85–6, 95
Davies, Paul 161
de Gandillac, Maurice 61
Deguy, Michel 58, 60, 164
Deleuze, Gilles viii, 102, 178
  *A Thousand Plateaus: Capitalism
    and Schizophrenia* 102
de Man, Paul 23
Democritus viii, 80–3, 172
Derrida, Jacques
  Adieu: To Emmanuel Levinas 8,
    97
  "The Animal That Therefore
    I Am" 15, 116, 153–4
  "Aphorism Countertime" 96
  *The Archaeology of the
    Frivolous* 2
  "At This Very Moment in This
    Work Here I Am" 8, 24, 76
  "Autoimmunity: Real and
    Symbolic Suicides" 6–7,
    138–9
  "Cartouches" 8